Mr. Monk
and Philosophy

Popular Culture and Philosophy®
Series Editor: George A. Reisch

For full details of all **Popular Culture and Philosophy®** books, visit www.opencourtbooks.com.

Popular Culture and Philosophy®

Mr. Monk and Philosophy

The Curious Case of the Defective Detective

Edited by

D.E. WITTKOWER

OPEN COURT

Chicago and La Salle, Illinois

Volume 46 in the series, *Popular Culture and Philosophy*®, edited by George A. Reisch

To order books from Open Court, call toll-free 1-800-815-2280, or visit our website at www.opencourtbooks.com.

Open Court Publishing Company is a division of Carus Publishing Company.

Library of Congress Cataloging-in-Publication Data

Mr. Monk and philosophy : the curious case of the defective detective / edited by D.E. Wittkower
       p. cm.—(Popular culture and philosophy ; v. 46)
    Includes bibliographical references and index.
    ISBN 978-0-8126-9674-5 (trade paper : alk. paper)
    1. Monk (Television program) I. Wittkower, D. E., 1977–
  II. Title: Mr. Monk and philosophy
    PN1992.77.M595M72 2010
    791.45'72—dc22

                                        2009040544

To the number 10. A nice, round number.

Contents

He's a Real Character: Monk's Competition

He's . . . Not Like Everyone Else: The Spiritual Side of Adrian Monk

Our Hour Isn't Over Yet, It's Only Been Fifty-Eight Minutes: Monk in Therapy

Mr. Monk Meets Alexander the Great

D.E. WITTKOWER

Wasps don't care about me. I'm not sure that they care about anything, really. They have their waspy business, I suppose, which seems to involve hovering around in mid-air, directly between me and the door that would allow me to get back inside where it's safe. But if one should land on my arm, it would sit there, its impossibly thin, barbed, machine-like legs gently sticking into the outermost layer of my skin, its thorax smoothly moving in and out with its respiration, moving the stinger closer and further, closer and further, in a steady, calm and unconcerned rhythm. To the wasp, a sting would be a quick thing with no consequences or importance; something it really might as well do, just in case I'm a threat of some kind. To me, a sting would mean a severe allergic reaction and a trip to the hospital—frightening, painful, and expensive, even with my health insurance.

The most frightening thing about the wasp is this: it doesn't care. Even death doesn't really mean anything to it. It has little sense of individuality or self-preservation. It has nothing to lose. I can't even threaten it meaningfully. I'm completely helpless before it, because it doesn't care about me or what I do.

The whole world is like that wasp. It doesn't care, either. It's got its business, I suppose, but the cycles of life come and go, and we individual living creatures are simply and constantly along for the ride, tossed about in its surf; taken up to the crests of waves or pulled down into the undertow with a terrifying and meaningless impartiality.

What can we do? We cannot negotiate with, bargain with, or threaten the world. All we can do is create some order, some structure and meaning within our lives, and hope that brute uncaring reality doesn't step in to squash our careful and rational plans with an airplane accident, or snakebite, or wasp-sting or something else. And, though we know that the world may put an end to us at any moment, we try to just ignore that possibility and pretend the world makes sense and cares about us. Of course, those of us who are rational, like Monk—we know better. No one seems to care, but we do, and we may be wrong . . . but we don't think so.

Mr. Monk and the Lost Cause

Mr. Monk is a hero, of a kind. He comes upon difficult challenges and uses his virtues to overcome them. But *Monk*, the show, is also about Monk's constant, daily struggles—struggles against fear and disorder, in which he always fails. Worse yet: he *must* always fail, precisely because he's struggling against fear and disorder. The hero stories help us pretend that the world that really *has* order and meaning to it—the good man wins, talent and work succeeds, and evil is overcome. They are stories of the world as we wish it was, and the world we seek to create. But Monk's hopeless struggles— these tell us of the world as it *is*.

Stories about hopeless struggle against the world are just as ancient as stories of heroic overcoming, and there is a basic human need for both. Consider, for example, קֹהֶלֶת (*Ecclesiastes*):

> All the rivers run into the sea, yet the sea is not full; unto the place whither the rivers go, thither they go again. All things toil to weariness; man cannot utter it, the eye is not satisfied with seeing, nor the ear filled with hearing. That which hath been is that which shall be, and that which hath been done is that which shall be done; and there is nothing new under the sun. . . . I have seen all the works that are done under the sun; and, behold, all is vanity and a striving after wind. That which is crooked cannot be made straight.[1]

These teachings are considered wise. But they are not exactly *popular*. They remind us of what we try to forget, that the world will take everything put together and rend it asunder, and that all our successes are transient and trivial. And *Ecclesiastes* also tells us, oddly, that we should enjoy these meaningless mortal

---

[1] *Kohelet* (*Ecclesiastes*) 1:2–4, 7–9, 13–15. Jewish Publication Society translation.

things anyway! But how can that work? If we know that "that which is crooked cannot be made straight," why not instead give up on righting the wrongs of the world and setting things in order?

Monk helps to tell us how to live with wisdom but without resignation; how to live while accepting that there is no hope, that is, how to live without simply denying reality, and without being simply frozen in inaction. He shows us the glorious, hopeless, and happy-enough life of a *Sisyphus.*

Mr. Monk and the Large Rock

Albert Camus wrote *The Myth of Sisyphus* in 1940. Europe had been thrown into a feeling of meaninglessness—Europeans had though of themselves as the most civilized and humane peoples in the history of this world, and yet had been at the center of the largest and most lethal war ever fought: the Great War (now, sadly, called World War I instead).

In the midst of this cultural despair, Camus wrote of Sisyphus. According to one version of the Greek myth, Sisyphus had been punished by the gods, who forced him to spend eternity rolling an enormous rock up a steep hill. Upon reaching the top, the rock would roll back down the farther side, at which point Sisyphus would begin his task again. In this eternal and hopeless struggle Camus saw a parable of the impossibility of human progress, for all of the things that make sense in human terms are exactly those which the world denies and destroys. All that human life builds, time takes away. Yet there's little else to do except to strive for human goods—love, success, respect, honor, and justice—even though the procession of generations have the same chance of success as the rock staying at the top of the hill.

And so, to imagine a human life worth living—unless we simply deny the reality of an uncaring world—we must, Camus said, imagine Sisyphus *happy.* Imagine him standing at the apex of his tortuous hill trying to position his rock at the top. Can we imagine that he smiles as he watches the rock borne downward by gravity, destroying the result of his hard work? Can we imagine Sisyphus feeling good when the breeze breaks through the oppression of the hot sun as he walks down his hill? Does he find a small and quiet satisfaction in his own perseverance as he puts his shoulder to the rock once again?

Mr. Monk and the Life Worth Living

To put Camus's question another way: Although he knows that filth will find its way there again, does Monk feel satisfaction in using a wipe? Can we imagine that Monk smiles as he looks upwards and sees that his ceiling, again, requires vacuuming? When he touches the lamppost, surely he knows that touching it means nothing, and will change nothing (for him as little as for the lamppost), but can he still take pleasure in doing so?

I think the answer to these questions has to be a clear and unequivocal "yes!" and, for that reason, Mr. Monk is as inspiring and affirming an example as Camus could ever have hoped for. He shows us how to imagine Sisyphus finding happiness despite his knowing that life is meaningless. Whose life, after all, is more meaningless than Adrian Monk's? He has lost the great love of his life to a death for which he can find no explanation. He is driven constantly by compulsions which he knows are irrational, and the product of a disorder. And his talent at catching murderers is always overshadowed everywhere he goes—airplanes,[2] peaceful country retreats,[3] a vacation resort[4]—by evidence that murder is a constant fact of human life, and that his efforts in law enforcement are as unlikely to change the world as sweeping up dirt in the forest. As Monk says in "Mr. Monk Can't See a Thing," "There's never hope"—and, later, "Hope. I hate hope's guts."

But although he may not always admit it to himself—when asked, for example, if he's been in a coma for the last ten years, he says "I wish"[5]—and even though his will falters from time to time[6], he clearly finds enough of value in his meaningless life to keep going from day to day. And if *his* life is worth living, then life must be worth it in general. The proof is in his compulsions, where his desires, values, and strivings are at their most meaningless, and the pain he undergoes at its most extreme. He engages in his compulsive behaviors in the face of not only an uncaring, unfixable world, but an uncomprehending and judgmental society. Here, not only does he know that his efforts are hopeless, but they actually drive others away from

---

[2] "Mr. Monk and the Airplane."
[3] "Mr. Monk Gets Cabin Fever."
[4] "Mr. Monk Takes a Vacation."
[5] "Mr. Monk and the Really, Really Dead Guy."
[6] "Mr. Monk Takes His Medicine," and "Mr. Monk and the Daredevil," for example.

him as well. But this is where he shows his greatest strength—in his insisting to live in the way he chooses and feels is right, even though people think he's crazy because he worries all the time, about things that they don't even pay attention to! Here, he might remind us of another inspiring Greek figure: Diogenes of Sinope.

Mr. Monk Eats Onions

Diogenes of Sinope looked at society around him, and saw the same kind of truth expressed in *Ecclesiastes*. He shunned social conventions, and claimed that even the simple and rustic life of ancient Greece was concerned with meaningless and unnecessary rules of behavior. Diogenes chose to live in a large barrel and to eat mostly raw onions, in order to show the Greeks that all their niceties and civilized ways were nothing but vanity, and an absurd and prideful denial of our simple nature. And for this, he was called a dog rather than a man, and it's from the Latin version of this title of disrepute—the Latin for "dog" is *cynicus*—that we get our English word "cynic."

Diogenes the Cynic lived like a dog, surely enough, but he was also a cynic in our modern sense of the word. He denied that his fellow men lived lives in accord with nature and reality, and tried to set an example. But his quest, he knew, was hopeless, and would not be understood by most of those around him. He is said to have wandered through the marketplace with a lit lantern at mid-day. When asked why he carried a lantern, even in the brightest sun—not an unreasonable question—he replied that he sought an honest man.

And so Diogenes the Dog lived much like Adrian Monk. He lived a simple life; his barrel and onions much like Monk's shirts, tweed jackets, and pot-pie-Tuesdays. He followed his goal of rationality and righteousness, his lantern carried at mid-day like Monk's constant investigation of every suspect, every date of Sharona's,[7] and every janitorial staff member,[8] seeking consistency, regularity, and reason. And he lived as an outsider within his society, refusing to ignore those things he found hateful simply because no-one else seemed to care.

---

[7] "Mr. Monk and the Candidate" and "Mr. Monk Takes a Vacation," among others.

[8] "Mr. Monk and the Big Reward."

Alexander the Great, who swept through and conquered much of Ancient Greece in the fourth century B.C.E., sought out Diogenes, having heard much of his wisdom (despite having heard everything else about him as well). It is said that when he came upon Diogenes, lying by the side of the road, he stood over Diogenes, surrounded by his most elite and honored Persian soldiers, and, with the full force and wealth of the Persian Empire at his disposal, asked Diogenes if there was anything that he could do for him. Diogenes said, "Only this: get out of my sun." By saying this, Diogenes showed that he was free from all desires that could be provided by social, political, or economic power, but wished only what even Alexander the Great could never provide: the ability to lie in the sun like any dog might. And Alexander, much to his credit, saw the great wisdom and strength of Diogenes's conviction, and that his commitment to his personal beliefs had freed him from the pointless worries and desires of other men. He is reported to have said, "If I were not Alexander the Great, I would wish to be Diogenes the Dog."

Mr. Monk Takes Up His Wipe

And so too should we all, if we are not Alexander the Great, wish to be Diogenes the Dog or Adrian the Defective. What strength there is, and what honor, in the steadfast refusal to care about what others say is important, and to live according to one's own views of right and wrong! To have so much to one's own life is surely enough, even if one remains committed to an impossible ideal that no-one else understands.

And what else is there to do, for one who can see the world for what it is, but refuses to accept the world in its ways? We may see that "under the sun, the race is not to the swift, nor the battle to the strong, neither yet bread to the wise, nor yet riches to men of understanding, nor yet favour to men of skill;" but that instead "all things come alike to all; there is one event to the righteous and to the wicked; to the good and to the clean and to the unclean" (*Kohelet* 9:11, 9:2). Seeing this, it is hard to imagine not taking up arms against the disorder, uncleanliness, and injustice of the world; Camus even writes that our knowledge of the need to risk our lives to help others is not at all heroic or praiseworthy, but is as simple a matter as "knowing whether two and two make four."[9] But to continue always to do so, without falling into despair—while it may be a simple thing—is a difficult thing.

And still more to do so with the knowledge that we will fail! In trying to order and clean the world, we seek to make the world into an orderly and ethical place. Monk knows that by solving one crime, he might be able to prevent a murderer from killing again—but there are always more murderers, always more crime, and his efforts can never stop that. In the same way, Monk knows that the ceiling will always get dirty again, and one day he'll pass away, and whoever lives there next will probably make the place a sty. Even the simple striving for decency and order requires great courage and conviction, as Monk shows us in his quiet and sometimes absurd courage—whether its courage in trying to stop a dangerous criminal, or in trying to get the window clean even though everyone is staring.

Camus once said, in an address to a group of Dominican Monks, "I share with you the same revulsion from evil. But I do not share your hope, and I continue to struggle against this universe in which children suffer and die."[10] It seems like it would only be reasonable to stop a struggle when there is no hope of success. But how can you stop a struggle—hopeless as it certainly is—against murder, war, pestilence, and disorder, while still remaining decent and humane? Mr. Monk does exactly what we all should do, if we can find strength enough to be decent human beings: he refuses to listen to claims that he should "be reasonable" or "accept reality," but is instead steadfast in his conviction, ready always to take up his task, wipe in hand.

---

[9] *The Plague* (Vintage), p. 132.
[10] *Resistance, Rebellion, and Death*.

I Just Solved the Case

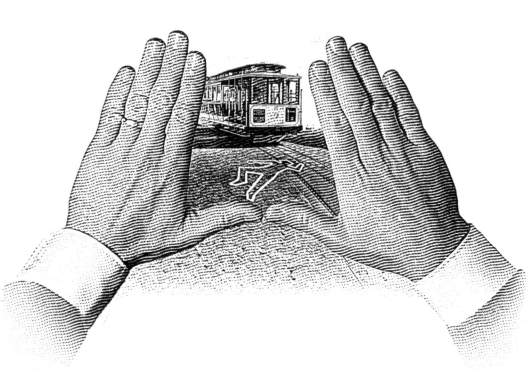

How Monk Thinks

1
Mr. Monk and the Phenomenological Attitude

TALIA WELSH

In "Mr. Monk Gets a New Shrink," as in most episodes, it is Monk's incredible perceptive powers that solve the case. Monk notices not only what a very attentive detective might capture—such as the fact that the carpet was just vacuumed and the vacuum bag is empty—but he *also* notices that a small decorative rock has been moved. What strikes the audience and Dr. Kroger is how astounding it is that Monk would remember such a small detail. Dr. Kroger comments, "It's amazing that you remember one particular rock," to which Monk replies "Well, I've been staring at it for nine years; you know, gift . . . curse . . ."

But what is really amazing here? It certainly isn't strange to look at something for nine years. We don't move around constantly and we tend to keep the same things for long periods of time. Like many writers, I stare out the window into my yard when I am trying to come up with something good to say. I think of my grandparents who spent forty years in a house, looking out a kitchen window to a small yard and alley. Would they have noticed a small two-inch rock in the garden that was removed? Would I notice if the lawn timbers were moved a few inches one way or another? Why didn't Dr. Kroger, for instance, who likely logged many more hours looking out into the courtyard, notice the misplaced rock?

Why *does* Monk see the misplaced rock? And why *don't* we see it? The much-studied phenomenon of *selective attention* illustrates how we selectively ignore visual data that contradicts our normal experience. Selective attention underlines how we often fail to pay attention to the "corners" of our experience. For example, Levin and Simons discovered in a 1997 study that most people failed

3

notice the change of an actor in a film. When an actor (not a famous one) was replaced by another actor (again not famous but also not similar in appearance to the original actor) who continued to play the same role, most people didn't notice the change had been made. It seems as long as we get that the actor is the "boyfriend" or "evil genius" we will not pay attention to the switch.[1] When we read about studies like this, we're sure that *we* would notice the switch, but many of us really don't!

Imagine you're standing in a public area and an interviewer approaches you and asks you innocently if you would answer a few questions. Agreeing, you start responding. After a few minutes, a couple of workmen walk between you and the interviewer carrying a large door. Following the briefest of pauses to allow the door to move past you, the interviewer politely finishes the survey and thanks you. What is difficult to believe is that most people will *not* notice that when that door was passed in between, the interviewer was switched with a different person.[2] We find such experiments disturbing—most of us think we really do see what is happening right in front of us! Test subjects are incredulous when they are told what happened but laughingly accept it when shown a video of themselves in the test situation.

In one of the funniest selective attention studies, subjects are asked to watch a short film with a number of people in white and black shirts passing a ball back and forth between each other. Typically, the "test" is to count the number of times the ball is passed. Intent on counting, most test subjects do not see a person in a gorilla suit, or a girl with a parasol, walk on screen.[3] (You can see examples of these tests on YouTube by searching for "visual attention test.") What will surprise you, having now read about these studies and being prepared, is that it seems *impossible* to not notice the gorilla-suit clad person, but most test subjects really don't.

Why is there this curious "blindness" in our attention? It's because what we "see" is more than what is visually in front of us.

---

[1] D.T. Levin and D.J. Simons, "Failure to Detect Changes to Attended Objects in Motion Pictures," *Psychonomic Bulletin and Review* 5 (1997), pp. 501–06.

[2] D.J. Simons and D.T. Levin, "Failure to Detect Changes in People in Real-World Interactions," *Psychonomic Bulletin and Review* 5 (1998), pp. 644–49.

[3] R. Becklen and D. Cervone, "Selective Looking and the Noticing of Unexpected Events," *Memory and Cognition* 11 (1983), pp. 601–08.

We don't just "take in" what appears to our senses and then decide what it means. What we see is very much influenced by what we expect, both consciously and unconsciously. In selective attention studies, we find that we tend to not be aware of changes that do not seem possible. The French phenomenologist Maurice Merleau-Ponty said that "The normal person *reckons with* the possible, which thus, without shifting from its position as a possibility, acquires a sort of actuality."[4] We think that we are blank slates, and when we have a new experience, we are open to whatever appears to us. But actually, we come to even innocuous experiences with baggage. We exclude data that doesn't make sense. It is just weird to imagine an actor changing mid-role, and so we ignore that data. It's nonsensical for people in gorilla suits to be walking around. We tend to ignore the non sequitur because it's not a real, living possibility for us.

If I enter into a room spoiling for a fight with my husband, I will certainly find one. If I venture into the world, assuming there is, or is not, a divine hand behind it, I will surely be confirmed in my assumption. If Captain Stottlemeyer enters the crime scene in "Mr. Monk and the Very, Very Old Man" assuming a 115-year-old man could not have been murdered, he will not be open to the possibility that a homicide occurred. The studies in selective attention tell us not just that our opinions and cultural heritage can influence how we interpret the world, but also that we have a psychological predisposition to ignore some elements of our perception and register others. But in order to be a great detective we must follow Sherlock Holmes's prescription that "It is of the highest importance in the art of detection to be able to recognize, out of a number of facts, which are incidental and which are vital."[5]

Unless I'm Wrong, which, You Know, I'm Not . . .

In Edgar Allen Poe's story *The Purloined Letter*, a letter that contains scandalous information about a French royal personage has been stolen. The police are aware of who took the letter and even know where it is. However, despite exhaustive searches of the

---

[4] Maurice Merleau-Ponty. *Phenomenology of Perception* (Routledge, 1996), p. 109.

[5] Sir Arthur Conan Doyle. "The Reigate Puzzle". In *The Treasury of Sherlock Holmes*. (Wilder, 2007), p. 251.

apartment with every means of technical and professional skill, they cannot find the letter. After hearing this tale from the prefect of police, C. Auguste Dupin, the celebrated investigator of the story, concludes that the letter isn't hidden there, but must instead be there *in plain sight* and, under the guise of visiting the thief, finds the letter in open view. Dupin points out to his unnamed narrator that the police are unable to find the letter not because it is hidden from view, but because they can only see the world from their perspectives. They can only search under the supposition that something important would be hidden from view because *they* would hide such an important letter. They cannot distance themselves from their prejudices about what a criminal "should" do.

In crime scene after crime scene, Monk enters into a room crowded with other experts but, like Dupin, he perceives the clues that slip by everyone else. Monk's talent is characteristic of any great detective: he sees what others pass over. Monk's uncanny perceptual talents provide the tools to crack the case, but often the ability for these talents to shine requires a constant management of Monk's extraordinary distractibility. Dirt, real or imagined, ordinary disorder, and any suggestion of asymmetry, all take Monk's mind away from the task at hand. Indeed, Monk often seems more occupied with restoring clean order to his environment than with helping to solve a homicide. Only due to the constant chiding of Sharona, Natalie, and Stottlemeyer is Monk able to solve the crime.

Would Monk's crime-solving abilities be stronger without his obsessive-compulsive tendencies? They are closely intertwined, or perhaps one and the same: Monk is distracted by things that we would likely ignore, but it is *because* he is distracted by so many seemingly inconsequential things that he notices incongruous elements that solve the cases. Monk really does perceive (not just *see*, but *perceive*) more than the rest of us.

The show *Monk* invites us to try and look both more closely and more broadly; to free ourselves from our own tendency to focus on what we think is present and relevant, rather than what is actually in front of us. Examples like the selective attention experiments show that we sometimes ignore big changes that are right in front of us. We "zone out" when traveling in a car, and when pressed with a question such as "Did we pass Main Street?" we're unable to say. Or alternatively, when we're in a tedious meeting, we might be unable to recall what has just been said even if we can hear the speaker quite clearly. In phenomenology, we call this the "natural attitude."

Phenomenology is a tradition in philosophy guided by the investigations of the German philosopher Edmund Husserl (1859–1938), who wanted to start with everyday, natural experience instead of abstract, philosophical theories. This focus on experiences, such as these experiences of selective attention, helps explain why most people are both conscious and not conscious of what they see and hear, just like the prefect of police in *The Purloined Letter*, or someone not paying attention to a boring speaker, or the driver who does not remember where she has just been. Phenomenologists try and set aside how we think things are, and what we think we experience, by taking up a "phenomenological attitude." In the phenomenological attitude, we approach the situation as unencumbered by preconceptions, perceptual or conceptual, and try to see things as they immediately and actually appear. When I zone out driving to work, I am thinking about something other than driving and thus my perception has faded into the background. In the phenomenological attitude, I want to be aware of all aspects of my experience not just those that seem the most important or catch my attention.

The phenomenological attitude does not replace the natural attitude. Zoning out in a boring meeting is surely a survival skill, not just a habit. Monk's life demonstrates the consequence of being unable to leave the phenomenological attitude and return to the natural one. When Monk remains unable to distance himself from the commonplace disorganization we encounter, his inability to leave the phenomenological attitude is both impractical and pathological. His powers of perception come at a price: he is unable to "turn off" seeing dirt and disorder and he is incapable of shutting down the endless stream of his own neurotic thoughts. His colleagues find this seeing and caring about the mundane disorder of the immediate situation annoying and distracting. Because Monk sees everything, hears everything, he is both a surprising genius and a pathological obsessive.

What Really Happened

Monk would see the change in selective attention studies; he would notice the new interviewer or new actor and puzzle over the incongruity. Monk's cognitive wiring is such that he is constantly being drawn to things that the rest of us pass over without notice. But how do those of us without his talents make sure to not fall into habitual ways of seeing—or not seeing, as the case may be? Phenomenology's answer to the philosophical problem of how to separate out truth from predispositions, expectations, cultural assumptions, and perceptual errors is to start out by not worrying about the truth at all. Instead, start by providing a careful description of what you experience and "bracket," or put to the side, any concerns with what should be true or what you expect to be true.

The father of phenomenology, Husserl, called upon us to return to what we experience more carefully, to what he calls going "back to the things themselves."[6] Phenomenologists make explicit what normally remains hidden from conscious awareness, because we are blinded to change or overly influenced by our cultural opinions. Phenomenologists strive to move from the "natural" attitude to the "phenomenological" one. In the natural attitude, we are like the other characters in *Monk*, in the phenomenological attitude we perceive the crime scene as Monk does. Our instinctive tendency is to stay in the natural attitude and not examine our opinions, beliefs, and habits that shape how we perceive others and the world around us.

In religious or political beliefs, we often find people who hold views opposite to ours to be stubborn and unreflective because they think they know the truth. We find those who cling so stubbornly to their "clearly false opinions" to be very frustrating. People tend to strongly defend their own views by excluding ones that disagree with them. We often accept only data that confirm our culturally-trained views, and exclude data that contradict them. As George Carlin once asked, regarding how each of us reflexively fails to understand the views of others as potentially valid, "Have you ever noticed that everyone who drives slower than you is an idiot and everyone who drives faster is a maniac?"

When we speak to someone who is very closed-minded, we have the impression of never being able to break that person's foolish self-certainty. How can this ignorant person not see how wrong she is!? But we can also ask the other side of that question. Why is

---

[6] Edmund Husserl, *Ideas: General Introduction to Pure Phenomenology* (Collier, 1962).

anyone "open-minded"? Why do philosophy at all? Philosophy asks us to be uncertain, to ask lots of questions that don't have obvious answers. It ruins our previous ideas and is cruel enough to not always replace them with comforting alternatives. The path of an open-minded person is not necessarily a happy one. Why not just stay in the natural attitude with our prejudices and beliefs that make us content? If ignorant, prejudicial beliefs help support a sense of self-satisfaction and have deep cultural and psychological roots, why would anyone want to call them into question? Phenomenology argues that the experience of the "foreign" causes us to leave the natural attitude and move toward the philosophical. For example, I can't help but question my own religious belief when I meet a reasonable intelligent person with a different one. This causes me to turn back on my own beliefs and see them *as beliefs* instead of as facts.

While religious and political views provide the ground for heated philosophical debates, the move to a phenomenological attitude can also be the simple experience of understanding that others do not see the world as I do. My first philosophical experience was when I was five. I had a pair of Charlie Brown snow overshoes. On the toes of the boots, the left had written "Good" and the right, "Grief." I remember standing in the snow, realizing that if I wasn't me, standing staring down at my toes, but was standing in front of me toe-to-toe, "Good Grief" would be upside down and I couldn't read it. While of course my thoughts about the matter were pretty minimal, it did provide a brief glance that my world is a world *for me*. I have a *perspective*. My world is not necessarily everyone else's world. I can only perceive *my* world; I cannot perceive *the* world.

At first this seems worrisome, since it is often the case—as with political views, for instance—that perspective seems to be *the problem*. It seems that if we could "get outside" our perspectives and really see the truth, we would find true knowledge. An absolute faith in the sciences, or *scientism*, holds a similar view. What is really true is something that will not permit a point-of-view; it would be something that would see something from all sides, all possibilities, at once. Phenomenology argues that this is based in the supposition that truth must be somehow without a perspective (or "objective"). It argues that a careful examination of our experience shows us that we have no reason to believe this.

Zen Sherlock Holmes Thing

When noticing a small change, Monk is struck by the way it is an
unharmonious fit within a larger landscape—a disruption. But
Monk does not, as one would in the natural attitude, assume that
certain disruptions are more or less relevant. He brackets out the
value-laden idea of what should and shouldn't be significant.

The murder that precipitates each episode is the most obvious
of disruptions in the characters' lives. The supporting characters
focus on the murder. If it is the police, such as Stottlemeyer and
Disher, they try to solve the homicide. If it is the criminals, they are
concerned with covering it up. What makes Monk different is that
he gives attention to seemingly unimportant details in the room and
in the victim's life. He has bracketed out any ideas about what the
murder should mean and sees the situation for what it really is.

In "Mr. Monk and the Garbage Strike," Monk is able to start solving the case by realizing that the union boss could not have possibly have killed himself because the wing-back of his chair would
have limited the movement of his right arm, and, in addition, why
would a suicide victim wipe off the prints from his bullets? The
solution often hinges on Monk's ability to put himself in the position of either the criminal or the victim. To say that the most truthful view would be to have no point-of-view would mean Monk
could not perceive the strangeness of the alleged suicide.

We cannot understand human experience without understanding human partiality and perspective, thus a God's eye "scientific"
view from nowhere could never explain how we always approach
a situation from somewhere. In the phenomenological attitude we
are asked to bracket our beliefs, or to put aside our preconceived
ideas, habits, and beliefs, and examine what experience really
teaches us. Monk shows us a phenomenological viewing of the
crime scene—as Sharona calls it in the first episode Monk's "Zen
Sherlock Holmes thing"—in his use of his hands to "frame" what
he is looking at while slowly walking around the room. He is taking in the entire scene, including the perspectives of the perpetrator and the victim. Monk is in the phenomenological attitude when
he considers both the chair of the union boss as well as how the
union boss would have acted in that chair. Stottlemeyer stays in the
natural attitude since he can only see what he, Stottlemeyer, finds
normal and natural. Monk is able to realize that the scene has different perspectives.

In our natural attitude, much of our experience is largely passive and unconscious except for the object of our attention. I don't think about all the various things in the yard—the rocks, the grass, the trees—when I am looking at a bird at the bird feeder. I am fully aware only of the bird. In order to engage in phenomenology, I have to make a conscious decision to not depend upon my unconscious and habitual beliefs, even those about the nature of the material world (Husserl, *Ideas*, §27). In Gestalt psychology, which deeply influenced and was influenced by phenomenology, we refer to the figure-background aspect of our perception. When one looks at a common optical illusion what is striking is that the same visual data produces two different perceptions that cannot be reconciled.

Take the above common optical illusion: either you see a vase or you see two faces, but you cannot see both at once even though the image does not change. Optical illusions present these kinds of either-or scenarios because our minds cannot find an "interpretation"—the image has no context, no supporting background to tell you if it is two faces or a vase. If a body was drawn attached to each face, the strength of the vase image would disappear. In perceptions that do not immediately challenge us, such as the perception of a room, we find that we tend to fixate on certain objects—the television screen, our dog, the painting—and do not pay attention to the other parts of the room. The rock Monk sees, Dr. Kroger also sees, but for Dr. Kroger it remains in the background, whereas Monk draws the background to his conscious awareness.

What is unusual about Monk is his ability to seemingly give equal cognitive weight to all aspects of what he experiences and to not give priority to the "obvious" object of focus. He engages in the phenomenological attitude in his "Zen Sherlock Holmes thing" by seeing what is really present rather than what we are predisposed to believe or ignore. In "Mr. Monk Goes to a Fashion Show," Monk finds out that the suspect cannot read English and questions how someone illiterate in English would have known to not use the door with a sign notifying that it will trigger an alarm if opened. What stumps Stottlemeyer and Disher in these cases isn't that they don't have access to the same sensory data as Monk, but that they can't seem to "perceive" its relevance. Monk notices how a criminal would have seen the situation; he would have read the sign unthinkingly and not used the door even though the fire escape was closest to the murder. The murderer's use of the English language was just background for him—he was busy thinking of the alarm as a problem, and never thought that his demonstration of English-language competence would be what would bring him down in the end.

No Exit from the Phenomenological Attitude

In "Mr. Monk and the Garbage Strike," Monk knows that the "suicide" is actually a murder, but lies about this in an attempt to end the strike that so disturbs his obsessive need for cleanliness. His disorder might open his eyes to clues that remain unbeknownst to others, but it ties him to them, not letting him distance himself from the immediate givens of his world. As we are constantly reminded in the show, Monk's abilities are also his "curse." Despite the value of being able to focus on all the details of a scene, from the smallest of rocks to the most obvious of emergency exits, Monk's curious talents have a dark side.

For one, it is extremely unpleasant to talk to a philosopher, or a police consultant, who cannot help but be skeptical about every undefended claim and fault. Socrates was finally prosecuted for this irritating quality of not permitting those with influence to pass off their opinions as knowledge. Even though a phenomenologist strives to capture in a description of experience what often goes unnoticed, most exit phenomenology when getting up from the desk. While it is frustrating to the subjects in selective attention studies to be later shown that they ignored a very obvious change in their perception (by showing them a video of their interview, for instance), this ability to not have to be aware of every change is what allows us to be normal and functional. It would be impossible to hold down much of a job if every time one noticed a small amount of dirt one was driven to distraction until it was cleaned.

The only way Monk can work is to have a full-time assistant at his beck and call 24/7. Monk presents us with an example of what a phenomenologist might be like if she were never able to leave the phenomenological attitude and return to the natural one. If we were trapped as careful observers of our experience, never able to return to the rest of habitual opinions and selective attention, we would drive ourselves and others to insanity.

The opening credits of the first show ("Mr. Monk and the Candidate") show Monk talking to himself during his obsessive getting-ready rituals (his socks in Ziploc baggies, brushing his teeth, hanging clothes) as if he were speaking to Dr. Kroger. In his monologue, Monk says familiar pop psychology types of affirmations "you can't sweat the small stuff" and "I'm going with the flow." He knows he suffers from his peculiar perceptive abilities and knows if he could only stop "sweating the small stuff" or ignoring everything he experiences, he would be happier.

In certain episodes, Monk's disorders cause him to have partial or complete breakdowns that require the assistance of his therapist, Dr. Kroger or later Dr. Bell. In the first season ("Mr. Monk Goes to the Asylum"), Monk is committed to a psychiatric hospital after he shows up at Trudy's old house, unaware of his behavior. While committed, the psychiatrist, Dr. Lancaster points out that Monk might be using his surprising analytical powers as props to hide his problems. Although it turns out that Dr. Lancaster is guilty of murder and imprisons Monk, Monk says almost ruefully when the doctor is arrested that "except for the murders and you trying to kill me, you really were the best doctor I've ever had."

Dr. Lancaster's interpretation is that Monk uses his "gift" to not have to form close relationships with others. Certainly his compulsions often ruin moments of normal human interaction—he is unable to focus on conversations if his hands feel dirty or something is out of place, and in "Mr. Monk and the Marathon Man," his badly-timed use of a wipe leads to several people assuming he is a bigot. Monk's sex life is non-existent since Trudy's death, a theme that receives a fair amount of attention in some episodes. Monk is even unable to *discuss* their past sex life much less have a sex life. In "Mr. Monk and the Paperboy," Dr. Kroger says, "Adrian, we can talk about your sex life with Trudy or we can sing show tunes until this session is over. It's your choice." It is then that we discover that Mr. Monk appears to be a fan of the classic Lerner and Loewe musical, *Camelot*.

These biographical stories provide us with a clue into an aspect of Monk's own limited perspective of his own life, despite his extraordinary openness to not being predetermined in his analysis of a crime. He's unable to integrate the importance of emotion in his own life and this makes him unable to enjoy the company of others. The neurologist Antonio Damasio's compelling book, *Descartes' Error: Emotion, Reason, and the Human Brain* (Penguin, 2005), explores patients with brain damage that compromises their ability to feel emotion. Such patients do not, as we might expect, find themselves in a Spock-like world where they are able to conduct themselves in a purposeful rational manner. Instead, they are strongly unable to function successfully in the world because they are unable to choose what is relevant and what is not in a situation. They have no perspective, no vantage point. At work, for instance, they will occupy themselves for hours with a relatively unimportant task instead of prioritizing the more significant tasks first. Maurice Merleau-Ponty also discusses such cases of brain damage in his *Phenomenology of Perception*, in particular the case of Schneider, whose injury caused a host of disabilities, including an inability to properly structure the world through empathic connections to others. Schneider is curiously unable to have any kind of ambitions or plans that would normally guide someone's life even though his intelligence is undamaged.

The "error" of Descartes that Damasio discusses, and Merleau-Ponty explores phenomenologically, is the misconception that reason provides us with the most authoritative structuring of our world and experience. Emotion, it has been long argued, leads us away from the truth because it tends to persuade us to think, do, and believe the wrong thing. But, we find that a person without an emotional compass cannot engage with the world in a meaningful, purposeful manner. Everyday tasks are almost insurmountable, interpersonal exchanges mysterious and frustrating. Damasio and Merleau-Ponty point out that reason isn't sufficient to provide us with a true knowledge of the world because it takes an "objective" stance that removes the narration we need in our lives. Reason by itself can only give us a world of sensory data without coherence or meaning.

Monk is able to perceive the emotional structuring behind the criminal's motive for homicide, but he refuses to allow emotional connections to structure his own life (except in the direst cases when he must overcome his disorder to save his friends' lives). Thus, Monk could possibly remain even closer to his phenomenological attitude if he would bracket his insistence on structuring the world according to phobias and rules of tidiness and instead be open to the way in which emotion plays a role in his life. Monk should be careful not to fall into his natural attitude of seeing emotional connections as "distractions." But it remains questionable whether such a move would make Monk a better detective, even if would make him a happier man.

It's a Gift . . . and a Curse

Is the curse the price of the gift? On the one hand, without his disabling obsessions, Monk could better see how his own life is structured by background emotional bonds. Yet, on the other, it seems that his talents come from his inability to leave the phenomenological attitude and return to the habitual, natural one. Monk complains in "Mr. Monk and the Other Woman" that "It doesn't make any sense" to which Stottlemeyer replies, "Does everything have to make sense, Monk?" For us, everything does not need to make sense. Most people are not constantly troubled by incongruous change, uneven books, and inconsistent behavior. In order to allow for the background of emotional connections that shape our experience to come to light, we have to allow others elements to return to the background. I cannot form a bond with a friend if I cannot stop thinking about the dirt on her shoes. I must allow the dirty shoes to recede from my awareness and concentrate on what she is telling me. But Monk seems unable to let the sensory background fade and let the emotional one come forward.

Monk's characteristic reply to Stottlemeyer's question, "Does everything have to make sense?", is "Well . . . yeah, it kinda does." The price he is afraid to pay for the loss of "sense" is the loss of his perceptive abilities. Even though Monk suffers from his disorder, he is in a bind: given his guiding ambition is to become a police officer again, he cannot lose too much of the "curse" or he will lose his unique talents. In the tradition of great private investigators and detectives of print and film, the road of genius is a solitary one where the gifts that solve cases isolate and exclude one from the illogical, emotional, and habitual lives of others. Monk's phenomenological perception marks him as different for better and for worse. As in Poe's poem, ever since his childhood, Monk has encountered a world that is different from our own:

> From childhood's hour I have not been
> As others were; I have not seen
> As others saw; I could not bring
> My passions from a common spring.

(EDGAR ALLEN POE, "Alone," 1829)

2

Mr. Monk Has an Epiphany

NILS CH. RAUHUT

All great detectives—whether fictional or real—have a remarkable ability to uncover the truth. They succeed in this even if the evidence is scant and the villains are brilliant in covering their tracks. Although great detectives are able to get to the truth under challenging circumstances, they do not all employ the same method of inquiry. Different detectives follow their own style of reasoning, and Adrian Monk is no exception. His work too is characterized by his own unique logic of discovery, distinct from that used by other great detectives. And, as we'll see, a bit more difficult to pin down than you might expect!

Let's start by clarifying the expression "logic of discovery." Consider one of the most famous detectives of all times: Sherlock Holmes. When it comes to the logic of discovery, Sherlock Holmes is, in many of his cases, the perfect example of what I would like to dub an "Eliminatist." Holmes himself describes this method to Watson in the novel *The Sign of the Four*. He says: "How often have I said to you that when you have eliminated the impossible, whatever remains, *however improbable*, must be the truth?"[1] The major steps in the eliminatist logic of discovery can be summarized as follows:

1. Consider all possible suspects (no matter how innocent they seem).

2. Collect and analyze all available evidence.

---

[1] *The Sign of the Four*, p. 111.

3. Eliminate possible suspects in the light of the evidence.

4. Continue this process of elimination until one suspect is left over.

Eliminatism is a style of criminal discovery that has similarities to early twentieth-century attempts to explain the logic of scientific progress. The philosopher of science Karl Popper famously claimed that science progresses through the falsification rather than confirmation of hypotheses.[2] Popper's falsificationist view of scientific progress looks a lot like the eliminatist model of progress in criminal investigations. Eliminatism also starts by considering a wide range of bold and imaginative hypotheses, and then submits these hypotheses one by one to a rigorous falsification process.

The falsification of hypotheses is often based on an argument style that is called *reductio ad absurdum*—that is, to show that a supposition must be false, because its truth would imply a contradiction. Eliminatist detectives seek to discover *reductio ad absurdum* arguments for as many suspects as possible. The eliminatist model of discovery culminates in a final deduction that allows the detective to eliminate all but one person from the list of possible suspects. This final deduction which leads to the identification of the criminal often takes place during a social event in which all suspects are present, and the way in which this is done can become one of the trademarks of famous detectives—Nick Charles in *The Thin Man*, for instance, or Nero Wolfe, with his habit of inviting groups of people to meet together in his brownstone, before accusing one of them of murder.

The eliminatist method considers each and every person connected to the crime as a possible suspect—regardless of whether a person *appears* guilty or innocent. Great eliminatist detectives consider everyone to be a potential criminal even if they have a stellar social reputation and an apparently watertight alibi. What matters in the investigation is evidence. Only if the evidence makes it clear that a given person could not have committed the crime will the eliminatist consider someone to be innocent, often leading to surprising and unexpected conclusions.

The eliminatist methods solves cases in a step-by-step fashion. As the story unfolds and as the detective is able to eliminate sus-

---

[2] Karl Popper, *The Logic of Scientific Discovery* (Routledge, 2002).

pects from the list of possible perpetrators he thereby continually comes closer to the final solution.

Monk versus Sherlock Holmes

In several of his cases, Monk's attention to detail allows him to eliminate hypotheses from further consideration. In "Mr. Monk Gets Stuck in Traffic," Monk notes that the crashed Volkswagen that was supposedly driven by Steve Marriott never passed him and Natalie. Monk also observes that there are no skid marks and that the transmission of the car is in neutral. Based on these observations, Monk falsifies the hypothesis which is maintained by the police; the crash was not an accident, it was murder. Similarly, in the episode "Mr. Monk and the Bully," Monk is able to show that if his old nemesis Roderick Brody had indeed been the killer of Douglas Fendle he would have used a gun rather than a steak knife.

In these and similar situations Monk falsifies hypotheses with the help of *reductio ad absurdum* arguments. However, just like good detectives, we too should avoid drawing hasty conclusions on the basis of preliminary evidence: even though Monk, in some of his cases, eliminates hypotheses from further consideration, it would be a mistake to classify his method as eliminatist. Further reflection makes it clear that there are a few fundamental and significant differences between Monk's method and eliminatism.

First, Monk never starts his investigation by considering all possible suspects. In many of his cases, as for example in "Mr. Monk and the Genius" or "Mr. Monk and the Magician," Monk quickly narrows his investigation to one particular suspect. The main question Monk investigates is often not the question "Who did it?" but rather "How did he do it?" This style of inquiry is at odds with an eliminatist model of discovery which requires, as we have seen, that each and every person connected with the crime is regarded as a possible suspect.

Second, Monk does not proceed in step-by-step fashion, continuously eliminating possible suspects and thereby gradually coming closer to the solution. Instead, Monk solves his cases in one fell swoop based on one crucial insight which allows him to apprehend the truth of the case instantaneously.

Finally, it is one of Monk's trademarks that he refuses at times to eliminate a suspect from consideration although the evidence strongly suggests that he ought to do so. In "Mr. Monk and the

Astronaut" Monk refuses to eliminate test pilot and national hero
Steve Wagner as a possible murder suspect although Wagner can
firmly establish that he was in space during the time of the murder
of his former girlfriend Joanne Raphelson. Monk has a hunch that
Wagner's the guy, even though Monk has of yet no or very little
evidence that supports this conclusion. Monk's refusal to eliminate
Wagner as a possible suspect is at odds with eliminatism.[3]

Monk does not reason like Sherlock Holmes. He does not follow an eliminatist model of criminal discovery. This does not mean
that Monk never falsifies and refutes hypotheses. He does do so in
several of his cases. However, falsification and refutation of
hypotheses and suspects only play a preliminary or a marginal role
in his overall logic of discovery.

Monk and CSI

If eliminatism does not capture the essence of Monk's logic of discovery, how else ought we to think of his investigative style? We
have seen that eliminatism resembles Karl Popper's logic of scientific progress. If Monk's logic is not like Popper's, it might be the
case that Monk's investigative style should be understood along the
lines of those philosophers of science who opposed Popper. Carl
Hempel[4] and Rudolf Carnap[5] are two prominent philosophers who
stressed the role of confirmation rather than falsification in the logic
of scientific progress. The essential steps in a logic model of criminal discovery that stresses confirmation rather than falsification can
be roughly described as follows:

1. Consider all available evidence (no matter whether it seems
   important or not).

2. Pursue the hypothesis that is best supported by the evidence.

3. Confront suspects and witnesses if the best supported theory
   contradicts their testimony and give them a chance to reveal
   a more truthful story.

---

[3] And, as we'll see in "Mr. Monk and the Contradiction," this might also be at
odds with the Law of Non-Contradiction.

[4] Carl Hempel, "Studies in the Logic of Confirmation" *Mind* 54, 1–26, 97–121.

[5] Rudolf Carnap, *Logical Foundation of Probability* (University of Chicago
Press, 1962).

4. Continue this process of confirmation until one theory is completely confirmed and the truth is revealed.

A good example of a detective who follows this confirmation style of criminal discovery is Gilbert 'Gil' Grissom from *CSI: Crime Scene Investigations*. Grissom, a trained entomologist, understands himself as a scientist. He is a master of finding and analyzing crime scenes and he's firmly committed to letting the evidence speak for itself. He does not jump to hasty conclusions and he always trusts evidence more than human witnesses.

Should we understand Monk's logic of discovery along these lines as well? The answer is a clear "No." We have already seen that Monk, at times, refuses to eliminate suspects in light of the evidence. But Monk also, at times, refuses to accept the theory that's best confirmed by the evidence. In the episode, "Mr. Monk Falls in Love," for example, there's plenty of evidence that Leyla Zlatavich has killed the Butcher of Zemenia. There is a hatpin, a charm bracelet, a motive, and a confession by Leyla that she has committed the murder. In spite of all this massive evidence against Leyla, Monk refuses to believe that she is guilty—and it turns out that he's right. The murder was in fact committed by Leyla's mother. This example illustrates that it is difficult to think about Monk as a classical confirmationist. There are times when Monk refuses to accept well confirmed theories.

We don't want to overstate this point. Monk's method clearly involves confirmation of theories. In the episode "Monk and the Genius," for example, Monk is convinced that chess master Patrick Kloster has poisoned both of his wives. Although Monk is firmly convinced that this is the truth, he does not rest until he can confirm this with evidence. This is also a standard feature of Monk's procedure in other cases. Monk is not finished with a case until he is in a position to confirm his hypothesis beyond reasonable doubt with crystal clear evidence. However, what distinguishes Monk's use of confirmation from the classical confirmationist is that confirmation does not guide Monk's search for the truth. For Monk, confirmation of his theories happens at the very end, *after* the truth has *already* been discovered.

Monk's Logic at Work

The fact that Monk's logic is neither eliminatist nor confirmationist suggests that Monk employs his own unique style of reasoning. In order to understand his investigative style more clearly it might be best to analyze a typical Monk case in more detail. In the episode "Mr. Monk Fights City Hall," Monk is able to solve the case by realizing that newspaper reporter Paul Crawford must have thought that city councilwoman Eileen Hill was pregnant and that this is the reason why he killed her. He comes to this insight by realizing that during an earlier interview Crawford, when asked whether Councilwoman Hill might have gone to a bar after her last meeting, had said "No, she wouldn't be drinking now." At the time, Monk did not pay much attention to the unusual phrasing of the sentence. However, as he is talking to Councilwoman Hill's new secretary, Maria Schecter, who is eight months pregnant and who declines Monk's invitation to go drinking, Monk realizes what Crawford really meant by the sentence.

What is especially interesting about this episode is Crawford's reaction to Monk's revelation that he is Eileen Hill's murderer. Crawford says to Monk with incredulity: "You don't like how I phrased that answer. What kind of evidence is that?" As a matter of fact, Paul Crawford is right about this. Monk's insight by itself is not really evidence. Monk couldn't get Crawford convicted on the basis of his insight, and no one else present seems particularly convinced by this observation either. This is the reason why Monk proceeds to confirm his allegation by quickly producing additional evidence that can be verified by others. Among other things, Monk grabs Crawford's necktie and reveals that it is of the same expensive and rare brand as the necktie that was used to strangle Councilwoman Hill. But Monk is producing this additional evidence primarily for the sake of others, to allow them to catch up. He himself doesn't seem to need the additional evidence since he has already solved the case on the basis of his epiphany.

The description of Monk's reasoning in the episode "Mr. Monk Fights City Hall" allows us to state a rough outline of the crucial stages in Monk's criminal methodology:

1. Monk experiences an epiphany (Epiphany Stage)

2. The epiphany allows Monk to solve the case with absolute certainty.

3. Monk presents evidence that proves to other that his solution is correct (Evidence Stage).

Monk's epiphanies are the most distinctive feature in his logic of discovery. Monk solves his cases with the help of sudden insights that allow him to grasp the truth instantaneously. In the episode "Mr. Monk Fights City Hall," for instance, Monk suddenly grasps what Paul Crawford meant by the phrase "No, she wouldn't be drinking now." This insight allows him to crack the case. Epiphanies like this one, which are triggered by accidental associations between apparently disconnected events, play a crucial role in each and every of Monk's cases. This is the reason why I would like to dub Monk's method "Epiphanist." Having given a name to Monk's logic and having highlighted the central features of his logic of discovery helps, however, very little in furthering our understanding of how his methodology actually works. What logical role do these epiphanies play? Should we interpret these epiphanies as simple hunches, as perceptions or perhaps as rational intuitions?

A Brilliant, Sick Mind

What exactly happens in Monk's mind when he experiences these epiphanies? Even people who work closely with Monk seem, at times, to be attracted to the idea that Monk has mysterious and supernatural abilities. For instance, in the episode "Mr. Monk and the Other Detective," Captain Leland Stottlemeyer says to Monk: "You know there are times when what you do appears like magic to me." However, attributing supernatural cognitive abilities to Monk makes it impossible to regard Monk as a great and admirable detective. Detectives are great because they can solve crimes with the same tools of thinking that are available to all of us and not simply because they have access to supernatural cognitive abilities. We should adopt a supernatural interpretation of Monk's cognitive abilities only if no other more naturalistic and rational explanation is available. Can we make sense of Monk's epiphanist methodology without evoking supernatural cognitive powers? I think we can.

Here's the thing: Our current reconstruction of Monk's method is still incomplete. According to our current model, Monk's epiphanies are the first step in Monk's methodology. They appear to happen instantaneously and out of the blue. If we understand Monk's epiphanies in this way it is no wonder that they appear like supernatural cognitive abilities. In reality, Monk's epiphanies do not happen out of the blue and they do not form the first step in his methodology.

The first step in Monk's logic of discovery is Monk's ability to register anomalies. When Monk investigates a crime he notes carefully every event that strikes him as odd. We can think of these anomalies as 'open why-questions'. To clarify, let's return to "Mr. Monk Fights City Hall." As Monk is investigating the murder of councilwoman Eileen Hill, he carefully notes everything that strikes him as unusual and which he thinks stands in need of explanation. He notes that it's odd that Councilwoman Hill has hired an obviously incompetent secretary. He notes it as odd that this secretary got the job in response to an advertisement in a Lamaze class and that she was only interviewed for five minutes before her drug test. He also is puzzled that there are positive pregnancy tests in the apartment of Councilwoman Hill although she is found not to be pregnant after all. Finally, he notices that Paul Crawford phrases one of his answers to the police in an unusual way. Being aware of all these anomalies is the first step in Monk's methodology. His epiphanies form the second step. What happens to Monk during these epiphanies is that he suddenly becomes aware that one and only one theory can explain every anomaly in the case. We can summarize this new way of understanding Monk's methodology in the following way.

1. Monk carefully takes note of all anomalies in a given case.

2. Monk experiences an epiphany that makes him realize that one and only one theory can explain all anomalies [Epiphany Stage].

3. The epiphany allows Monk to solve the case with absolute certainty.

4. Monk presents evidence that proves to others that his solution is correct [Evidence Stage].

This expanded model of Monk's logic of discovery eliminates the need to appeal to supernatural cognitive abilities. When Monk experiences an epiphany he all of a sudden realizes that one theory explains every single anomaly in a given case. It's true that these sudden insights are very often triggered by lucky associations, but what is happening in Monk's mind is perfectly ordinary. He realizes in one moment that one, and only one, theory can explain everything that stood in need of explanation.

Our analysis of Monk's reasoning clarifies why Monk is a genius. What distinguishes Monk from ordinary people is his ability to notice anomalies. Most people would not have noticed that it is odd that the new secretary of Councilwoman Hill got her job in response to an advertisement in a Lamaze class. Monk, however, is a master in spotting these oddities. Monk's extraordinary abilities as a detective are essentially linked to his obsessive-compulsive disorder. Monk is able to spot anomalies so easily because his mind demands order in everything. Monk is bothered by any form of chaos. For him, any open why-question and any puzzle is a form of disorder that needs to be overcome. Monk's need to solve his cases is rooted in his desire to impose order onto the world. His mind cannot rest until all open questions have been explained and answered. As outsiders we are inclined to regard his extraordinary ability to remember every single anomaly as a gift, but for Monk it is actually a curse—Monk's search for the truth is part of his battle to stay sane.

Moreover, our model of Monk's reasoning can explain why Monk's epiphanies are not proper evidence. When Monk solves a case he is able to see that one theory can explain all anomalies in a case. However, ordinary people are not aware of all the oddities in a given case. This explains why Monk's epiphanies are inherently private and cannot be corroborated by others. Only he can see that his theory can answer all open questions. This is the reason why he follows the epiphany stage by producing additional evidence that can be confirmed by others. He is able to do this because he has already found the truth.

Is Monk's Certainty Justified?

Monk's logic of discovery is essentially linked to his epiphanies. After Monk has experienced an epiphany, he's absolutely certain that he has found the truth. This is surprising. Philosophers have had notorious difficulties in finding certainty in anything. René Descartes, the great French modern philosopher, who made the search for epistemic certainty his main goal, concluded that he was certain that he existed as long as he thought, but he would have never been so bold as to conclude that anyone could be certain of his solutions to criminal puzzles. Is Monk's certainty about his epiphanies simply an act, or a mistake, or is he justified to be so confident in his solutions?

At first glance, there are excellent reasons to dismiss Monk's absolute trust in the reliability of his epiphanies as an act. For any given set of observations there's always more than one theory that can explain all the given observational data.[6] Suppose, for example, that you have observed swans in the United States for many years and that all the swans you have seen have been white. This observation can be explained by a number of different hypotheses. It might be the case that

1. All swans everywhere are white.

2. All swans in the United States are white, but they are black everywhere else.

3. All swans in the United States are white and swans in China are green and all other swans are red.

It's easy to see that we can produce infinitely many hypotheses that are consistent with the observation that all swans you have seen have been white. However, nearly all of these hypotheses, although compatible with the same set of observations, appear forced and not likely to be true. The reason for this is that we seek out theories not only because they are compatible with our observations but also because they are simple and intuitively plausible. Among all consistent hypotheses the idea that all swans are white is the simplest available explanation of why all the swans we have seen have been white. This is the reason we prefer this hypothesis over alternative ones. However, our preference for accepting the simplest explanation can also lead us astray. In certain situations—especially when we're dealing with criminal investigations—the simplest hypothesis is not guaranteed to be true. This shows that we have no epistemic justification to accept our conclusions with certainty. Even if one theory is compatible with all observations and even if we strongly prefer this theory to all other available ones we can never be absolutely certain that the theory is true.

This raises a fundamental epistemic worry for Monk's investigative style. When Monk experiences an epiphany he grasps that one particular theory explains all anomalies in a given case. But Monk

---

[6] As a matter of fact there are infinitely many theories that can explain a given finite set of observational data. See: Nelson Goodman, *Fact, Fiction, and Forecast* (Harvard University Press, 1983).

never considers alternative explanations that can also explain the observed anomalies. If Monk were to consider alternative theories he would have to choose between such theories in virtue of their simplicity, or some similar criterion. Moreover, if Monk were to choose among competing hypotheses he would not be justified to embrace his conclusions with absolute certainty. Yet, Monk never seems to choose among competing theories that have equal explanatory power. In addition, Monk is entirely happy to embrace and advocate theories that are extremely complicated and convoluted. Considerations of simplicity seem to be irrelevant for him.

Monk's refusal to consider alternative explanations and Monk's absolute trust in the truth of his conclusions seem epistemically irresponsible—that is, they seem to be irresponsible ways of seeking knowledge and forming beliefs. Can we defend Monk from this charge? I think we can. The crucial thing to realize is that Monk is not dealing with sets of observational data. Monk's epiphanies offer explanations to anomalies. But anomalies are not the same as ordinary observations. We should think of anomalies as puzzles or—to use a scientific term—as research problems. When Monk investigates a crime his obsessive mind is able to notice *all* unsolved and unexplained anomalies in a given case. His mind grasps everything that stands in need of explanation. This state of explanatory disorder is followed by Monk's sudden realization—during the epiphany stage of his method—that one theory can explain each and every anomaly.

The reason Monk is so confident that no alternative explanations are available is provided by a metaphysical background principle. Monk seems to hold that *only true theories* can explain *all* research problems. False theories, on the other hand, only offer partial explanations. This principle explains why Monk's epiphanies provide him with so much confidence. When Monk understands that one theory explains everything in a given case, he can be sure that he has found the truth because only the truth is able to explain it all.

Is this metaphysical background principle plausible? This depends on one's overall disposition towards the world. As long as one holds that chaos and confusions are only appearances and that the real world is perfectly ordered and fully harmonious, the principle is easy to accept. That the soundness of Monk's logic of discovery depends on the truth of such a principle and therefore requires a link between truth and order should hardly come as a surprise. After all, Monk's primary method—noticing and being bothered by anomalies—is based on his obsessive-compulsive search for *order* at least as much as it is motivated by a search for truth or justice; as for example, at the end of "Mr. Monk Takes Manhattan," where he seems more upset with the public urinator than with the murderer. Given that this fixation on the anomalous is at the heart of both his logic of discovery and his personal psychological struggle, at the heart of both his gift and his curse, it is hard to see how he could keep going from day to day without some implicit, deeply seated faith that we live in the 'best of all possible ordered worlds', namely a world in which one true theory offers complete and satisfactory explanations for each and every anomaly.

3

Mr. Monk and the Sinister Milk

MICHELLE GALLAGHER

Adrian Monk inhabits a complex, scary world. Menacing glasses of milk lurk in every kitchen, crooked paintings in every hallway, broken traffic lights on every corner. He is afraid most of the time and his fears overwhelm his rational nature. Though he is aware on some level that these fears are unreasonable (Mr. Monk is a smart man, after all!), he nonetheless avoids the milk, straightens the painting, and waits at the crosswalk for the broken light to say 'Walk'. Most of us, at one time or another, have had an unreasonable fear: of spiders; of flying; of public speaking; and so on. But most of us (hopefully!) are not the tangled mass of internal contradictions that Monk appears to be.

When we're in the grips of a feeling we know is unreasonable, it can seem as though we are literally of two minds. When you look at Monk, you can see the internal struggle written on his face. Witness Monk, distracted by a gut-wrenching fear that his stove might be on ("Mr. Monk and the Candidate"). His insides churn. He's trying to explain why the murder victim wouldn't have been a smoker, but he can't. Thoughts of the stove possibly being on distract him. He knows very well that the murder investigation is important. He has no reason to think the stove might be on. Nonetheless, the desire to run home and check the stove's knobs paralyzes him. He strikes the classic Monk wince of agony. Time stops. This time?—Success! The investigation can continue.

Who among us has never felt the menacing presence of just such a fear? And when has this fear ever cared about such eminently reasonable thoughts as air travel safety statistics or reassurances that someone else has turned off the stove? Maybe the difference between thinking and feeling runs *so* deep that they are two fundamentally different kinds of things that can *only* interact by being in conflict. Those of us who have checked a lock five times in as many minutes before leaving for work could scarcely claim not to have a certain sympathy for this view. There's just no negotiating with the nagging fear of the door being unlocked. Even if we act on our rational nature and not our unreasoned fears, even if we manage to keep our hands off the lock, we may still have these extra feelings hanging on to us like barnacles—simply *attached*, serving no purpose but to torture us, making life miserable, and for no reason. On this bleak picture, reason's job is to silence or hamstring feelings and it does this through sheer, brute force.

But there is a way we talk which suggests that the difference between thinking and feeling might not be so hopelessly stark. We often use the word "feel" somewhat interchangeably with the word "think." "How do you *feel* about your chances of getting a raise?" "Given the current state of the economy, I don't *think* a raise is likely." When we talk like this, are we just being sloppy? Or are we right to treat the difference loosely, as we often do?

One philosopher who took this way of talking very seriously was David Hume. For Hume, there *is* no difference in kind between thinking and feeling. Hume thought that to believe something is to *feel* a certain way about it.[1] There's something promising about this suggestion. If we're right to use the loose talk, maybe there's room for negotiation between thinking and feeling after all. That could come in pretty handy. For example, I want to get on that plane. Mr. Monk wants back on the police force. If both of us could just talk some sense into our feelings, well, it might make these things a little more likely, and that would be a good thing for both of us. The plane might seem like an incredibly heavy and awkward piece of metal that gravity will accelerate towards a speedy and sudden return to earth where it will instantly become a grotesque hunk of twisted burning metal and plastic and flesh . . . but people fly all the time, right? And physics can explain that it really can stay in the air! That makes it safe, right? Right?

So *does* it make sense to say that thinking is just a species of feeling? And if so, how exactly would these negotiations between

---

[1] See Book I, Part III, Section VII of Hume's *A Treatise of Human Nature*.

our thoughts and feelings proceed? Is there anything we could do to make them a little more . . . successful?

Conflict Is Conflict

A natural reaction we might have to Hume's suggestion that thinking and feeling are the same kind of thing is that Hume's just plain wrong. Thinking and feeling are just different! "Thinking is the same kind of thing as feeling" sounds like the sort of crazy thing you could only find someone saying in a philosophy department, or, maybe, on the beach after soaking in too much sun. You might as well say that seeing is the same as tasting, or that up is the same as sideways. Why should we take this suggestion seriously?

If Hume were here, he would ask us to examine this reaction closely. Just because we have a reaction, doesn't mean we understand it very well. We should look at all of the available empirical data, "beat about all the neighboring fields,"[2] as Hume would say, before jumping to conclusions. Some of the data we find might be surprising. Ask yourself this: Does a conflict between a fear and a rational thought really look all that different from a conflict between two rational thoughts or two feelings? If these different types of conflicts feel similar, that would suggest a similarity in the underlying phenomena.

How does Monk feel in these situations? Reason suggests that the murder must be connected to a story in the paper, because the murderer stole the paper off of Monk's porch ("Mr. Monk and the Paperboy"). The murderer must have had a reason for stealing the paper. But painstakingly analyzing every story turns up nothing (sort of).[3] None of the news stories are connected to the murder. For now, reason is at odds with itself. It's going to take some serious wincing (and a good dose of depression) to solve the case.

Opposing fears conflict in the same way. Adrian suddenly realizes that a snake is loose at the crime scene ("Mr. Monk and the Very, Very Old Man"). Does he jump on the table despite his fear of heights? Or does he stand on the ground despite his fear of snakes? Actually, he jumps on the table because "Snakes trump heights." But not until the third snake. At first, he freezes, screws up his face. The motions he is able to make become characteristically stiff.

---

[2] See *Treatise*, Book I, Part III, Section II, paragraph 12.
[3] If you missed the episode, I won't spoil it for you.

Think about the way you feel, when you yourself are in the midst of one of these conflicts. Does the struggle between the *fear* of being late for work and the *fear* of the unlocked door feel different to you from the struggle between the *fear* of flying and the *rational thought* that flying is safe? Or does it feel the same? To me, and, I suspect, to Monk, it feels the same. Still, there is *something* distinctive about thinking, isn't there?

Do You Feel Me?

One way that thinking is supposed to be different from feeling is in what it produces. Hume wouldn't put it this way, but we might say that reason produces beliefs—mental representations about how the world is—that are either true or false. Feelings do not. When Mr. Monk reads the snake feeding schedule and learns that there are supposed to be three snakes in a cage where only two snakes are to be found, he comes to the conclusion that a third snake is on the prowl. He represents the house to himself as containing an un-caged snake.

There are various forms this representation might take. Mr. Monk might literally imagine a picture of a (no doubt gargantuan, venom spewing) snake in the house. He might be silently saying to himself "there is a snake in the house!" He might be on the lookout for snakes in the house and not in other places (say, safely contained in a bag). Or he might, in some other way, be actively of the mind that in this very house, there is a snake. However he's going about it, he is representing the house as having a snake in it. This representation is his belief. It's about the house, a snake, and their relative locations. It's either true or false. There is either a snake in the house or there is not. And it is the product of a bit of (deductive) reasoning.

Not all of our beliefs are the product of reason. Our senses can tell us that the world is a certain way. When Monk sees a cross hanging crookedly on the wall, he's paying attention to a feature of the world: the angle of the cross ("Mr. Monk and the Miracle"). He represents the cross as crooked. Still, our senses don't do all the work. Many of the things that terrify Monk are things he can't see. He can't see the germs on the stranger's hand, but he believes they are there. Whenever we cannot sense something directly, we must rely on our reason to generate our beliefs.

Feelings, on the other hand, don't produce beliefs, though they may depend on them. Feelings are attitudes we have about how we believe the world to be. The angle of the cross makes Monk uncomfortable. The looming presence of a third snake terrifies him. If Monk didn't believe the cross was crooked, he wouldn't be anxious about it. If he didn't believe that a third snake was in the house, he wouldn't feel the terror. Feelings are the *result* of beliefs, while thoughts are the *source* of them.

If we took all of Monk's beliefs away from him, would he still have these tense feelings? It's hard to imagine Monk without any anxiety. Knowing Monk, he is always nervous about something or other. We've actually seen Monk with amnesia ("Mr. Monk Bumps His Head") and, yes, he's still on edge. It's just not clear that he's on edge about anything. As it turns out, some of our feelings are *about things*, and others are *just* ways that we feel.

There's a What-It's-Like

Some feelings are like heartburn: they influence what we do and they are important to us, but they don't have much structure or content to them. They don't represent something in the world as being a certain way; they just are a certain way. Heartburn, for example, is what it's like to have the sensation of stomach acid burning the esophagus. It's a bad way for an esophagus to feel, but it's not exactly a feeling *about* the esophagus. I can have heartburn even if I've never heard of an esophagus. I can even mistake the feeling for a heart attack. Feelings like heartburn don't come with any information as to what they're about, because they're not about anything. They're just raw feelings. Monk's generalized anxiety might be something like this.

Other feelings do have structure. My fear of dogs is not just a feeling of acid building, which I might confuse with a heart attack. It's *about* dogs. Still, structured feelings are like raw feelings in that there is such a thing as "what it's like" to have them.

According to Hume, beliefs are like the second kind of feeling. There's a "what it's like" to have them, and that's crucial to what they are. But they are also about things.[4] He claims that a belief is nothing but a *feeling* that some representation of the world is a *true* one. For example, my belief that 'the snarling German shepherd running towards me is dangerous' is a feeling that a very real, angry

---

[4] See *Treatise*, Book I, Part III, Section V, especially paragraph 5.

German shepherd coming towards me really does pose some threat. If this were not a feeling of mine, if there were nothing it was like to be believe that the German shepherd is dangerous, I wouldn't be able to take heed of my belief and, say, call out for help. My belief in that case would be like an unnoticed yard sign, "Danger! Beware of dog!" The sign only moves me if I see it before I see the dog.

An obvious question, and a question many have asked, is: What does it mean for something to feel true? Actually, we can say quite a lot about what it feels like. A representation of the world feels true if it has a certain force to it that a mere daydream or idle fancy doesn't have.[5] When I'm daydreaming, I can, at least temporarily, represent the world as being any way I like. I can envision a purple sun, a unicorn, or a city of gold. If I think hard enough, I can even imagine the possibility of the highway lying open before me, devoid of traffic, in the middle of the day. For one shining moment, I can almost see a clear path ahead to my exit. But reality comes crashing in. Luckily for the car ahead of me, I can't hold on to the 'open road' fantasy for long. It doesn't feel real, and as well it shouldn't.

Because they feel more forceful than idle fancies, beliefs have a much different effect on my daily activities. I stop my car, instead of hitting the car in front of me, and I feel the surge in my chest as I realize I've been drifting away. When Monk asks a suspect where they were at the time of the murder, the suspect feels far more nervous and strange when he answers with a lie than he would if he had said something he believed to be true.

Feeling Our Way Through Things

If Hume's right, it's not so strange that a conflict between a fear and a belief can feel similar to a conflict between two different feelings or two different beliefs. After all, according to Hume, when a belief conflicts with a fear, that's just two different kinds of feeling coming into conflict.

That is not to say that there is no *problem* when beliefs and other kinds of feelings conflict. As we all know, acting on feelings other than our beliefs often produces undesirable results. I am sit-

---

[5] See, for example, Hume's discussion in §39 of Section V, Part II of his *Enquiry Concerning Human Understanding*.

ting at a poker game and I do a bit of calculating. I figure out the odds of my getting dealt an ace are one in fifty-two. Those aren't very good odds at all. Nonetheless, I feel lucky. I just have a hunch that an ace is about to be dealt and I bet accordingly. The next card? Not an ace. I just lost my money and that's a problem. But what was wrong with going with my gut? Why should I act on my beliefs and not on any of these other kinds of feelings that might be hanging around (such as that I'm feeling lucky tonight)?

We judge people like Monk harshly when they look at a man who was in a coma at the time of the crime and based on nothing but a hunch say, "He's the guy." ("Mr. Monk and the Sleeping Suspect"). But Monk's gut feelings at least, usually turn out to be correct. The guy in the coma did plant the bombs. Still, we wouldn't close a case just based on Monk's gut feeling. Why is that?

And what people have thought is that the process of thinking *matters*. Thinking, as a process, is better suited to guiding us towards the truth and towards right actions than any other process. To think, we have to do some logic, figure out what causal forces are at work in a given situation, weigh probabilities. The end result of thinking is a feeling, a belief, but the process itself is not just the winds of emotion sweeping us away to conclusions. That wouldn't be a process helpful for getting to the truth of things at all. What is this process? And why does it work?

Thoughts in Motion

When Hume thinks of thinking, he thinks of representations following each other in a sequence. And there are two ways this happens. One way is somewhat random. Some thoughts just seem to come to mind unbidden. It's really hard not to think of anything. Try it. Or rather don't try it. If you try too hard, you're liable to wind up accidentally thinking of something. This is the familiar stream of consciousness. Let me try it right now:

red	kitten	bird	twee	truck	robust	egg	yogurt	white
	fairy	wings	grey	suit	Monk	eyebrow	case	

At first glance, the list looks arbitrary. But if we look closer, we can see some order to the chaos. Some of the words are about things that resemble each other. "Egg" and "yogurt" resemble each other insofar as they are white. Some words on the list are about things that are contiguous. They are always found together. "Fairy" and "wings." And some words are related causally. Birds tweet. That's what they do. Monk solves cases. That's what he does.

So there's a method to the madness even though I wasn't deliberately choosing what to think about. Hume recognized three methods to the madness of non-deliberative thought: resemblance, contiguity, and causation. A modern psychologist could probably tell you about more ways thoughts are related to each other. But what's important isn't the list of ways thoughts are related. What's important is that there are "gentle forces of attraction" at work in our minds that we don't have complete control over.[6] I assure you, I did not want to think of yogurt. It's just something that happens from time to time, particularly when I'm already thinking of things that are white. For Monk's sake, I'm just glad I didn't think of milk instead. These ways that thoughts are naturally attracted to each other turn out to be very important for the way we think and the success of our thinking.

The other way thoughts follow each other is with deliberation. I can bring any representation of the world to mind I like. I am free to think about a pink elephant, even if I am not naturally led by gentle forces of attraction between thoughts. There. I've just done it. I've thought of a pink elephant. I can rearrange my thoughts as well. I can go ahead and add a dinner jacket to my mental image of a pink elephant. So how does belief get into the picture? All we've done so far is describe some of the order and disorder in sequences of thoughts.

Heavy Thoughts

Well, remember, we said that beliefs are not just representations of the world. They are forceful-feeling representations of the world that have effects on our lives. What Hume has to explain is where this force comes from and what happens when opposing forces collide.

Some representations just come with that force because of the structure of their contents. Here's an example that would surely bother Monk. 'A bent antenna is not straight' ("Mr. Monk Gets

---

[6] See *Treatise,* Book I, Section IV.

Cabin Fever"). This isn't a thought we could be moved off of. Not being straight is part of what it is to be a bent antenna. If someone asks me whether a bent antenna could be straight, if I'm going to be honest, I have to say no. I might be mistaken about whether my own car antenna is currently bent or straight, but not about whether a bent antenna could be straight. If it's straight, it's not a bent antenna. And, actually, this idea is so forceful in my mind, that if I were going to lie, I'm not even sure what I'd say instead.

We can look at a number of such representations and make comparisons between them. We could represent lots of antennas, bent at different angles and mentally line them up in order of decreasing straightness (and increasing annoyance to Mr. Monk). This representation is of the most bent antenna, that representation is of the least bent, and so on. When we're doing that, we're engaging in a process of reasoning, the conclusion of which will feel certain. It *will* be certain too. It will be certain because the relationships between the structured contents just are what they are. The most bent antenna could not be the least bent, because of what it is. It will feel certain because relationships which *are* certain have an irresistible influence on my thoughts. I don't have the power to think that a bent antenna could be straight, not even for a moment.

One limitation on this process is that no matter how well we compare thoughts, this won't get us beliefs about anything except those thoughts. It won't get us out into the world. No amount of examining and being aware of the structure of the contents of my representations will tell me whether my car antenna is actually bent. That force has to come from somewhere else.

Obviously, some things I can just see or otherwise sense. For example, I can just run outside and inspect my car. Oh good, it's straight. Monk would be proud. And try as I might to see a pink elephant in a dinner jacket in front of me, my computer screen with this document open keeps getting in the way. My representation of the pink elephant that I don't see doesn't have much force, but my representation of these words on this page do.

Repetition

So there are at least two sources of force for beliefs: my senses (or other immediate perceptions) and the structure of the contents of my representations. Most beliefs, however, require something more. Monk's fear of the germs contaminating all hands but his own, remember, isn't a fear of germs he's actually seeing. Nor could he have concluded that germs are on anyone's hands just by thinking about what germs are. After all, just after Monk has used a wipe, his own hands are relatively germ free. The nature of germs does not by itself guarantee that anyone's hands will be covered in them. Yet, Monk believes in the germs and this belief generates a fear. Where does the force of that belief come from?

What Hume suggests is that the primary source of force for these kinds of beliefs is *repetition*.[7] I don't have to see the sun rise this morning to have the belief that it did. I have seen the sun rise before. In seeing it, I couldn't help but represent the world as having in it a glorious, rising sun. In fact, and this is important, *every* time I have gazed to the east in the morning and my view has been unobscured, I have seen the sun rising.

The force of my earlier experiences of sunrises gives some oomph to the sunrise of tomorrow that I am merely contemplating. Each sunrise I have seen in the past gives my representation, now, a tiny bit of oomph. All those tiny bits of oomph added together make it extremely difficult to think that the sun might not rise in the future. I can represent the world that way, but only fleetingly. And this representation doesn't cause me to do anything. Instead, I plan to live tomorrow in a world with a sun.

In my case, I have seen (barely!) enough sunrises to know that once again, today, it happened. The sun rose. I don't have, nor should I have, any doubts about this. Even a philosopher couldn't seriously doubt it. They might, for a moment, doubt it during a fit of philosophy while locked up in a musty office. (Don't let this happen to you!) But when the philosopher comes home, the day's thinking done, and settles in to watch an episode of Monk, even she does not doubt in the slightest that tomorrow the sun will rise.[8]

Of course, every day I see the sun, I believe that the sun I see that day is the exact same sun that I have seen every other day. But repetition doesn't require that. The gentle forces of resemblance, contiguity and causation are enough to get things going. The spider you saw under your bed on Tuesday is probably not the same spider you saw there on Wednesday. Still, the repeated seeing of

---

[7] This is a central doctrine of Hume's. For one of his cleanest expressions of it, see *Enquiry*, §36 of Section V, Part I.

[8] This echoes Hume's sentiments on backgammon in the concluding section of *Treatise*, Book I.

spiders under your bed gives you a belief about the next spider, the one you aren't seeing now. The spiders resemble each other closely enough to give oomph to your representing the space under your bed as containing spiders. They all spin webs. They all have eight legs. It's close enough. The more times you look under your bed to find a spider, the more you will believe that a spider is there now, even if you haven't looked.

As for myself, I don't see a spider under my bed every time I have to get something out from under it, thank goodness. But sometimes I do. I have had repeated experiences of both finding spiders under my bed and not finding them. Both kinds of experiences have an influence on my beliefs. Both have their proper influence on the representation of the world under my bed. Consequently, I kind of think there is probably a spider under there right now, but possibly there is not. But probably there is.

Sometimes most of the weight of experience falls on one side and we can still be wrong. When Adrian's childhood bully, Roderick Brody, hires Monk to find out if his wife, Marilyn, is cheating on him, Monk gleefully takes the case because Brody's suspicion is all he needs to form a belief that the wife is cheating. Monk acts on that belief, and takes the case, because he wants to humiliate the bully. "She's cheating on him . . . It has to be true, it's always true" ("Mr. Monk and the Bully"). In Monk's experience, whenever someone asks the question "Is she cheating on me," it turns out to be true. And so Monk believes it and acts accordingly. In this case, Monk's wrong. Marilyn was not cheating on Roderick. That can happen. Repeated experiences don't make us infallible, but they do determine many of our beliefs, at least according to Hume.

Repetition

But if Hume were right, why would I be terrified that the plane I am about to board will crash? I have seen and heard about planes landing safely over and over again. It's not just the vast majority. It's almost every commercial passenger plane that has ever taken off. With, and here's the rub, *some rare exceptions*. With most of the force lined up on the side of "this plane will safely land" and almost none on the side of "this plane will crash," why am I still afraid that the plane will crash? And why isn't that fear a small one, proportional to the tiny possibility of disaster?

Here's what happens. My mind dwells on those rare exceptions, particularly when I'm at the airport surrounded by the sights and sounds of air travel. I can think of nothing else, nothing but the plane I'm about to board coming apart in mid-air. And even though I'm not seeing or reading about an actual plane crash, and even though the greater number of experiences is on the side of the plane landing safely, I'm not paying attention to those safely landed planes. Their force isn't having the effect on me that they might and should, because I'm not even thinking about them. I'm stuck on planes crashing. If you keep repeating to yourself, "The plane is going to crash. The plane is going to crash. The plane is going to crash," eventually, because of the repetition, you will almost come to believe it. Unfortunately, while repetition of experiences has the most influence on our feelings, other kinds of repetition also have an influence. This is what trips up Monk.

One of Monk's characteristic behaviors is looking at all of the facts. We think of Monk as the kind of detective who examines all the evidence of a case in excruciating detail. This is a key tool in his devising cunning solutions. However, truth be told, Monk dwells on the negative. He is constantly searching out facts about things he would be afraid of and constantly obsessing about those infinitesimal possibilities of the occurrences of fearful events. Because Monk's attention is focused on the events he fears, his belief that these things will happen grows ever stronger and the fear of them ever greater. Often times, we see Monk lost in his own mind, unable to properly experience the world around him. When the homeless men enter Monk's apartment, all he can think about is the possibility of them leaving a biological mess on his floor ("Mr. Monk and the Miracle"). His gaze casts about, searching for places they might touch with their contaminated hands, step on with their muddy feet, or worse. None of these things are happening. None of them are things Monk has likely even seen happen in the past. However, all of his focus is on these possibilities.

On the face of things, it looks like if Hume's theory of belief were true, then Monk should believe that all the things he fears will really come to pass. But Monk shows at least some signs of not believing them. He often listens when others tell him that his actions are unreasonable. He works against his fears by seeing his psychologist. He even goes to a new psychologist when he hears word that alternative methods might be more effective at curing his obsessions ("Mr. Monk Gets Hypnotized").

The thing is, Monk is capable, from time to time, like the philosopher who exits her study, of stepping back and not focusing only on those unlikely events that generate his fears and attract his attention. Sometimes he might actively do this, like when he decides that he needs to see his psychologist right away. Sometimes the force of the many repeated instances of watching people drink milk without anything bad happening to them must exert itself even despite his greatest focus. At these times, reality comes crashing in, like the highway during my fantasy of the open road. And at least for a moment, Monk gets a glimpse of the world as it truly is, or at least acts as though he does. But like that, it's gone.

If he for an instant thinks of the small possibility of the feared thing happening, his mind can focus on nothing else. Even though the snake is not underfoot, it might as well be for Monk. There is no chance of fooling Monk with a bag empty of snake. Even if he saw the snake in the bag, Monk would not go back in the house without a healthy dose of coaxing. To him, the house is a snake house. To be feared.

Step Back

So, what can we, and Mr. Monk, do about this? What's the practical lesson here? Instead of concentrating hard on the worst possibilities, we can try to look at all of the possibilities, good and bad, that we face each day. Instead of feeding our fear with repeated thoughts, we can widen the scope of our view and come to a considered judgment which we can then act on.

Is this difficult? Just ask Monk. Since his wife died, tragically, his mind is constantly on worst-case scenarios. Feelings have a kind of inertia that can be hard to overcome. But, like Monk, we can do our best to act on our beliefs, and to fix our attention on all the possibilities around us, not just the worrisome ones. Of course, we don't all have a Natalie and a Captain Stottlemeyer to remind us of what we should be focusing on. Much of the time, we have to do it ourselves.

What really will happen if you get in front of the audience and make that big presentation? What will happen if you back out? How likely is the worst outcome? The best? We fear that the presentation will go poorly and maybe it will, but probably it won't be that bad. It's up to us to use our imagination in this way, to develop the right beliefs and act on them.

I'd like to think that Monk could do it too, that he could make it on his own, even though his fears and his tendency to focus on what he's afraid of are stronger than most. Now that *Monk*, the series, has come to an end, and Monk (tragically) doesn't have to entertain us anymore, he will finally be free to take the wider view. He can concentrate on all of the minutiae he encounters, the frightful and the inspiring alike, to his heart's content. Maybe someday, long after the final credits roll, he will even sit down, relax and slowly enjoy a tall, cool glass of milk.

He's the Guy

What Monk Is Made Of

4

Mr. Monk and the Virtuous Habit

LINDA LEVITT

As *Monk* began its fourth season in 2005, USA Network unveiled the "Characters Welcome" campaign. The tagline fits series on the network that feature protagonists like Adrian Monk, Gregory House, and Shawn Spencer: unique characters who defy social norms with their quirky, often socially-challenging behavior and their unparalleled brilliance. Viewers are accustomed to the idiosyncrasies that make Monk this kind of character: his insistence on using antibacterial wipes after shaking hands with strangers; his need to right anything out of order, from window blinds that are askew to a disorganized closet; and his lengthy list of fears that interfere with his professional and personal life. As Monk tells Captain Leland Stottlemeyer, "It goes: germs, needles, milk, death, snakes, mushrooms, heights, crowds, in that order."

Monk's obsessive-compulsive disorder plays out both painfully and humorously. His need for order and control can provide comedic moments, like when he sets a coaster under the saucer for a coffee cup, or cleans the kitchen of Lieutenant Adam Kirk while stopping by his house to ask him a few questions. He's socially awkward and damaged, but brilliant. Many who encounter Monk for the first time tend to dismiss him, placing him outside of social norms because of his unusual behavior and his inability to effectively relate to other people. Monk is judged and ostracized not only by strangers by also by police officers who watch his curious methods of investigation. Monk's anxiety and tension are palpable, and it's difficult for officers to reconcile his great intellect with the awkward mannerisms of the so-called "defective detective." Yet when Monk solves a crime, he typically earns the respect, if not the awe, of those who listen while he describes how a particular homicide was committed. That sense of awe only furthers Monk's outsider status, as it provides more evidence that Monk is simply not like other people.

Even Monk's relationships with those closest to him—his assistants Sharona Fleming and Natalie Teeger, as well as Stottlemeyer, his former partner on the force—are fraught with strangeness as they try to compensate for Monk's social shortcomings. There are a handful of exceptional circumstances in which people who meet Monk accept him at face value, leading to encounters that surprise both Monk and the audience. Sheriff Margie Butterfield is smitten with Monk in "Mr. Monk Visits a Farm," even after she's been briefed on Monk's OCD by Lt. Randy Disher. In "Mr. Monk and the Lady Next Door," Marge Johnson doesn't hesitate to befriend Monk, who is standing uncomfortably at an intersection, waiting for the "Walk" sign to light up, granting him permission to cross. After acknowledging that she herself is seen by the local police as "just a crazy old coot," she simply hooks arms with Monk and encourages him to "be a pirate" as they cross the street together. Marge does not judge Monk, as so many others do.

Monk's personal habits and his crime-solving techniques defy norms. He sees things no one else seems to see until he explains them, and solves crimes no one else can. Yet Monk is not only a quirky character, he is also a man of character, whose virtue and morals are at the center of who he is.

A Blessing and a Curse

Before his wife Trudy's murder, Monk's professional life as a police officer was one of character: a member of the force takes an oath and is expected to uphold ideals of virtue, integrity, and courage. Monk is ravaged by Trudy's death. He could not prevent it, he could not solve it, and his everyday life is completely undone in her absence. The conflict between who he was and who he has become plagues Monk, who finds himself unable to act instinctively as he once did. Monk is devastated when he allows a suspect to run past him near the beginning of "Mr. Monk Takes His Medicine"—an event that leads him to try medication to better manage his OCD (although the results are not what he hopes for).

Aristotle can lend insight into Monk's conflict and the resolution he desires. We live in an Aristotelian world: although Aristotle lived from 384 to 322 B.C.E., Aristotle still has a tremendous influence on our contemporary perspectives. He studied, taught, and wrote about everything from the natural sciences and physics to rhetoric and ethics. Like Monk, then, he knew something about everything. As Captain Stottlemeyer says of Monk, "He has an encyclopedic knowledge of the strangest, most arcane things" ("Mr. Monk Goes to the Carnival"). Monk, like Aristotle, is compelled to figure out how things work. He also has an extraordinary capacity to remember things, from the minutiae of everyday life to details of significant events. His memory, Monk says, is both a blessing and a curse. It is also both part of what makes him a character and part of what makes up his character.

Aristotle believed that individuals fundamentally want to find happiness and live a good life, and that we can find happiness through our virtuous character—the moral and ethical principles we establish for ourselves and live by. Aristotle believed that philosophical endeavor should be a common pursuit: don't we all want to understand what happens in the world, why it happens, and our place in it? Spending time thinking about how we conduct ourselves and live in concert with others is valuable because it is a path to improving our lives.

Aristotle's idea of happiness is not necessarily a state of joy but rather a fulfilled life in which you live up to your potential, which is the highest goal of being human. And what sets humans apart from other animals is our ability to reason, so it follows that reason is fundamental to living well. Reason also leads us to moral virtue: through reasoning, we come to understand what is right and good. Our virtues are revealed in our habits, as how we act in the world is a reflection of what we think. We develop these habits through experience, in two ways: first, careless acts can be instructive about future actions and we learn (hopefully) from our mistakes; and second, the more often we act virtuously—courageously, for example—the more accustomed we become to doing so. So the virtuous person, acting with practical wisdom, will act without harm to others or himself, and with goodwill in mind; and virtuous actions lead to virtuous habits, which leads to becoming a virtuous person.

The virtuous habit is also an expression of balance, finding a mean between excess and deficiency. With regard to relating to others, for example, Aristotle sees friendliness as the mean between being obsequious, which is excessive, and standoffishness, which demonstrates deficiency. As Monk works through his social awkwardness, finding the right mean is a particular challenge.

Doing Good and Being Good

For Aristotle, a person's character is reflected in both thought and action. Thinking virtuously must precede acting virtuously, but virtuous thought does not necessarily always result in virtuous action. Monk thinks virtuously, but his fears keep him from acting. Aristotle claims that it is immoral not to act when we know we should, whether in defense of someone who needs support or to right what we perceive as wrong. Monk has knowledge of virtue, he knows what is right, but his anxiety makes it difficult for him to take right action, even though he knows what he should do.

Monk's struggles between what his moral compass tells him and the phobias that keep him from acting create an emotional connection for the audience. These struggles also often create a good deal of the humor of the show. In the pilot episode, "Mr. Monk and the Candidate," Sharona is taken hostage by a suspect being pursued by Monk, Stottlemeyer, and other members of the police force. Monk knows he must follow the killer and try to save Sharona, but he must fight against his misgivings about descending into the germ-filled sewer. Rather than feeling angry or disappointed with Monk, the audience is able to have empathy for him. This is possible in part because the scene becomes comedic as Monk maneuvers down the ladder, trying to protect his hands from contact with germs, only to splash down into the filthy sewer.

Aristotle would see Monk's occasional inability to do what he knows is right as a sign of weakness of will—the Greek word is *akrasia*. His inability to act in accordance with his beliefs makes it difficult for Monk to think well of himself and enjoy his life, which would be the result of virtuous action. In Aristotelian terms, *akrasia* is a sign of unwillingness rather than a lack of ability, but it plays out as inaction regardless of its cause. Those who are close to Monk know that his inaction is rooted in fear and not lack of concern, and they don't view Monk as immoral, although *akrasia* is still a kind of failure—a man of character, we think, does the right thing, even when it is difficult, unpleasant, or filthy and germy.

Having virtue should lead us toward happiness, but throughout the series, virtue creates conflict for Monk. In "Mr. Monk and the

Bad Girlfriend," his suspicion that Captain Stottlemeyer's girlfriend has committed murder is the cause of a moral dilemma. Stottlemeyer should be the pinnacle of virtuous character—how could he be in love with a murderer? To suspect Linda Fusco is to call Leland's character into question. Monk confronts the captain when the evidence strongly suggests that, as Monk says, "she's the guy":

> **MONK:** This isn't easy for me.
> **STOTTLEMEYER:** (*raising his voice*) Oh really? Well, what is? You're talking about the woman I love, Monk.
> **MONK:** I know. I know.
> **STOTTLEMEYER:** I think I know what's going on here. You look at me and you can't stand it. I have what you want. The badge, a woman, a life . . .
> **MONK:** That's true.
> **STOTTLEMEYER:** This is not my problem, Monk, this is your problem. You deal with it.

Stottlemeyer angrily tells Monk that for old time's sake, he'll forget the incident ever happened. Yet even after Monk shows how Linda Fusco murdered her business partner and she is led away in handcuffs, Stottlemeyer doesn't apologize to Monk. An unspoken aspect of the relationship between these two men is that while they recognize each other's weaknesses, they also see each other as men of character. Stottlemeyer's apology would take something away from Monk. Although the badge, the woman, and a normal life are locked in Monk's past, to retract his statement would mean that Stottlemeyer believes Monk isn't capable of restoring his life, or his career. Getting his badge back would mean regaining both his virtue and his manhood, and would be public and institutional affirmation that he is a man of character.

What Appears to Be the Case, and What Others Overlook

The badge is a sign of character. A police officer's badge is a symbol of dedication, bravery, courage, and duty. When Monk lost his badge, he lost a core aspect of his identity, not only professionally but also personally. As the series begins, Monk is gingerly stepping back into his professional life by serving as a consultant. His reputation—for both his brilliant detective work and his OCD—precede him. In the opening scene of the pilot episode, Monk and Sharona are at a crime scene, the home of a woman who has been murdered. Monk is distracted, thinking he's left the stove turned on at home. Sharona pulls Monk aside and tells him, "Forget about the damn stove, okay? You are on a job here. You're a private consultant. . . . You've got to shut up. The department thinks you're nuts. You're never gonna get reinstated. You're never gonna get hired. We're both gonna be unemployed. Do you understand the importance of what I'm saying? Now, pull yourself together. Concentrate. You'll be brilliant. You're brilliant." Sharona plainly lays out the circumstances: Monk must control his OCD if he hopes to have members of the police department focus on his strengths rather than his shortcomings. She also reminds him of his virtue, encouraging him to focus on what he knows.

Monk's desire to be reinstated to the police force is mirrored by Lt. Randy Disher's crisis of confidence in "Mr. Monk Visits a Farm." After bungling an arrest, Randy's self-assurance is destroyed and he decides to resign, taking up residence on the farm he inherited from his uncle. Monk figures out how Randy's uncle was murdered, but Oates, the farmhand, convinces Monk to try to let Randy solve the case, knowing it will restore his confidence. Randy has been listening to motivational CDs while he sleeps, and in the early hours of the morning Monk turns off the CD player and tells a sleeping Randy how the murder occurred. The next morning, Randy calls the sheriff and, following Monk's typical scheme, lays out the story, beginning with Monk's trademark phrase, "Here's what happened." In a moment of doubt, Randy turns to Monk, who encourages him to continue. The suspect is arrested, and Randy returns to the police department, once again self-assured.

Randy's self-doubt relates to Aristotle's three artistic proofs in persuasive speaking: *ethos*, the appeal of the speaker's character; *pathos*, the emotional appeal to the audience; and *logos*, the rational appeal of the message. *Ethos* requires the speaker to have credibility, which Randy lacks. If the audience is skeptical about a speaker's trustworthiness or doubts his intentions, the speaker is less likely to have his message well received. We are far more willing to listen to—and believe—speakers we respect. We see Monk's *ethos* when it is more difficult for Randy to convince the sheriff of the suspect's guilt than it typically is for Monk. Monk doesn't have the badge, as Randy does, but he has earned his credibility through solving dozens of seemingly unsolvable murders.

Logos, or logical reasoning, is fundamental to Monk's detective work as well as his persuasive abilities. In "Mr. Monk and the Candidate," he runs through a series of assertions: the murderer was tall, he was a smoker, he waited in the victim's house, and he was looking for something, perhaps on the victim's computer. Somewhat surprised by Monk's statements, the officer on the scene asks for clarification:

> **LT. GITOMER:** I'm sure that you're right, but how do you know all that? I mean, about the computer . . .?
>
> **MONK:** It's patently obvious, isn't it? There are no prints on the keyboard, not even hers. Why? He used it, he wiped them clean.
>
> **LT. GITOMER:** Right, and you said that he was tall.
>
> **MONK:** The victim's short, maybe 5'4". Look at the chair. It's lowered almost all the way.
>
> **LT. GITOMER:** We've been here all morning and nobody even noticed that.

Monk's *logos* is often strongest when his reasoning enables him to see what others overlook, as is often the case.

Pathos is the third artistic proof, which Natalie uses to persuade Monk to support her decision to continue in her run for the school board despite attempts on her life ("Mr. Monk and the Election"). She explains that in the investigation following the death of her husband Mitch, a Navy pilot, he was accused of cowardice, and she feels she must be courageous to maintain her daughter's respect. Natalie appeals to Monk's sense of compassion as well as his belief that courage is a virtue.

Despite the credibility Monk earns from Stottlemeyer and Disher, his OCD and phobias still stand in the way of him rejoining the force. In "Mr. Monk Goes to the Carnival," Stottlemeyer testifies before the review board considering Monk's reinstatement. The captain has confidence in Monk's ability to be a good detective—to solve difficult crimes, to demonstrate the honor and loyalty expected of a member of the police force, and to be an exemplary citizen. But Stottlemeyer can't recommend Monk because he doesn't trust his ability to carry a gun and provide the necessary support for another armed officer. He doesn't doubt Monk, he doubts his illness. Although he's devastated by Stottlemeyer's decision, in later seasons of the series, Monk may begin to agree that he did do the right thing by not recommending him for reinstatement. Monk may not get his badge back, yet his work as a consultant and his interactions with other people improve his quality of life and begin to restore his sense of self. His actions are better aligned with his virtues, leading Monk toward a more fulfilled life. Being able to act without thinking, rather than being rendered unable to act by his fears, becomes more of a habit.

The Pleasure of His Company

While Monk learns how to contend with Trudy's death, her absence is a continual presence in his life. He cannot regain what he's lost, but he's found reason to go on with his life, difficult as it may be. In "Mr. Monk Goes to the Ballgame," Monk has a candid, intimate conversation with a professional baseball player, Scott Gregorio, who is mourning the murder of the woman he loved. Monk tells him, "When Trudy fell in love with me, I was a detective. I was on the street, breaking cases. So I keep working. I keep trying to be the man she loved. That's all you can do. Be the man she loved." Monk determines that Gregorio's lover was killed to distract him from his quest to break a season home run record. Monk and Sharona are in the locker room when the baseball player is interviewed after failing to break the record. Glancing over at Monk, Gregorio tells the reporters, "I met a man recently. He's become a good friend. He reminded me there are a lot more important things in life than baseball. What matters most are the people you love. Being true to them or their memory. That's the real ballgame. My friend isn't giving up on that, and neither am I."

For Gregorio to call Monk a good friend is an overstatement. He uses the term casually to describe the honesty he shared with Monk and the solace Monk provided. Yet the detective doesn't have friends, save for the close circle of those with whom he works. When Marge Johnson seeks out his friendship, Monk thinks there must be a catch, since no one would simply want to be his friend ("Mr. Monk and the Lady Next Door"). Not only is Monk a challenging companion, he also lacks the trust needed to develop strong interpersonal relationships.

Like Monk, Aristotle had few close friends and was difficult to get along with, as seen in his relationship with his teacher Plato, who he constantly disagreed with. Aristotle pursued his interest in friendship as part of his study of ethics. What brings people together, and why do we pursue friendship with certain people but not others? What can we gain, and what can we give? Aristotle believed that friendships form around one of three aspects: goodness, utility, or pleasure. In friendships based on goodness, we find virtue in another person and choose to spend time with them in order to exercise our virtues and theirs.

Monk's friendships are largely based on utility: what binds him to other people is the benefits each can gain from the relationship, rather than the pleasure to be found in each other's company. Friendship based on utility might seem contrived or lacking deep emotional connection, yet that doesn't detract from the value of such friendships.

Monk's relationship with Captain Stottlemeyer is grounded in utility: that Monk solves cases for the department serves them both. The department gets the arrest, and Monk develops a new career as a consultant and is able to regain his sense of self-worth. Early in the series, Monk's relationship with the captain is tenuous as best: Stottlemeyer finds Monk difficult to contend with and resents him solving cases the police department should be able to manage on its own. "Mr. Monk and the Three Pies" shows that the captain's friendship with Monk extends beyond utility. At the crime scene, Stottlemeyer is brusque and dismissive, trying to get Monk to leave since he hasn't been hired on the case. By the time the case is solved, the captain's perspective softens. The murder suspect, who lives next door to Monk's childhood home, has set the house on fire and Monk courageously saves his agoraphobic brother Ambrose from the blaze, leading him out of the house after years of being homebound. Stottlemeyer sees the love between the brothers, and sees the risk Monk is willing to take for another person. Monk is made a bit more human in that moment, and the captain sees his goodness and virtue.

Sharona aspires to a friendship with Monk based on pleasure, in which two people enjoy pursuing a common interest or activity. In "Mr. Monk and the Candidate," she tells her date that a sense of adventure—feeling like Lois Lane—is the primary benefit of working for Monk, but dealing with his phobias at times outweighs the pleasure she gains. Their relationship is also based on utility, as Monk needs Sharona in order to function in society. She is the intermediary between him and other people, facilitating his awkwardness and making it possible for him to do the work he does.

Sharona gains financially as well, as being Monk's nurse and assistant is her job.

Natalie, however, has a different relationship with Monk. While their friendship is primarily rooted in utility, there is a common sense of virtue shared between them. When Monk first offers Natalie a job, she declines. She accepts the offer after Monk chooses to save her daughter Julie's fish instead of grabbing a priceless, stolen moon rock when both are dropped by the suspect he is pursuing. Natalie says only one other man would do such a thing: her husband Mitch. She sees the goodness in Monk, and develops her friendship with him for the mutual pursuit of virtue made possible through their relationship.[1]

You Don't Have to Be Like Him to Like Him

Rhetoric and poetics are among Aristotle's significant philosophical interests and legacies. Aristotle believed theater was fundamentally about *catharsis*, the purification or emotional cleansing that we experience at the end of a drama. In order for catharsis to take place, the audience must have a connection with the characters in a performance. Our appreciation of a television series or film often comes from its characters and how we relate to them. We laugh when they laugh, we cry when they cry, and we cheer them on when they face challenges. Through identification, audience members can try on different identities as we imagine ourselves standing in the shoes of the characters we admire, as well as those we despise.

Jonathan Cohen maintains that there are four aspects to identification: sharing the character's feelings, sharing the character's perspective, sharing the character's goals, and losing your own sense of self while being absorbed by the plot.[2] Identification with Adrian Monk is more complicated than identification with other TV protagonists. It's difficult to share Monk's perspective. We may not readily relate to a man of such extraordinary intellect, yet Monk's social shortcomings make it possible for us to identify with him in

---

[1] See "Mr. Monk Makes Some Friends" for a different and more extended discussion of Aristotle's view of friendship.

[2] J. Cohen, "Defining Identification: A Theoretical Look at the Identification of Audiences with Media Characters," *Mass Communication and Society* 4:3 (2001), pp. 245–264.

spite of his uncommon brilliance. An intense sense of pathos is created for the audience as we watch Monk try to piece his life back together. In this context, Monk's unease and impatience are not only tolerated but enable the audience to feel affection for him.

There are times when Monk's lack of consideration poses a challenge for identification. He tends to be self-involved, as a result of both his phobias and logic that guide his actions in the world. For example, in "Mr. Monk on Wheels," Monk is unrelenting and rude toward Natalie, as he holds her responsible for his having been shot in the leg. His expectations for her help far exceed his usual demands, and he seems unaware of it. In scenarios like this, it's difficult for the audience to identify with Monk. Instead of feeling empathy toward him, we are more likely to feel empathy toward Natalie, who bears the brunt of Monk's anger and frustration.

Conversely, the conflict Monk experiences in "Mr. Monk's Other Brother" creates identification with and compassion for the detective. When Monk's half-brother, Jack Jr., escapes from prison and breaks into his apartment, he is faced with a moral dilemma: do obligations to the law outweigh obligations to family, especially when the family member in question is one without a close bond, and a criminal? But Jack Jr. comes looking for help, and it is precisely the kind of help only Monk can offer. More than providing him with a hideaway, Jack Jr. wants Monk to solve the murder of the prison's social worker, for which he is being framed. It's likely than many viewers have, to a lesser degree, faced similar circumstances. We can understand Monk's feelings as well as his motivations. Although harboring a fugitive is illegal and unethical, Monk wants to help his half-brother, despite his constant doubts about Jack's honesty. He grapples with understanding his familial relationships, which have not been easy: his father abandoned him, his mother was detached and controlling, and his wife was murdered. Throughout the series, Monk works to resolve his difficult past, trying to unlock doors toward a happier future.

In identifying with Monk, viewers wish for his wellbeing, that he can find happiness in his life. This might seem impossible. Monk himself doubts the possibility of contentment and is terrified when he sees a note in his file in Dr. Kroger's office that he reads as "No hope" ("Mr. Monk Gets a New Shrink"). The audience experiences pathos, fearing along with Monk that the psychiatrist thinks his patient is a hopeless case. When Monk finally has the opportunity to raise the issue, Dr. Kroger tells him, "I would never say that about anyone, especially about you." He recalls that he wrote "N. Hope," an abbreviation for New Hope, where Monk's father was born. Viewers who identify with Monk may feel relieved not only for him, but for themselves, with Dr. Kroger's assertion that there are no hopeless cases. Aristotle's work on character shows that there's hope for Monk, that it's possible for him to move from *akrasia* to a state of balance and contentment by acting virtuously.

Monk is a man of virtue, and his struggles to be virtuous are essential to the audience's appreciation of the series. The desire to live a fulfilled life by thinking and acting with virtue is part of the human condition. By watching Monk work through both his conflicts and his moments of contentment, viewers can reflect on their own ethical perspectives. The audience's identification with Monk can be ennobling: not only can we imagine ourselves as both clever and virtuous, we can also forgive ourselves for our foibles and shortcomings, as we forgive Monk for his. Through identification, we can see ourselves as characters with character.

5
Mr. Monk Makes Some Friends

MICHAEL DODGE

MR. MONK: Hey thanks. Thanks for killing me.
CAPTAIN STOTTLEMEYER: Hey, that's what friends are for.

—"Mr. Monk Is on the Run"

Here's the thing . . . what exactly is friendship? I feel fortunate to have the friends that I have, but I sometimes wonder what it really means to be a friend.

Luckily, I'm not alone. The perplexities of friendship have eluded many, despite earnest efforts to identify its true meaning. The nature of friendship has been the subject of discussion among philosophers for millennia, and to date no one has found a definitive explanation. But what Plato and Aristotle lacked, Adrian Monk makes up for in spades. Fans of *Monk* know that the Defective Detective always solves the case, and that nothing can evade him for long. Monk's obsessive-compulsive behavior makes him a prime candidate for solving the mystery of friendship. Simply put— he's the guy.

To understand Mr. Monk's perseverance and dedication to the people in his life is to truly understand the nature of friendship. We laugh at the agitation Monk's friends endure while dealing with the defective detective's quirks, but these oddities only serve to endear him further. Like Monk's deductive abilities, his friendship is unique and irreplaceable. Aristotle might ask whether Monk's friends attached themselves to him for his utility as a detective (and paying boss), or as an inherently valuable person. Montaigne might see Monk as the kind of friend so important that he's like a square tomato—delicious symmetrical perfection. Armed with only his mind ("it's a gift. . . and a curse") and an impeccable shirt (approved by Inspector #8, of course), Mr. Monk can help us answer our question.

It's true that Monk finds it difficult to accept friendship from those that offer it ("Mr. Monk and the Lady Next Door"), but his hesitation tells us a great deal about the vulnerability we feel in opening up to new friends. We could also ask if Monk's love for Trudy, and his dedication to her even after her death, is an example of the ultimate friendship ("Mr. Monk Meets Dale the Whale"). Monk's quirks make us wonder if his friendships are one-sided, or whether he's the ideal friend—a perfect 10. Monk's compulsions may irritate those around him, but his relationship with Natalie, Sharona, the Captain, and Randy reveal everything we need to know. The nature of friendship may be difficult to understand, but if we put Monk on the case, he'll figure it out. When he does, we'll put it in a baggie, label it, and hand him a wipe.

Monk Discovers Friendship—With a Little Help

With all the mess of the world to sort through, how would Monk go about solving the case of friendship? To help suss it out, Monk could turn to a number of philosophers who have discussed the subject. Using his trademarked "Zen Sherlock Holmes Thing," Monk would tell us that friendship is perhaps best understood as the product of three major components: mutual caring, intimacy, and shared activity.[1] Investigating friendship requires us to examine these three components by applying the wisdom of philosophers who have commented on the nature of friendship. The views of Plato, Aristotle, Seneca the Younger, Francis Bacon, and Michel de Montaigne, just to name a few, are helpful in understanding whether Monk's relationships with those around him are true friendships, or if they are something else entirely.

Philosophers or not, most people think of friendship as an intuitive thing. We think we know our friends are indeed friends because of how we interact. Monk is no different in that regard. Monk's obsessive compulsive disorder, along with his litany of phobias (312 of them, according to "Mr. Monk and the Daredevil," including heights, milk, dentists, germs, disorder, mud, and touch-

---

[1] Bennett Helm, "Friendship," *The Stanford Encyclopedia of Philosophy (Fall 2008 Edition)*, <http://plato.stanford.edu/archives/fall2008/entries/friendship>.

ing), may make it more difficult for him to connect with others, but he nevertheless manages to collect a good number of people he can justly name as friends. Indeed, his unique problems make him a prime candidate for the study of friendship—if Monk has a friend, then we can see more clearly what makes a relationship of that kind work than we could with the average person who claims to have numerous friends of varying importance.

The most obvious component of any friendship is mutual caring. I care about my friend for her sake, and she cares about me for my sake. I hope that my friend is in good health, that she is happy, and that she is successful in life. Ideally, my friend reciprocates those feelings. The most important thing here is that I care for my friend because of who she is, and not because of what she can do for me. She is a companion, not a simple acquaintance. Monk's friends show the same level of concern for him. As an example, when Sharona left Monk to go back to New Jersey, Monk was crippled by the loss, and when he finally came back to work, Stottlemeyer pulled him aside to tell Monk that he had been worried about him ("Mr. Monk and the Red Herring"). Monk shows the same concern when he worries for Stottlemeyer after hearing that the latter had been shot ("Mr. Monk Takes His Medicine").

Friendship, however, is more than simply caring for one another. It also matters how intimate one person is with the other—not in an erotic sense, but rather in the deeper sense of one who cares for another *more* than he would for a simple acquaintance. When Monk was placed on suicide watch after learning that his flaws were even worse than Harold Krenshaw's ("Mr. Monk and the Daredevil"), Natalie and Stottlemeyer took turns staying up with him all night. Their connection to Monk is so deep that they daren't leave him for fear of what he might do.

Intimacy is not always so forthcoming, however. Sometimes it needs to be developed. For example, when Natalie and Monk were involved in a traffic accident ("Mr. Monk Gets Stuck in Traffic"), Monk never asked how she was. Natalie had to wonder whether Monk would be there for her if she needed it, so she told Monk that "it's a two-way street, Mr. Monk. We have to be there for each other." Monk replied, "I'll be there." Later, when Natalie was hanging off of the back of the construction truck driven by the killer, Monk risked his life during a dangerous car chase to shoot the hydraulic lift of the truck and save Natalie. Natalie asked Monk, "You unbuckled your seatbelt?", to which Monk replied, "Two-way street."

Indeed, the intimacy of friendships allows us to behave in ways we may not have thought possible. For instance, Monk was able to overcome claustrophobia to help a friend in "Mr. Monk and the Magician." Realizing that his friend, the affably loquacious Kevin Dorfman, had been murdered by the magician, The Great Torini, Monk allowed himself to be placed into a cramped prop during a live magic performance. Monk was terrified of being closed up in such a small space—even before he was placed in a coffin and buried alive ("Mr. Monk vs. the Cobra"); an experience that would make anyone claustrophobic! Despite this, Monk went along with the stunt in order to gain evidence that the stage prop had been used to store heroin. This discovery was important because Dorfman had uncovered evidence that could have exposed the trafficking, and it provided the impetus for Torini's actions.

What about shared activities? One wonders how Monk's friends can be said to share anything with Monk at all, considering his case-solving methodology almost seems to be a one-man act. Additionally, his compulsions also appear to set him apart. Neither Stottlemeyer nor Sharona, for instance, brush with the Gertler 4000, vacuum their ceilings, or polish their light bulbs. However, people don't need to share every activity to be friends—they only need to share enough activities to become closer to one another. For Monk, this means solving case after case (over one hundred at this point) with the San Francisco Police Department, helping them see what they could not see on their own. Even more mundane tasks can help cement friendship, like helping Stottlemeyer wipe smudges off of his new car ("Mr. Monk and the Three Julies"), decorating a Christmas tree with Natalie and Julie ("Mr. Monk and the Secret Santa"), helping Natalie explain the nature of love to Julie ("Mr. Monk and the Birds and the Bees"), or even listening to angst-ridden music from the *Randy Disher Project*. These activities are done not because they *have* to be done, but because they are motivated, at least in part, by the desire to do something with one's friend in furtherance of that friendship.

"It's What Plato Called the Great Cosmic Swirly. There's No Escaping It."

Monk hit the nail on the head when he noted that there was no escaping Plato's cosmic swirly ("Mr. Monk and the Bully"). Among Plato's (428–328 B.C.E.) philosophical exploits was a study of friendship. In his dialogue *Lysis*, Plato uses Socrates, the great gadfly of Athens, as a tool to understand the nature of friendship. Socrates asks some young men to help him understand friendship, and after a multitude of questions have been answered, it appears that neither Socrates nor the men really know what friendship means. The men admit to having friends, but Socrates leads them further and further down the Great Cosmic Swirly.[2] But where Plato left off, Monk can pick up—with a little help from Aristotle (384–322 B.C.E.). Aristotle wrote extensively on the subject in his *Nicomachean Ethics* and the *Magna Moralia*. In fact, he considered friendship of such importance that he wrote that "without friends no one would choose to live, though he had all other goods."[3]

Here's what happened: Aristotle argued that there were three kinds of friendship: those of utility, of pleasure, and of virtue. A friendship of utility is one in which the people involved associate with one another because they get something out of the relationship. This is only a shallow form of friendship. When Monk was duped into believing that Hal Tucker wanted to be his friend ("Mr. Monk Makes a Friend"), he was unwittingly being used to cover up Hal's crimes. When the usefulness of Monk's friendship ceased, so too did the friendship itself. Contrasting Hal's duplicity, Natalie tells Monk that she's his friend. Monk, however, suspected an ulterior motive, and told Natalie that she was his friend only because he pays her. Natalie quickly corrected Monk, informing him that he doesn't pay her *that* much. Natalie is Monk's friend *in spite* of their work relationship—not because of it.

Friendships based on pleasure are defective for similar reasons. This kind of friendship is based on an ephemeral pleasure I get out of another person. It's like enjoying the company of the popular guy at work or college, and taking every opportunity to inform others that he's your friend, only to cease associating with him as his popularity wanes. If I associate with someone because he makes me laugh, so long as the pleasure I feel from the humor continues,

---

[2] "Well, Lysis and Menexenus, we have made ourselves rather ridiculous today, I, an old man, and you children. For our hearers here will carry away the report that though we conceive ourselves to be friends with each other—you see I class myself with you—we have not as yet been able to discover what we mean by a friend." Plato, "Lysis," in *Collected Dialogues* (Princeton University Press), p. 168.

[3] Aristotle, "Nicomachean Ethics," in *The Complete Works of Aristotle* (Princeton University Press), p. 1825.

so too does the "friendship." In a sense, this is a superficial relationship. If my friend ceases to make me laugh, I no longer get pleasure from the affiliation, and the friendship comes to its end. This is not to say that utility and pleasure are undesirable qualities in a friendship, but rather that utility and pleasure alone are insufficient for true friendship. Utility and pleasure friendships both suffer from the fault of basing their existence on what can be gained from another, rather than the equal exchange of virtue between the two individuals.

Aristotle's third kind of friendship is more lasting. Friendships of virtue are those that are based on the character of the people involved. As Artistotle put it,

> Perfect friendship is the friendship of men who are good, and alike in excellence . . . Now those who wish well to their friends for their sake are most truly friends; for they do this by reason of their own nature and not incidentally; therefore their friendship lasts as long as they are good—and excellence is an enduring thing. (p. 1827)

Monk is fortunate to have individuals of this sort in his life. Stottlemeyer, Sharona, Natalie, and Randy all care for Monk in this intimate way—the virtuous friendship. They care for Monk for his sake, both because of his excellence, and also because of their own. Another aspect of a virtuous friendship is that it subsumes, or includes, the effects of the other kinds of friendship. Monk can experience the utility and pleasure of having a friend like Stottlemeyer, and vice versa, since a virtuous friendship will be both useful and pleasurable in addition to being lasting. A virtuous friendship is intrinsically valuable, like the number 10, or a meal served with each item on its own plate—something that is important and good, not because it's useful for something else, but just for its own sake.

"That's Strange. Why Would He Need a Mirror on the Ceiling?"

Monk's lack of knowledge concerning man's lascivious pursuits notwithstanding ("Mr. Monk Meets the Playboy"), his curiosity serves to bring the concept of mirroring to the forefront. Aristotle was fond of this metaphor, and in fact argued that the true friend is a mirror by which one may judge oneself. Since we are all biased and chained by our own passions and opinions of ourselves, we turn to our friends to reflect to us the right character by which we should live our lives. Just as our friends were attracted to us because they found us to have an excellence of character, they also serve to remind us of the good within us when we might otherwise go astray.

This is the highest function of the virtuous friendship—friends mirroring one another in order to help each other maintain a state of good. Friends are so important to living an ethical life that one cannot maintain excellence without them, "for the friend is, as we assert, a second self."[4] For a person to know himself, he must have friendship, since without a friend, one cannot see into the mirror, and therefore cannot see the truth. The philosopher Francis Bacon held a similar belief, noting that impartiality requires the good counsel of friends.[5] Bacon recognized another benefit to having a friend as a second self—"that this communicating of a man's self to his friend works two contrary effects; for it redoubleth joys, and it cutteth griefs in halves" (p. 71). And who wouldn't benefit from a little redoubling and cutting from time to time?

Not only do friends share activities with one another, they also share happiness, and alleviate each other's pain. This effect might seem obvious, but it deserves reflection, and it serves as a potent factor in forming and sustaining friendship. Monk benefited from this on many occasions. Both Sharona and Natalie kept Monk stable in situations where otherwise he would have lost control. They were able to comfort him whenever he mourned Trudy, and they celebrated his success with him after every case he solved.

Building on Aristotle's foundation, the Stoic philosopher Seneca the Younger (who is still pretty old—4 B.C.E.–65 C.E.) also examined the nature of friendship. Like most Stoics, Seneca was concerned with living an ethical, self-sufficient existence. Stoicism is a philosophy of life intended to lead a person to an independent, fulfilled state in life where one obtains the status of a sage, or wise man. Such a man is perfectly content, like Monk in a sterile computer

---

[4] Aristotle, "Magna Moralia," in *The Complete Works of Aristotle* (Princeton University Press), p. 1920.

[5] "And certain it is, that the light that a man receiveth by counsel from another is dryer and purer than that which cometh from his own understanding and judgment, which is ever infused and drenched in his affections and customs." Francis Bacon, "Of Friendship," in *Friendship* (Albert and Scott, 1890), p. 73.

"clean room" ("Mr. Monk and the Garbage Strike"). Seneca reflected on the concept of friendship as an exercise in conforming oneself to the Stoic lifestyle. He shares some of Aristotle's views, but disagrees strongly on others. He agrees, for instance, that friendship cannot be formed with the goal of gaining something for oneself:

> Anyone thinking of his own interests and seeking out friendship with this in view is making a great mistake . . . a person adopted as a friend for the sake of his usefulness will be cultivated only so long as he is useful.[6]

Hal Tucker was one such "friend," cultivating Monk to his own ends. Even Marci Maven, Monk's perennially obsessed fan, expressed her disdain for him once the pleasure of being with him soured ("Mr. Monk and His Biggest Fan," although, it seems, she regained her obsession with Monk by the time "Mr. Monk's 100th Case" rolled around). Seneca also agreed that the virtuous friend is absolutely trustworthy. He argued nothing should be held back from a friend—the friend will be loyal if treated as such. However, Seneca also warned that it is crucial to judge a man before making him your friend.

> Think for a long time whether or not you should admit a given person to your friendship. But when you have decided to do so, welcome him with heart and soul, and speak as unreservedly with him as you would with yourself. (p. 35)

She may not have realized it, but Natalie followed Seneca's advice when she first met Monk. Originally, she employed Monk's help in investigating why burglars had twice invaded her home ("Mr. Monk and the Red Herring"). It seemed odd that both men had been preoccupied with Julie Teeger's fish tank. Monk agreed to help (after offering her a job as his assistant), and discovered that by a curious set of circumstances, a highly valuable moon rock had been placed in the fish tank. After the episode's antagonist manages to steal the moon rock (along with the fish), Monk pursues him, eventually catching up just in time to see the fish and the rock spill to the ground. Despite his aversion to touching a fish, Monk saved it, rather than the rock, because he knew how important it

---

[6] Seneca, *Letters from a Stoic* (Penguin, 2004), pp. 49–50.

was to Julie. This had a profound impact on Natalie, who told Julie that only one other man would have saved the fish instead of securing a rock worth millions—her father. After judging the quality of Monk's character, Natalie then accepted the job as his assistant, and the rest is history.

Seneca differed from Aristotle in that where Aristotle thought friendship was essential to a virtuous life, Seneca believed a person needs only himself to be content. However, Seneca was far from advocating a life without friendship. He argued that there is pleasure in finding and keeping friends. Friendship should be pursued for better or for worse, and one should not look for friendship only when there is no chance of bad things happening. In this sense, friendship is a gift, and a curse. Seneca also noted that friendship is something that is worthy of pursuit for its own sake, and that making friends is a skill that can be improved by effort, much as a sculptor improves his art by the act of sculpting. Though a man does not need friends to be happy, neither does he wish to be without them.

Bread and Butter

Though Monk would benefit from consulting the wisdom of the ancients, he may find a better fit with the philosophy of Michel de Montaigne (1533–1592). A statesman and thinker of the Renaissance, Montaigne is best known for popularizing the essay as a form of writing. In fact, Montaigne contributed to the study of friendship through his essay, "On Friendship." For Montaigne, true friendship is a powerful, deep, and abiding force. He thought that true friendship was so rare that fate creates it only once every few centuries. Like Aristotle and Seneca, Montaigne also believed that friendship based on pleasure or profit is inferior to the real thing. True friends become so intimate that it is difficult for them to tell where one begins and the other ends.[7] Of all of the friendships in

---

[7] "In the friendship in which I am talking about, souls are mingled and confounded in so universal a blending that they efface the seam which joins them together so that it cannot be found. If you press me to say why I loved him, I feel that it cannot be expressed except by replying: 'Because it was him: because it was me'. For the perfect friendship which I am talking about is indivisible: each gives himself so entirely to his friend that he has nothing left to share with another." Michel de Montaigne, *On Friendship* (Penguin), pp. 9–10, 15.

Monk, only one comes close to the depth Montaigne described—Monk's love for Trudy. Monk's one passion (beyond that of a germ-free world) is his devotion to Trudy. Even years after her death, Monk still mourns her. He wears his wedding ring, and often stares at her pictures. For Monk, Trudy was his second self. She was his mirror, and he judged his life by the reflection he saw in her face. When Monk was buried alive, suffocating in a coffin, it was the image of Trudy that comforted him, and she guided him to make a decision that he knew was right (giving up Trudy's office to help pay for Natalie's expenses). Monk loved her so much that he had nothing left to give to another, even though he has tried ("Mr. Monk Falls in Love").

Before Trudy succumbed to her injuries from the bomb that destroyed her car, she uttered the words "bread and butter." Monk tells us that whenever he and Trudy had to part ways, even if only briefly, she would say bread and butter. She meant that they belonged together, and that they could never be separated for long. When she spoke those last words, she was telling Monk that they had to let go for a while, but that they would be together again eventually. This was more powerful than any love, because it went beyond simple passion, and it connected Monk and Trudy as if they were one person.

It's Time for the Other Walkie-Talkie

Monk once told Dr. Kroger that Jack Monk, Adrian's father, had given his son a walkie-talkie for Christmas ("Mr. Monk and the Man Who Shot Santa"). When Kroger started to say how fun those could be, Monk sadly noted that his father had given him only one walkie-talkie, since Monk had no friends. I think it's time for Monk to get another one, as it's obvious he has many friends now.

It's obvious because the things he does for the people around him are things that one would only do for a friend. When Randy's gambling addiction landed him in serious debt with a Vegas casino, for instance, Monk risked becoming addicted himself in order to save his friend ("Mr. Monk Goes to Vegas"). Monk has looked out for Stottlemeyer on several occasions as well, helping him with marriage problems ("Mr. Monk and the Captain's Wife"), and risking their friendship by devastating Stottlemeyer with the news that the woman he loved was a murderer ("Mr. Monk and the Bad Girlfriend"). Monk's virtue makes him a natural, if unconventional, friend. His courage, tenacity, and eccentric compulsions have carved out a unique set of people who help Monk make it through the day. His complicated life demonstrates the fascinating ability of friendship to overcome great adversity, and this is exactly why Monk, with the help of a philosopher here or there, is the perfect detective to help us understand the nature of friendship. If anyone can figure it out, he can. Simply put—He's the guy.

6

Mr. Monk Takes On the *Übermensch*

COURTLAND LEWIS

> In his own way, given what he had to deal with, he was the bravest
> man I ever knew. He was a yardstick for me, of both detection and
> character.
>
> —CAPTAIN LELAND STOTTLEMEYER ("Mr. Monk Goes to Mexico")

It might not be obvious at first glance, but Mr. Monk, whom we lov-
ingly refer to as the "Defective Detective," is the greatest kind of
human there can ever be! We see examples of such greatness from
the very first season all the way through to the final season. For
instance, in "Mr. Monk Goes to the Carnival" we see Mr. Monk
climb a Ferris wheel in order to save Sharona from a murderer; and
in "Mr. Monk Is Someone Else" we see Mr. Monk go undercover,
stand up to Captain Stottlemeyer, and risk his life to singlehandedly
entrap a mob boss, in order to save a complete stranger.

Viewers are left wondering: how can Monk overcome all of his
many fears and psychoses to do such things? Granted, it takes a lot
for Mr. Monk to perform such tasks, but in both of these examples
we see Monk rising above what is expected of him as a character
and what we would expect from most "normal" people. The type
of "rising above" that Mr. Monk exhibits here and throughout the
series has a philosophical corollary in Friedrich Nietzsche's concept
of the '*Übermensch*' (often translated as 'Overman' or sometimes as
'Superman').

The '*Übermensch*' is a type of person who has transgressed, or
risen above, the common state of being human to become the greatest kind of man there can be, and Mr. Monk "takes on" this idea in
two ways. First, he takes on the *Übermensch* by representing it, just

as Tony Shalhoub takes on the characteristics of Mr. Monk to portray him on TV. In this first way, Monk serves as an example of the
Übermensch and how one should think of Nietzsche's concept of
human nature.

Second, Monk takes on the *Übermensch* by challenging what
kind of person is an '*Übermensch*' and the way in which we typically think about superior and inferior people. In other words, this
second way challenges our own understanding of human nature.

What does the character Monk represent? This isn't an easy
question to answer, for different readers will inevitably have different interpretations. It's true that there are certain things about
Monk's character that we should all be able to agree upon: he is a
brilliant detective, he has certain phobias and psychoses that hin-
der his ability to interact with others in a "normal" way, and among
other things, he has an undying love for his deceased wife Trudy.

All of these things, however, are merely facts about Mr. Monk.
Though we may agree on these facts, we may still disagree about
what exactly Monk is supposed to represent. For some, Monk represents the power of love, for others he represents an outsider who
struggles to survive in an uncaring, and oftentimes cruel world.
These different explanations of what Monk's character represents
makes the character of Monk dynamic, and allows viewers to
engage with Monk on a personal level by using him to facilitate the
exploration of their own hopes, fears, loves, desires, and anxieties.

In other words, we see a little of Monk in ourselves. So, any
attempt to categorize what Monk represents will always fall short
of completeness, because all explanations are related to our own
particular perspectives. However, we should not let this shortcom-
ing inhibit our exploration, for it is this type of exploration that
makes philosophy so much fun.

One way of answering the question about what Mr. Monk represents is to see what Monk teaches us about human nature.
Human nature is a popular topic for both contemporary and
ancient storytellers, and the topic of much debate among philosophers. The latter typically use calm objective reasoning to explore
the issue; while the former typically use such things as film, television, and stage to stir up the subjective passions and intuitions of
viewers. The Greek philosopher Plato (427–348 B.C.E.) thought that
the poetry of storytellers could never produce any knowledge
about human nature because of its reliance on the passions of individuals, which change as quickly as Monk solves crime. Plato main-

tained that only calm, rational, philosophical reflection can lead to any real understanding of human nature. Friedrich Nietzsche, on the other hand, sees the passions of individuals as being crucial to understanding human nature, and any attempt to explain human nature without the passions is doomed to fail. Since what Monk represents is tied directly to the particular perspectives of each individual, understanding what Mr. Monk tells us about human nature requires a more Nietzschean approach.

The Choices Mr. Monk Makes

To understand Nietzsche's *Übermensch*, we first need to know a little about existentialism. Jean Paul Sartre (1905–1980) coined the term 'existentialism' to describe the idea that your choices determine who you are and what sort of meaning your life has. For Sartre, humans are born without an essence or meaning, and it is not until we begin making choices that our essence, meaning, and purpose comes into being. In other words, as Sartre describes it, 'existentialism' is the claim that "existence precedes essence."

Sartre's claim might not seem that radical at first, but it is. Take, for instance, the wipes that Mr. Monk is always using. Even though they can be used for a variety of unintended purposes, they were created with a specific purpose in mind. Some inventor had the idea for portable little pieces of paper or cloth that are capable of killing germs and preventing disease, and then took the time and energy to create such a thing. Sartre says of such artifacts that their essence is defined by a creator prior to their creation, and therefore their essence precedes their existence. Stated differently, the essence of what it means to be a wipe existed in the mind of a creator before it actually existed as a physical wipe. The wipe, and any other artifact, has its meaning determined by its creator and it can never rise above this predetermined meaning.

Humans, as opposed to created artifacts like wipes, exist prior to having an essence. For Sartre, humans are not created by a God with any specific purpose in mind, and because of that, humans must determine their own essence. They do so by making choices, and it is these choices that fill one's life with meaning and determine what the essence of each particular person is. Monk, for example, found himself in a situation where the love of his life and the one person who seemed to understand him was brutally murdered. This experience caused Monk to mentally break down, and for several years he was unable to make any choices. Eventually, however, Monk imbued his life with meaning by choosing to find out who was responsible for Trudy's death. His life, now, is driven by and guided by his desire to find Trudy's murderers, and living a well-ordered life helps him achieve this. Even though he is motivated by the goals just mentioned, his life is still ultimately determined by the choices he makes. Monk chooses to clean his home, sanitize himself after touching others, straighten things, and ensure that things are balanced and numerically even. These are not simply side-effects of his obsessive compulsive disorder, for we see he chooses to overcome his "disorder" all of the time. For instance, he chooses to keep his coffee table at an angle because it reminds him of Trudy ("Mr. Monk and the Very, Very Old Man"); when he tries to make friends Monk is surprisingly capable of "dirtying" his house and "hanging-out" ("Mr. Monk Makes a Friend"); and he chooses (with some persuasion) to drink water from a stream in the woods when he is lost ("Mr. Monk Gets Cabin Fever").

The entirety of Mr. Monk's choices combine to create the essence of the character called Monk, and as a result, we know who Monk is. Of course, in Monk's case the reader will have to suspend reality to some degree, for the character of Monk was created in the minds of Andy Breckman and David Hoberman. Even so, Tony Shalhoub, and countless writers and directors, have made several decisions over the years that make Monk a unique individual.[1] Also, watching TV itself is a suspension of reality, and while watching it we don't see Monk as a creation of a few individuals; rather we see Monk as a real person, who faces many difficult decisions, and *chooses* to engage the world in which he lives in his own unique way. We see Monk as a real person, one whose essence is determined by the choices he makes.

"I've Been Smokin' THE TRUTH, *MAN!*"

Even though Nietzsche lived and wrote before Sartre was even born, he is considered an early existentialist. He is an existentialist because of the importance he places on how choices determine the

---

[1] For a fascinating discussion of the dynamic relationship between actor and character, take a look at Leonard Nimoy's *I Am Spock*.

meaning of each individual's life. Like many existentialists, Nietzsche does not exactly rely on arguments. Instead of fancy arguments he uses aphorisms: short, concise statements meant to convey a thought-provoking idea. The following three passages are good examples of Nietzsche's aphorisms:[2]

> The errors of great men are venerable because they are more fruitful than the truths of little men.
>
> *Shedding one's skin.* The snake that cannot shed its skin perishes. So do the spirits who are prevented from changing their opinions; they cease to be spirit.
>
> Do you want to walk along? Or walk ahead? Or walk by yourself? One must know *what* one wants and *that* one wants.

These aphorisms are open to different interpretations, but even so, there is something in them that is intuitively truthful, and it is because in his aphorisms Nietzsche tells us he strove to "say in ten sentences what everyone else says in a book—what everyone else *does not* say in a book."[3] With Nietzsche, he often achieves his goal, but he sometimes achieves it at the price of consistency. What the reader of Nietzsche quickly finds out is that strict logical consistency is not one of his major concerns, and therefore, the reader must learn to engage the material subjectively by filling in gaps and interpreting how the material is to be understood and applied to the reader's life.

The presence of inconsistencies should not bother the reader, for we enjoy seeing the same sort of inconsistencies in Mr. Monk. Mr. Monk requires everything be straight and in its place, yet he refuses to straighten his coffee table. These sorts of things draw us to Monk and make us want to see and know more. By trying to understand Mr. Monk a little better, we indirectly challenge how we see others who are different, which indirectly challenges our own understanding of human nature. This more Nietzschean way of stirring up personal passions about human nature is a key feature of storytelling, and it's a more fruitful way of engaging viewers because it's complex—just like real life.

---

[2] All of these passages can be found in *The Portable Nietzsche*, edited by Walter Kaufmann, pp. 30, 92, 472.

[3] Friedrich Nietzsche, *Twilight of the Idols*, "Expeditions of the Untimely Man."

One of Nietzsche's greatest commands (and an inconsistent one at that) is that one must become what one is.[4] What does it mean to tell us to become something that we already are? Inconsistencies aside, this command is at the heart of Nietzsche's existentialism, for it commands us to make decisions about who we want to be, even though our choices are limited by the outside forces that try to corral us into to being something else, like society, morals, and physical impediments. But all this really shows is that, like Mr. Monk, we can be raised in a less-than-perfect home, where our father left, our mother died, and where our brother has his own set of crippling phobias; yet, our life is still shaped by the decisions we make: like going to school, dating and marrying, joining the police force, and becoming a private investigator. A simple look back at Mr. Monk's life shows us that he had a lot to rise above, and that so far, he has been successful because of the choices he made.

Next, for Nietzsche, man is simply a tightrope between beast and *Übermensch*. In other words, man is a transition and must be passed over and left behind. What Nietzsche means by this is simply that most humans get caught up in the morality, values, and desires of the day without ever challenging whether or not such things should be accepted. Nietzsche maintains that we must challenge all of these things in order to achieve our full potential. Achieving this potential means that we become more than human, we become super-human. The type of life that the vast majority of people live doesn't meet Nietzsche's standards of what it takes to be an *Übermensch*. Instead, most people belong to the herd. The herd is the Court of Public Opinion: it is the mass of unthinking followers of trends, public figures, and fads. The herd is made up of common humans and must be transgressed in order to achieve the full potential of human greatness: the *Übermensch*. Nietzsche's claim is that there is a type of human existence that is superior to common human existence, and this superior existence is one of freedom from the values, thoughts, and desires of the masses, who merely function according to a herd mentality.

To achieve this freedom, we must reject all received values about what is right and wrong, institute our own value system, and then hold ourselves accountable for living according to those values. This is a major task, and only a few people have ever achieved such a state, according to Nietzsche. For Nietzsche, however, this

---

[4] Nietzsche, *Ecce Homo*, "Why I Am So Clever."

reevaluation of values is necessary for becoming the *Übermensch*, and from watching *Monk* it is apparent that Mr. Monk is successful at achieving this task.

It's a Bird! It's a Plane! No, It's Mr. Monk!

Unlike most of us, Mr. Monk has this super-human ability to achieve what Nietzsche prescribes. Mr. Monk's behavior exemplifies a person who is able to set his own values and then follow them. Here are three examples.

- First, he has insane standards of cleanliness: he flosses his teeth hourly ("Mr. Monk Flunks Traffic School," in Natalie's blog), and he places used tissues in baggies within baggies ("Mr. Monk Stays in Bed").

- Second, Mr. Monk has incredible mental abilities: he remembers everything that ever happens, and he is the greatest detective since Sherlock Holmes.

- Third, Mr. Monk is relentless in his search for finding truth, both in the case of Trudy's death and for all other crimes.

All of these examples, and the many more that are not mentioned, show that Monk has a super-human ability to set values for himself and then hold himself to those values.

Of course, being able to set one's morals and values, and being able to abide by them, produces the side-effect of being separated from others, which is another component of being an *Übermensch*. This separation causes the *Übermensch* to become a "true" individual, who stands alone in relation to the masses. Monk renounces the ways of "normal" society in order to live in a world that is well-ordered, well-maintained, and truthful. He detests the ways of the world, because they are cluttered, dirty, and full of deceit.[5] Monk is guided by his own set of standards, and because of this, he sets himself apart from the rest of society as "the new, the unique, the incomparable."[6] Monk recognizes that he is different than most

---

[5] See the chapters "Mr. Monk Meets Alexander the Great" and "Mr. Monk and the Bodhisattva Ideal" for other, closely-related interpretations of the kinds of claims about value and meaning implied by Monk's constant striving for order, and how it separates him from others.

[6] Nietzsche, *The Gay Science*.

people and even takes pride in it. In "Mr. Monk and His Biggest Fan," after Natalie says, "After all, you're only human," Monk replies, "Hey, there's no need for name-calling." Monk sticks out like a kangaroo in a dinner jacket no matter what the situation or place, and this is due to his living according to vastly different standards than everyone else.

This separation is a key aspect of being an *Übermensch*, but the way in which Mr. Monk separates himself from others also challenges us to rethink our understanding of human nature and what it means to be an *Übermensch*. Most of the characters on the show see Monk as inferior, but as we all know, he is superior in many ways—and in ways that are more important than the ways in which he is inferior! The superiority that Mr. Monk has, however, has nothing to do with any physical domination, which has been the classic way of representing the *Übermensch*.

Can Mr. Monk Really Be the '*Übermensch*'?

Nietzsche claims that individuals like Julius Caesar, Leonardo da Vinci, and Jesus of Nazareth are examples of *Übermenschen*, so any comparison of Mr. Monk with the *Übermensch* must address the fact that Monk seems to be that odd man out on this list. The fact that Monk has not ruled a powerful nation, been a great inventor or painter,[7] or served as the cornerstone of a religion should not dissuade the reader from accepting Monk as a modern-day representation of the *Übermensch*. But it does challenge this interpretation.

A cursory look at the character Monk implies that he is dysfunctional. However, the more we watch, and the more we get to know Monk, the more we see that he is a highly complex character who doesn't easily fit the description "dysfunctional." In fact, Mr. Monk is highly functional—just not in the same way that everyone else is. He solves incredibly difficult criminal cases, maintains a personal regiment of cleanliness and orderliness that most of us would fail at, and though he seems to be plagued by the fear of almost everything, he is typically able to rise above all of these fears—at least when he wants to.

All of the above features suggest that Monk is a superior type of human being: the *Übermensch*. Now, the idea that Monk is

---

[6] Arguably, Monk might be considered a great painter; see "Mr. Monk Paints His Masterpiece."

"superior" might strike some readers as odd, especially since society typically paints people with phobias and psychoses as "broken." What is more, most of the characters on *Monk* see or act as though Monk is inferior—except with regard to his reasoning, perception, and memory. *Monk* shows viewers every week, however, that these preconceived notions of human nature and what it means to be superior are mistaken. To get a better sense of this, let's look at the relationship between Mr. Monk and Captain Leland Stottlemeyer.

Monk is an obsessive compulsive, phobia-ridden detective that never forgets anything and crushes the hopes of all criminals that have the misfortune of having him on their cases. Captain Leland Stottlemeyer is a stressed-out, can't-win-for-losing captain of the San Francisco police department, who is divorced, aided by the incompetent (but lovable) Lt. Randy Disher, and is totally dependent on Monk to solve San Francisco's toughest crimes. Of course, there are other characters like Natalie Teeger, Dr. Kroger, Dr. Bell, Sharona, and the always-present-in-spirit Trudy, and each of these relationships have their own quirks, but there is an important connection between Monk and Stottlemeyer that deserves special attention.

Beginning with Stottlemeyer, we can see there is a strong physical resemblance between him and Nietzsche. In the face, they look almost identical: they both have large moustaches that cover most of their mouths, they have intense eyes, and both have a well-defined forehead. In fact, if one were trying to describe what Nietzsche looks like, one could easily say that he looks like Captain Stottlemeyer. From the character traits pointed out above, however, it's obvious that Stottlemeyer can't represent the *Übermensch*, because his life is in such disarray: he seems to be completely lacking in the strengths that the *Übermensch* and Monk both share.

So, why is there a character that so resembles Nietzsche physically but is so dissimilar philosophically? Ignoring the fact that it is probably pure coincidence—facts aren't always the most interesting aspects of things—the only reasonable answer is that the relationship between the inferior Stottlemeyer and the superior Monk suggests a new understanding of what it means to be an *Übermensch*. Stottlemeyer is supposed to be superior. He is the quintessential man: he is successful as Captain of the San Francisco Police Department, he is strong, has power, and even gets to carry a gun, which gives him the ability in certain circumstances to decide whether a person lives or dies. However, when we compare Stottlemeyer with Mr. Monk, we see that Stottlemeyer isn't as superior and Monk isn't as inferior as might first appear. Stottlemeyer even admits this in "Mr. Monk Goes to Mexico" when he says, "He was a yardstick for me, of both detection and character." What we see is that Stottlemeyer is the quintessential man for the herd, and the herd is more concerned with following orders than challenging themselves to become something greater than what they are.

Monk is supposed to be inferior; he is the "defective detective" who requires the constant help of others to survive in the "jungle out there." But to viewers it's obvious that Monk is the superior one. He isn't in charge of anyone, except *maybe* Natalie, he lacks physical prowess, and he doesn't carry a gun. Even with these "shortcomings" he is the one who has set himself apart from the herd to become superior in his reasoning skills, personal habits, values, powers of observation, and ability to remember. If it were not for Mr. Monk's help, Stottlemeyer's career would be less-than-forgettable. Monk is the superior person who solves the crimes, holds himself to the values that he himself has prescribed, refuses to give up on finding Trudy's killer, and continually overcomes his fears and phobias. These are the things that set Monk apart from the herd and from Stottlemeyer, and they are what make him an *Übermensch*.

Once we look at the comparison of Monk and Stottlemeyer we see that Monk is not only the *Übermensch*, but he also challenges us to rethink who can be an *Übermensch* and what the *Übermensch* should look like. The stereotypical portrayal of the *Übermensch*, as usually seen in sci-fi films, is a man who is buff, vicious, cunning, and mean, but Mr. Monk shows us that this portrayal is inaccurate. Monk shows us that the *Übermensch* can take form in all sorts of individuals, like himself, who has risen above the base nature of humanity, lives a life dedicated to truth, is kind and gentle, and lives by his on set of values. One doesn't need to conquer, kill, or destroy; rather one can fight for truth and justice, and a world that is a little cleaner, and still be an *Übermensch*.

Mr. Monk's Greatness

With all of this said, Mr. Monk still has room for improvement. He still has feelings of revenge, as seen in "Mr. Monk and the Bully," he still can be duped by false prophets, as in "Mr. Monk Joins a

Cult," and he sometimes seems ashamed of who he is, which are all signs of being all-too-human. But nowhere did Nietzsche say that the *Übermensch* had to be perfect. Transgressing the tightrope of humanity is a "dangerous going-across, a dangerous wayfaring, a dangerous looking-back, a dangerous shuddering and staying still."[8] One must risk everything in order to achieve this greatness. Mr. Monk certainly risks it all when he ventures out into the dangerous world, and he has lost nearly everything in the process. However, these trials and tribulations have merely made him harden his resolve to rise above the imperfect world in which he finds himself, which is exactly what Nietzsche meant when he said, "What does not kill me makes me stronger."[9]

Mr. Monk sets himself apart from the masses in his own unique way. While the herd is busy playing games, living falsely, committing crime, and trying to oppress others, Mr. Monk rises above such features of being all-too-human and lives a life as an *Übermensch*, in search of truth. It's this dedication to truth, and the values he sets for himself, that make Mr. Monk a shining example of the *Übermensch*.

Though we may not envy Monk and his quirky ways, we admire his strength and achievement, and there is a poetic beauty to the character and how he acts. From his undying love to the Zen-Sherlock-Holmes-thing, Mr. Monk touches a part of each viewer's heart in ways that we least expect. Though Monk's character challenges the way we think, it is a representation of the *Übermensch* that we can all relate to and sympathize with.

---

[7] Nietzsche, *Thus Spoke Zarathustra: First Part.*
[8] Nietzsche, *Twilight of the Idols.*

Unless I'm Wrong, and I'm Not...

Monk's Logic

7

Mr. Monk Isn't Himself

DANIEL P. MALLOY

There's only one Adrian Monk.

—Captain Stottlemeyer ("Mr. Monk Goes to Mexico")

Who is Adrian Monk? For any fan of *Monk*, the answer to this question is obvious enough. Adrian Monk is a former San Francisco homicide detective now working as an outside consultant as a result of the breakdown he suffered in the wake of the death of his wife Trudy. Mr. Monk suffers from obsessive-compulsive disorder and a long list of phobias including, but not limited to, fears of heights, flying, spiders, germs, frogs, and milk. This all seems distinctive enough, although we could go further in our description: Mr. Monk is this tall, weighs this much, bears a striking resemblance to actor Tony Shalhoub, dresses like so, behaves in this way, is associated with these people.

But some of these characteristics are more important than others. The description of the defective detective only becomes philosophically interesting when we start removing characteristics. For instance, suppose Monk forgets who he is—if he starts answering to the name Jerry and acts like he is a roofer, is he still Monk? Or suppose he overcomes all of his phobias, starts overlooking details at crime scenes, loses interest in solving cases, and refers to himself as "the Monk"—is he still Monk then? These scenarios, drawn from episodes of the show, all point to the philosophical problem of personal identity.

The problem of personal identity asks, "What makes Monk, Monk?" Which of Monk's characteristics is most important to making him who he is? The answer to this question is of tremendous importance for not just Monk, but for all of us. Life plans, responsibility for our actions, hopes and dreams for the future all depend on the idea that we are the same persons over time.

If I'm not the same person today as I was yesterday, then what I did yesterday doesn't matter to me today! If I robbed a bank yesterday, or had won some award, that would mean nothing to me today unless I am still the same person. Similarly, if the person I am tomorrow is not the same person I am today, then I don't have to worry about the consequences of my actions. I can go out on a massive bender without worrying about a hangover or waking up in an unpleasant place, like a jail cell, because the person who experiences those unpleasant consequences won't be me.

So what makes Monk Monk? Some say it is his physical characteristics—that guy is Monk because he looks like Monk. But he didn't always look like that, and probably won't in the future. More technically, we could say that Monk is Monk because he occupies the same body as Monk always has, but there are problems here too. Others claim that it is the memories that make the man. Monk is Monk because he remembers being Monk and remembers the things that have happened to Monk. But what if Monk loses his memory? If we accept the memory theory, then when Monk gets amnesia, he's no longer Monk. Still others argue that character and characteristic behaviors are the keys to personal identity. But then "the Monk" is not Monk in spite of looking like Monk and having his memories. Still others have argued that personal identity is simple and unassayable.

Mr. Monk Shares His Body

The common-sense response to the problem of personal identity is to fall back on bodily identity. Monk today is the same as Monk yesterday because they share the same body. There's something intuitively satisfying about this theory. It's simple and straightforward. This response seems particularly appropriate for Monk, given his concern for the integrity of his body. For example, Monk's reason for refusing medications that may help him suppress his neuroses is that he cannot stand the idea of "things" being inside him ("Mr. Monk Takes His Medicine"). Many of Monk's other quirks also point to a concern for the integrity of his body—his fear of germs, for instance. In spite of the appeal of the theory of bodily identity, it has some flaws.

A common problem with many theories of personal identity is the duplication problem. That is, most of these theories do not rule out the possibility of two distinct bodies having the same identity. Part of the appeal of the bodily identity theory is that it does seem to rule this out. But it doesn't. To see why, look at what happened the time when Mr. Monk briefly had a double.

In "Mr. Monk and the Actor," an actor played by Stanley Tucci studies Monk's habits and motivations in order to portray him in a TV movie. The actor in question, David Ruskin, is a method actor and is famous for becoming too involved in his roles. After playing an alcoholic, he checked into rehab—despite the fact that he never drank. This obsession with accuracy could be a dangerous thing in any case, but in Monk's case . . . well, just watch the episode, if you haven't already. For us, the interesting aspect of "Mr. Monk and the Actor" is the actor's desire to become Monk. Just because Ruskin looks like Monk, talks like Monk, and does the things Monk would do does not make Ruskin into Monk. So, we'd probably want to say that Monk's appearance and actions do not make him who he is, and it makes some sense to say that this is because, no matter how good a job Ruskin does, he still has his own body, and Monk has his, and they are different humans!

Suppose Ruskin took this desire as far as he could. He's pretty obsessive, after all. (Another thing he has in common with Monk!) Suppose he decided that in order to properly play Monk he had to inhabit Monk's body. Suppose he somehow had his brain transplanted into Monk's body—would he then be Monk? Of course not. And yet, in addition to thinking he's Monk and acting like Monk, the actor would have (most of) Monk's body! But still, he would not be Monk.

This objection to the bodily identity theory is easily answered: the actor in Monk's body removed an important part of that body. Bodily identity theory doesn't require that the body remain completely the same over time—just the important parts. Monk can get his hair cut without becoming a different person. He could likewise lose body parts and remain the same old Monk—Monk minus an arm or a leg would still me Monk. Even a heart transplant wouldn't alter Monk's identity. When, for instance, Monk's eyes are changed by the solvent in "Mr. Monk Can't See a Thing," robbing him of his sight, he remains the same Monk. But remove the *brain* and you remove the "Monkness" of Monk. So, bodily identity theory is really brain identity theory. As long as the brain remains untouched, Monk will be Monk. If our actor friend transplanted Monk's brain into his own body, then it would still be Monk just walking around in David Ruskin's body, and probably quite upset and unsettled about the whole thing.

But do we need the whole brain? Suppose it were possible to remove *part* of Monk's brain and replace it with the same part of Ruskin's brain. We could see why one might want to do this: Ruskin wants to know it's like to be Monk. Part of that experience would be having Monk's neuroses and his detecting abilities. So, we leave the parts of Monk's brain responsible for these alone, but remove the parts that process short- and long-term memories. Those parts we replace with the same parts from Ruskin's brain, so that when we reverse the procedure, Ruskin will remember inhabiting Monk's body. Now, Ruskin possesses most of Monk's body as well as a good portion of his brain: is he Monk? Nope. He's still Ruskin in Monk's body. Monk is now in Ruskin's body, or possibly resting comfortably in a vat in some mad scientist's lab.

One Body, Two Monks

Leaving Monk's brain alone doesn't guarantee Monk's identity either. As far back as John Locke (1632–1704), philosophers have speculated about the possibility of having two or more distinct persons inhabiting the same body. Locke says that consciousness is what makes a person. So, we can have two or more people inhabiting a single body, as long as each consciousness is separate. Whatever my body does when I'm asleep has nothing to do with me because I'm not conscious of it.

For us, this can be illustrated by recalling the time when Mr. Monk took his medicine ("Mr. Monk Takes His Medicine"). The result was a total transformation of Monk's personality. Monk became "the Monk." The Monk was everything Mr. Monk wasn't, but thought he wanted to be. Where Monk was timid, the Monk was reckless. Where Monk was careful, the Monk was careless. Anyone dealing with the Monk would swear that he was *not* Adrian Monk. Sharona even asks Monk at the close of the episode, "Are you, you?" implying that the Monk was, in fact, not Monk. If that's the case, then the theory of bodily identity has a problem. The Monk and Monk shared the same body *and* the same brain—so there needs to be some other or additional criterion of personal identity. So, given this example, it seems as if bodily identity cannot explain personal identity!

There are two possible objections to this use of this example that could defend bodily identity theory. The first says that while Monk acted differently while on his medication, he was still Monk. This seems valid, until we think about Sharona. Sharona did not treat the Monk the way she treated Monk. Nor did she hold Monk responsible for the way the Monk acted. And, of course, whatever criterion of personal identity we settle on, it will have to connect it to responsibility; an important part of what it means to be the same person over time is to be responsible for all the actions performed by that person. Since Monk isn't responsible for the actions of the Monk, it follows that he isn't the same person.

A second, more tenuous objection would hold that Monk's medication so altered his brain chemistry that, while it is true that Monk and the Monk were not the same person, this is not a problem for bodily identity theory because they were also not really inhabiting the same body! While this sounds like an attractive explanation in some ways, interpreting bodily identity in such a strict sense would make it virtually impossible to maintain a personal identity for more than a few minutes. Every time someone's brain chemistry changed in a significant way, there would be a new person. Would Monk angry be a completely different person from Monk sad?

One thing our consideration of bodily identity theory has pointed to is the importance of the brain in determining identity. Now the question becomes, what makes the brain so special? Monk's brain is more important to being Monk than his hair or his face or his hands, but why? The answer would have to be connected to some function of the brain, something the brain does that no other part of the body can do. There are many such functions performed by the brain, but there is only one that is closely connected to identity: memory.

Mr. Monk Loses Himself

After we have given up on bodily identity as the sole criterion for personal identity, the next theory that presents itself is the memory theory. According to this theory, Monk is Monk so long as he retains Monk's memories. This theory was first proposed by John Locke in his *Essay Concerning Human Understanding*. Locke says, "as far as this consciousness can be extended backward to any past action or thought, so far reaches the identity of that *person*; it is the same *self* now as then."[1] This theory seems even more apt for Monk than bodily identity theory, and more apropos for Monk than for the rest of us. After all, unlike Monk, most of us have huge gaps in our experiential memories. Experiential memories are distinguished from other kinds of memories, and it is only experiential memories that are tied to personal identity.

For instance, the memory I have of writing this chapter is experiential—I remember being there, before the keyboard, trying to think of how to explain things. But the memory I have of the theories of personal identity is not experiential. That is, it's not something that I've experienced in the same way that I experience eating breakfast in the morning or talking with my friends. Other sorts of memories are what we might call informational memories. It doesn't matter how many different people know about theories of personal identity—everyone on Earth could have the same information, and it wouldn't make them the same person. But if someone else remembered writing this chapter, then we would have a problem deciding which of us was me.

Now, for most of us, there are gaps in our experiential memories. How many people can recall what they had for lunch on this day five years ago? Or which pair of socks they were wearing when they first watched *Monk*? I couldn't, and I don't know anyone else who could either. Except Monk. Monk remembers everything. Monk can even remember his own birth, according to one of his sessions with Dr. Kroger ("Mr. Monk and the Naked Man").

The gaps in experiential memories that most of us have present some problems for Locke's theory. For example, look at what happened in "Mr. Monk Bumps His Head." In this episode, in spite of his excellent memory, the titular bump causes Mr. Monk to suffer amnesia. It doesn't help matters that Monk is in a strange place, disconnected from his friends and usual surroundings. Under the influence of one of the townspeople, Cora, Monk adopts the identity of "Jerry," a roofer. Although some aspects of this new identity don't make much sense—like why he is a roofer, since he is afraid of heights—Monk accepts it. "Jerry" begins to settle in to life as a small town roofer and part-time detective. According to Locke, "Jerry" is *not* Monk. Although he looks like Monk, has the same

---

[1] John Locke, *An Essay Concerning Human Understanding*, p. 302.

body as Monk, acts like Monk, and even has the same neuroses and fears as Monk, Jerry is a different person. So, when Monk's friends turn up and inform him that he is Monk, they are wrong. Jerry's Jerry, and Monk is Monk.

Perhaps this doesn't present a problem. We saw when we talked about the difference between Monk and the Monk, it's perfectly possible for two identities to share a body. But what about when there is no other identity? What happens when Monk simply forgets? If Locke is right, then Monk is not Monk when he forgets. Now, it's rare for Monk to forget anything, but he has been known to black out from time to time. In "Mr. Monk and the Rapper," for instance, Monk blacks out completely during his first meeting with Murderous. Monk keeps talking, answering questions, even accepting a job, but afterwards has no clear recollection of the meeting or remembers the meeting inaccurately. He thinks he declined the job. He even "remembers" Murderous and his crew taking the bad news very well.

So, we ask Locke, who accepted the job? It wasn't Monk, since he doesn't remember. In a situation like this, Locke would have us make finer distinctions, such as a distinction between Monk fully aware and Monk blacked out. Is Monk-fully-aware the same person as Monk-blacked-out? As Locke said, "if the same Socrates, waking and sleeping do not partake of the same *consciousness*, Socrates waking and sleeping, is not the same person."[2] But, if that's true, then we can't hold Monk responsible for what he did or said when he blacked out. So, in this case, Monk-blacked-out was hired to do a job and didn't do it. Monk-fully-aware did the job, but wasn't entitled to be paid for it, since he wasn't hired for it.

Locke's theory has had its share of detractors. Such is the life of a philosopher. Among these detractors, one of the most famous is Thomas Reid (1710–1796). In his essay, "Of Mr. Locke's Account of Our Personal Identity," Reid argues that we can't accept Locke's theory because it leads to contradictions. Reid offers this scenario: imagine a man at three stages of life. First, as a child he scrapes his knee. Then, as an adult, he is wounded in battle. Then, as an old man, he falls and breaks his hip. The injuries are not important—the memories are. The old man remembers being wounded in battle, but not the knee scrape. The adult wounded in battle

---

[2] *An Essay Concerning Human Understanding*, p. 308.

remembers the knee scrape. This means that the old man both is and is not the man who was wounded in battle. He's the same man, because he remembers being wounded, but he is not the same because he does not remember what the wounded man remembered. To illustrate Reid's argument using Monk, let's go back to our old friend Jerry. Jerry is not Monk because he doesn't remember being Monk. Later, after Monk has regained his memory, he seems to recall being Monk and being Jerry. That would mean that Monk at the end of the episode is Jerry and isn't Jerry. That's not possible—you either are someone, or you are not!

Mr. Monk Acts Strangely

There have been some attempts to answer Reid's objections by reformulating Locke's theory. Among the current attempts is the theory of *psychological continuity*, which is based partially on Locke and partially on Reid's contemporary David Hume (1711–1776). This is connected to memory, but not quite as stringent a criterion. It would allow, for instance, that Jerry is more or less the same person as Monk because he has many of the same characteristics and because he knows he's missing his memory.

When Mr. Monk lost his memory, he retained some key characteristics of his Monkness. Jerry may not have known about Monk's life, but he shared most of Monk's quirks, phobias, and skills. Let's not forget: Jerry the acrophobic roofer solved a murder. According to psychological continuity theory, this would be enough for us to say that Monk and Jerry were at least somewhat the same person. That phrase, "at least somewhat" points to one of the features of the theory that both allows it to overcome the defects of other theories but also makes it difficult for most of us to accept. Psychological continuity does not demand a permanence of identity. Instead, starting with Hume's insights in *A Treatise on Human Nature*, it accepts that Monk today is only more or less the same as Monk yesterday, and not quite the same as Monk last week, but still more similar to Monk last year than anyone else would be. In other words, psychological continuity theory allows for degrees of identity. Or, rather, says that personal identity is never a matter of exact similarity, but *always* is a matter of degrees.

Hume's theory is based on his criticisms of the idea of personal identity. In his *Treatise of Human Nature*, Hume searches for the basis of the idea of personal identity and doesn't find it. He says, "when I enter most intimately into what I call *myself*, I always stumble upon some particular perception or other, of heat or cold, light or shade, love or hatred, pain or pleasure. I never can catch *myself*."[3] Hume goes on to describe the self as "a kind of theatre, where several perceptions successively make their appearance; pass, re-pass, glide away, and mingle in an infinite variety of postures and situations."[4] So there is no identity properly speaking. Instead, there's a succession of what some have called "person-states" that are more or less closely related to each other, depending on how many other person-states there are between them. I'm closer to the person I was yesterday than I am to the one I was last year because there are fewer person-states separating the former than the latter.

There are a few objections to this theory, one of which we've seen before. The first objection is the problem of duplication. Take the actor again: at the climax of the episode, our thespian friend is acting more like Monk from a few years prior than Monk is. The actor is convinced that this episode's "the guy" is, in fact, the guy who killed Trudy. He is out to exact Monk's revenge. Monk talks him down. If we accept psychological continuity theory then the actor is, at that moment, Monk from several years prior. And Monk is someone else altogether. Allowing for degrees also allows for duplication, and one Monk is quite enough.

Mr. Monk Is Suggestible

We needn't go so far to pose problems for psychological continuity theory, however. We only have to ask one question: at what point does Monk cease to be the same person he once was? How much difference between Monk today and Monk yesterday is enough for us to declare that they are not the same? Several episodes help us illustrate this point. In "Mr. Monk Is at Your Service," for instance, the defective detective goes undercover as the new butler for Paul Buchanan. His mission is to gather evidence proving that the master of the house killed his parents. Instead, Monk gets so wrapped up in his new role that he ceases to work on the case altogether. The point is that in this case,

---

[3] David Hume, *A Treatise on Human Nature*, p. 180.
[4] *A Treatise of Human Nature*, 180.

Monk's behavior changes only slightly, but in a significant way. His attention to detail and even his phobias (some of them) serve him well in his new identity. But his sense of justice disappears entirely. So, is the butler still Monk in disguise? A psychological continuity theorist would have to say "sort of."

And maybe they'd be right. People act differently in different situations, and different jobs call for different virtues. As a detective, Monk needs his sense of justice. As a butler, he needs loyalty more. So, let's look at a situation where the degree of change is much greater. In "Mr. Monk Joins a Cult," Mr. Monk, well, joins a cult. Thanks to what Stottlemeyer calls his "suggestibility," when Monk goes undercover in a cult he quickly falls under the sway of the cult's leader, "Father," or Ralph Roberts (Howie Mandel). This brings about a complete change in Monk. He doesn't care about the case, or his friends, or his life, or even Trudy. Strangest of all, Monk feels . . . happy. So, with this complete change of character, Monk in the cult is *not* the same person as Monk in everyday life. That means that when his friends 'deprogram' him they are, in a way, committing murder.

And so, the psychological continuity theory doesn't work because it rejects from the outset precisely what we've been looking for: a criterion of permanent personal identity that can explain how it is that we are the same people even though we undergo change. Think about all the different adventures where Monk doesn't act quite like himself: "Mr. Monk Goes to the Office," "Mr. Monk Takes Manhattan," "Mr. Monk and the Employee of the Month," "Mr. Monk and the Kid," "Mr. Monk Makes a Friend," "Mr. Monk Paints His Masterpiece," "Mr. Monk Gets Hypnotized," and "Mr. Monk and the Lady Next Door" all display a Mr. Monk who is not quite Mr. Monk, but of course the main character is always Monk, and of course he is always the same Monk who was the main character in the episode before, and in the episode to follow. But neither memory nor bodily identity theories have been able to explain exactly why. We're faced with a situation analogous to one Monk occasionally finds himself in: knowing who committed the crime and why, but having difficulty working out the how. We know personal identities persist over time. The Monk we see in the final season of the show *is* the same person we saw in the first season. But *how* Monk *stays* Monk is difficult to pin down.

Mr. Monk Is Mr. Monk

Thomas Reid,[5] Bishop Joseph Butler,[6] and others contend that personal identity is just one of those things. That is, they argue that since personal identity is a fact, and since we can't seem to explain it in other terms, it must be "simple and unassayable," meaning that personal identity is known solely through experiencing it and can't be reduced to some other experience, like bodily integrity or the continuity of memory. It's no more possible to understand what makes Monk Monk, beyond the fact that he just *is* Monk than it is to explain a color wheel to someone who's been blind since birth.

The notion that personal identity is simple and unassayable doesn't satisfy me. Why not? Given the problems we saw in the likely suspects, it seems likely neither of these is "the theory." But a philosopher is a lot like a detective. We share the same goal: to discover the truth. Both employ similar methods: gathering facts and formulating theories, always remaining open to new evidence. From this perspective, the trouble with the simple and unassayable theory is that it refuses to formulate an actual theory of personal identity. The entire theory comes down to "People are who they are." This is the equivalent of Mr. Monk arriving at a crime scene, examining the body of a victim who was clearly murdered, and pronouncing that she "just died." People don't "just die." Nor are people just who they are.

I have presented some theories of personal identity, but there are others. It is not enough to declare personal identity "simple"— that is just a way of ignoring the problem. And this is not a problem we can ignore. Our identities, our senses of self are too important to be ignored. Additionally, this problem is too bound to questions of responsibility for us to bypass it. If Monk today is not Monk yesterday, then he doesn't get credit for solving that case. And if I'm not the same me that I was yesterday, then I don't get credit for writing this chapter—someone else did it.

---

[5] Thomas Reid, "Of Identity," in *Personal Identity*, edited by John Perry (Berkeley: University of California Press, 1975), pp. 107–112.

[6] Joseph Butler, "Of Personal Identity," in *Personal Identity*, pp. 99–105.

8

Mr. Monk and the Contradiction

NICOLAS MICHAUD

"It's a blessing… and a curse." Adrian Monk has made this statement many times throughout the course of his investigations. When you think about it literally, though, his statement is rather confusing—how can something be a blessing and a curse at the same time?

This statement of Monk's seems to violate at least one major logical rule: the Law of Non-Contradiction. In logic, the Law of Non-Contradiction is usually considered the strongest of all our logical rules. This law tells us that something cannot be both true and false at the same time. Monk uses rules like these to solve crimes. But, he also seems to ignore this rule when it comes into conflict with his own intuitions. It seems to me, given Monk's obsessive nature, that he should be unwilling to accept any contradiction, whatsoever.

Perhaps his statement that "it is a blessing and a curse" is not a direct contradiction; perhaps this confusing statement just provides us with an insight into Monk's conflicted nature. But, even if we give him the benefit of the doubt in that case, there are definitely times when Monk is willing to assert that someone is "the guy" even when this really imply a direct contradiction! So, there are times when Monk will admit that it is impossible and, yet, still argue that the impossible must be true.

In "Mr. Monk Goes Back to School" Monk asserts that the science teacher, Derek Philby, is "the guy" responsible for the murder of an English teacher. This seems to be impossible, however, because Philby was proctoring a standardized test during the time of the murder! When Monk asserts that Philby committed the crime

95

Sharona tells him "he can't be in two places at once. It's impossible" and Monk replies "I know it's impossible, but he's the guy." How can a mind like Monk's flout the impossible? This seems to imply that Monk is okay with the belief that Philby could both proctor the exam and not proctor it at the same time. How can he be so relaxed about a contradiction? Is it because he is confident that the seeming contradiction will resolve itself? Or is it because he knows something that we don't: namely, that the Law of Non-Contradiction is false?

First, I should do a bit more to explain this logical law. The Law of Non-Contradiction tells us that if something is true then it also cannot be false at the same time. In fact, Monk uses this logical rule and others regularly to solve crimes. For example, in the very first episode, he argues that an assumed suicide is actually a homicide. He makes the point by arguing that had it been a suicide—by taking an overdose of pills—the victim would have had a glass of water nearby, and there was no glass of water so it was not a suicide. If we want to formalize his argument, we could simply do this:

1. **If someone purposefully overdoses on pills, then they use of glass of water.**

2. **There was no glass of water used in this case.**

3. **Therefore, in this case, the person did not purposefully overdose.**

This seems like a pretty good conclusion given the evidence. But if we don't follow the Law of Non-Contradiction, then, #2 can be both true and false—there was no glass of water used *and there was a glass of water used*. It would seem that this possibility would throw all our logic out the window. Given that he recognizes the strength of the logic above, is it possible that such an analytic mind, like Monk's, could allow for a contradiction is his reasoning? It seems as if the writers who create Monk may have allowed for a grave error. Monk's very ability to solve crimes requires that he adhere to the Law of Non-Contradiction. And, given Monk's obsessive qualities, when Monk adheres to something he really sticks to it, there should be no allowance for even the mildest of contradictory statements.

It's Not a Contradiction, It's Just Messy

Let's consider Monk's statement regarding his abilities being a blessing and a curse. Well, first, let's be sure that Monk's statement is really a contradiction. A genuine contradiction requires that a statement *both* be true *and* false. Generally, when something is a blessing, it is not a curse. In fact, if "blessing" means anything, it seems like "not a curse" would be logically implied by any reasonable definition of "blessing," and similarly "not a blessing" seems a necessary implication of any reasonable definition of "curse." If something is a blessing and a curse it seems that what we are saying is that it is both a blessing *and* not a blessing. Recall, though that a violation of the Law of Non-Contradiction requires that the opposing statements be true at the same time. It maybe that his gift is both a blessing and a curse, but just at different times.

Perhaps all that he means is that sometimes it is a blessing, like when solving crimes, but at other times it is a curse, like when he's thirsty, and there is no Sierra Springs to be found. This may well be the case. And it seems as if this is a good and simple answer. The problem that I have with it is that his claim about it being a blessing and a curse is a general one. Monk seems to be stating that his gift is an actual blessing, not just "useful sometimes." If my intuition is correct and we don't read more deeply into what Monk really means, it seems as if he's saying that his ability are a blessing and a curse in its entirety or else he would say "it is a blessing *sometimes*, and a curse *sometimes*." Given Monk's obsessive nature it's likely that if he meant the second statement he would say so, for the sake of clarity.

Well, the other answer that we can try out is that a blessing need not be *only* a blessing. In other words, perhaps being a blessing doesn't mean that something is not a curse. So Monk isn't saying that his abilities are a blessing and not a blessing; he is just saying it is a blessing and, also, a curse. Maybe it is similar to a flavor that is both sweet and sour. But, does the word "blessing" really work like that? When we say "blessing" we mean "really good" and when we say "curse" we mean "really bad." So how can something both be "really good" and "really bad?" The very definition of "good" means "not bad." So, we are then stuck with the same problem. His abilities are both very good and very bad at the same time.

Either of the two answers presented seem possible, though I think the first answer is the cleanest. To be honest, I am not sure which is correct. Monk is probably just being unclear, which not only solves this problem, but also may solve many other problems in philosophy. Monk's statement, alone, that his abilities are a blessing and a curse is not enough to prove that Monk actually believes in true contradictions. Instead, he's likely just not being particularly clear when dealing with a possible contradiction. This may not be surprising, though. Think about how often Monk just follows his own intuitions and just "knows" that someone is "the guy." Monk can't give us more, or be clearer in those instances, but he knows the truth and he sticks with it.

This leads to the bigger problem. Monk is very willing to assert that something is true well before he has the evidence to prove it. Now, we may argue that his amazing brain has simply solved the crime before he can articulate it, but this seems unlikely as, often, he doesn't have all of the information necessary to solve the crime until later in the case. Even worse, Monk is willing to entertain contradictions until the case is solved, as if it is no problem at all.

In "Mr. Monk and the Astronaut," Monk's sure that a man who was in space during the murder committed the crime. The Astronaut, Steve Wagner, has an airtight alibi—he was in space during the time of the murder. Nevertheless, upon meeting Wagner, Monk is convinced that Wagner is the guy. Despite the fact that a man who is in space cannot also commit a murder here on Earth at the same time, Monk holds fast to his belief that Wagner is guilty. This seems impossible and a clear violation of the Law of Non-Contradiction! How can the murderer be on Earth committing murder and in space—not on Earth—at the same time?

Despite this impossibility, Monk ignores the contradiction and maintains, that Wagner's the guy. His intuitions alone seem to be enough for him to ignore the most fundamental law of logic. This is real problem. Imagine what would be happen if the rest of us were so willing to ignore the Law of Non-Contradiction just because of our intuitions. For example, imagine that you have an intuition that your lover was having a sex affair with a particular person last Thursday. However, much to your annoyance, your lover points out that he or she was with you all day last Thursday. Should you be willing to ignore the fact that it is impossible for your lover to do both just because of your intuition? How is what Monk does any better?

I'll concede this much to Monk: unlike us, Mr. Monk has always been right, and the contradictions are always resolved. His intuitions prove to be correct and the contradictions prove to be only contradictions in appearance. Even so, isn't he a bit too laid back about contradictions, even if he believes they will resolve? I don't know how comfortable I am with a crime solver who is willing to ignore the law that prevents him from believing I committed a crime in Paris when I was in London all day!

Take Two Contradictions and Call Your Analyst in the Morning

How can Monk deal with this, then? It seems that he has allowed a contradiction into his way of thinking. This is very problematic as his whole life revolves around following logical rules. If he is willing to ignore a contradiction solely due to his intuitions, how do we know that others aren't similarly true? Let your imagination go wild—blessings can be not blessings, murderers can be in space and not in space, the truth can be false, circles can be triangles, murder can be bad and not bad, and so on! So how do we stop it? Surly there cannot be true contradictions—a statement *can't* be true and false at the same time. Monk must be mistaken by allowing his intuition to flaunt contradictions.

The philosopher Graham Priest has made a living from arguing that there can be true contradictions. And so he would argue that Mr. Monk need not be failing in his logic at all. There are times when the evidence is such that we should accept contradiction rather than blindly follow the Law of Non-Contradiction. He argues that in some rare cases a statement can both be true and false *at the same time!* So, Monk's statement need not be a problem, even if it is a contradiction, if we can simply show that it is what we in the philosophical world call "a dialetheia." More importantly, seeming contradictions like "the man who was in space during the time of the murder on Earth is the guy" may be true if we have good reason to believe the contradiction is true. Perhaps our intuitions alone would not be enough to assert that a contradiction is true, but Monk's intuitions, which are always correct, may well be enough.

What, according to Graham Priest, is an example of a true contradiction? Here's one: "This sentence is false." This is often called the Liar Sentence. If the Liar Sentence is false, then when it says, "this sentence is false" it is also true, but if it is true then the statement "this sentence is false" is false, which makes it true, and so on. The Liar Sentence plagues philosophers. But Priest doesn't think it needs to be a problem, it is simply a dialetheia—a true contradiction. So perhaps Mr. Monk, like Priest, is onto something, he is just acknowledging that we should not let our assumption that all contradictions are false lead us to reject good evidence that a particular contradiction is true.

You probably want to object at this point. If there can be true contradictions, how can we tell if any particular sentence is actually true or actually false? How can Monk use his deductive skills to solve problems if any particular statement could be true, false, or both true and false? It would seem that any of the beliefs that he uses to solve crimes like "someone who overdoses on pills uses a glass of water" could be both true and false and so any conclusions that he reaches from that statement may also be true and false. How can we be sure that any true statement we make isn't also, at the same time, false?

Priest's the Guy

Priest thinks he can solve this problem too. Using the ideas of another philosopher, H.P. Grice, he thinks that we can differentiate between true statements and dialetheia. Grice's ideas work nicely with the way that Mr. Monk generally thinks. Monk doesn't say something unless he believes there is good reason to think it is true, even if he is unable to articulate all of those reasons at the time. In the same way, Grice thinks that we can solve some philosophical problems by recognizing that when we speak, we generally mean the strongest thing that can be interpreted from our statement. So Priest argues that we can know that something isn't a dialetheia because if I make a statement I will state that it is a dialetheia, if I believe it is a dialetheia. In other words, you never need to worry about a statement Monk makes being a contradiction because, if it is a contradiction, he'll tell you. He would never say, "John is the guy" unless he believes he is the guy. If Monk, thought, for instance, that John was both the guy and not the guy, then Monk, by Gricean rules would say so.

How do we know that people follow Gricean rules? We know this because if you wanted to tell me that you are reading a book you would not say, "I am reading a book or I am in Spain." It would be true to say, but you would go with the simpler, stronger statement, "I am reading a book," for the sake of clarity. In the same way Mr. Monk would simply state the contradiction if he had reason to do so. So this may be the case with his statement that his abilities are both a blessing and a curse. In this case, it would be inaccurate to say that it is a blessing and it would be inaccurate to that it is a curse, because both of these statements do not include all of the necessary information. Unfortunately, this does not solve the problems of contradictions.

Priest's Gricean move may help us rest assured that Monk would not state a dialetheia unless he believed it, but isn't it still a problem for Monk to be so relaxed about contradictions in the first place? How is Monk able to assure himself that any particular statement is not a dialetheia? How can he determine which facts are dialetheia and which are not? Usually, the foremost criterion that we use to determine if a bit of logic is a bad bit of logic is if it results in a contradiction. For example, imagine that Disher states that "John committed a murder in the USA yesterday." If Monk points out that John was in another country all day yesterday, we know that Disher must be wrong because John cannot both be in the country committing the crime and not in the country at the same time. So we believe that Disher is wrong because his conclusion—that John committed the crime results in a contradiction. But if contradictions can be true couldn't Disher simply reply to Monk, "Well maybe John was both in the USA and not in the USA at the same time?" If contradictions can be true, how do we prove Disher wrong?

Priest would likely have to reply that we only need worry about a contradiction being true *when we have reason to believe they are true*. In the case above, we have no reason to believe that John can both be in the country and out of the country at the same time. The problem for Mr. Monk still seems to remain difficult. There is a well-known dictum made famous by the character Sherlock Holmes which states "Once you eliminate the impossible, whatever remains, however improbable, must be the truth." (Nils Rauhut examines this maxim in Chapter 2 of this volume.) This is a pretty useful way of thinking when one is attempting to solve a crime. I wonder, though, can this still be a true statement in light of the possibility of true contradictions? What could be impossible if contradictions are true? How do we differentiate between things that are impossible and those things that we just assume are impossible because they are contradictions?

Here's How It Happened and Didn't Happen

At the end of the day, my mind is eased because Monk doesn't allow contradictions to exist unresolved. Eventually, in every case, his intuitions are proven correct and this is often because the tension caused by a contradiction is relieved due to new evidence. As a matter of fact, the contradictions that Monk seems to humor may well actually act instead to motivate Monk and the other investigators to solve the crime. In the case of "Mr. Monk and the Astronaut," Monk knows that Wagner's the guy and the fact that it seems impossible creates a tension that must be released. Stottlemeyer is often motivated by this tension. He knows that what Monk is saying seems impossible, but he also knows that Monk is never wrong. So he seeks a solution that both removes the contradiction and also meets Monk's intuitions.

If Monk was actually okay with contradictions, he would likely be able to walk away from the case saying, "Yes, he was in space and he committed the murder on Earth at the same time" and be done with it. Instead, he tries to figure out how Wagner was able to commit the murder even though it seems impossible. Despite Wagner's airtight alibi it turns out that he did commit the murder . . . without violating the Law of Non-Contradiction. Before he left, he set the victim's garage door to open and strangle her while he was in space. What we realize is that we were assuming something that was false—that Wagner must be on Earth to commit the murder—which resulted in the contradiction. Once we realize that Wagner could commit the murder while in space we no longer need to worry about the possibility of him being in space and not in space at the same time. Simply put, the contradiction is false. Wagner was in space and Wagner committed the murder.

Similarly, some philosophers believe that the Liar Sentence is also a case of not having all of the information. Perhaps we'll discover that sentences cannot refer to themselves or that the Liar Sentence is simply a false statement. What Monk's examples do for us is demonstrate that seemingly true contradictions are inevitably resolved. In every case, even when Monk is willing to allow for an impossibility, what seemed impossible is proved to be false. It may be that Monk never actually allows for contradictions. Instead, given his deductive powers, he uses contradictions as motivation to seek a solution. In the case of the homicidal astronaut, Monk had very good reason to believe that Wagner was guilty due to his observational powers. This truth resulted in a contradiction *that Monk had to resolve.* Monk continued to search for evidence and once that missing piece of information was found the contradiction proved to be false.

Priest would likely argue that I am cheating here a bit in order to avoid having to admit that some contradictions can be true. He might say that the Liar Sentence is special because it is true *about its own falsity.* Having said that, if I concede that there are true contradictions and that Mr. Monk indulges in them on occasion, I can't make sense of how Monk's crime-solving system works. Monk relies on a system of logic that negates impossibilities and requires that false statements be not true. The contradictions that he entertains are used as motivation to solve the crime—and thereby resolve the contradiction. If contradictions can be true then it seems as if Monk's means of solving crimes becomes far less certain, and one wonders why he doesn't simply accept the contradiction instead of being motivated to solve it.

It seems to me that, in Monk's case, that he does not actually allow for the belief that a contradiction might be true. Quite the contrary, in each case of a seeming contradiction, Monk is very motivated to resolve the contradiction. Although he's willing to admit that the impossible seems to be true, he does not stop there. He continues on the case until he can prove not only that a particular person is "the guy" but also demonstrate how the crime was committed, without contradiction. The worst Monk can be accused of is an occasional lack of clarity, as in the case of his gift as a blessing and curse. Which should be expected from someone who is both deeply conflicted and much smarter than the average guy. My reply, then, to Priest is a simple one in light of what we have learned about Mr. Monk. A sentence like the Liar Sentence is a crime that needs to be solved. Instead of agreeing that the contradiction is true, we should be motivated by it to figure out what the missing piece is. We might find that once we uncover that missing clue, it all makes sense and, the contradiction is resolved.

9

Mr. Monk Goes to the Library

JULIE KANE

> Whenever something not-horrific happens to me, I don't trust it.
>
> —"Mr. Monk and the Lady Next Door"

Adrian walks through the jewelry store; tilting his head and peering through fingers, he wiggles slightly as he moves his hands up and down, getting an altered view of the scene. This is what he does. This is how he works. At this point, it's sort of his shtick. We know that this is how he's going to work the scene—he'll filter out the clues, the one or two things that don't belong among the however many other variables in his view. How does he do it? How is he categorizing items so that he knows what belongs, what's happened, what's right, and what's wrong?

Monk's desire for order, his procedures that veer from the standard routes taken by his colleagues, even his personal relationships—all these have deep connections with tenets and historical facets of library cataloging. The need to divide and separate, to collect, and to create order out of chaos; these have occupied librarians and OCD detectives alike for eons. Monk, you'll see, is a modern-day Charles Cutter, shown up day after day by his flashier counterpart Melvil Dewey. Monk's detecting skills mirror the way we assign subject headings. He struggles constantly in his daily quest for control over his environment, while catalogers yearn for Universal Bibliographic Control. All in all, Monk himself could be described through cataloging.

Catalog librarians have been trained to use rules to categorize and sift; in this country they follow stringent rules laid down in *Anglo-American Cataloguing Rules, Second edition, 2002 Revision* (usually just called *AACR2*), very soon to be superseded by *Resource Description and Access* (*RDA*), they have the *Library of Congress Rule Interpretations* when they don't explicitly know how to follow up, and a wealth of sources to use for backup. Monk has Natalie, Captain Stottlemeyer, and Randy Disher, who's really just about as helpful as a brain-damaged Labrador—goofy and cute to have around, but not about to provide any soul-chilling insights. But Monk, it seems, manages to get the same kind of work done, even without our reference materials, rules, and procedures!

How many professions as a whole relate to Monk? A very good friend of mine regularly calls me Monk, with unrestrained glee in her voice. She's a licensed psychologist. This concerns me. (More for her paying clients than for myself, since I acknowledge my Monk-like qualities.) I'm primarily a catalog librarian by profession. What's a catalog librarian? You know how all libraries have these catalogs? They list every single thing in the library; every resource, with lots of information about each one, with a call number that tells you its location on the shelf, something about the topic, other relevant resources, subject headings, and all that good stuff? A catalog librarian figured out and wrote all that, coded it so that the computer could read it for your enjoyment, and did so according to rules that we all share and use consistently with one another.

I organize knowledge, and maybe that means that I inherently relate to the OCD way of life. Things bother me. Usually they're tiny inconsequential things—things that have absolutely nothing to do with my life or work. For example: it drives me to distraction that paper cups on television never have liquid in them. Watch for it if you've never noticed; I think you'll never be able to un-notice. It's not something that can be well-acted away—if there's no liquid, there's no weight! We notice! Why can't they put some water in there if they're worried about hot coffee-related lawsuits? Am I like Monk, foisting my overbearing peevishness on those around me? We both may *think* we're sharing righteous outrage and helpfully pointing out glaring inaccuracies, while we're *really* just annoying our friends.

I love Monk. He makes me happy. I can't help but smile back at him in the opening montage when he's so blissful in his hazmat suit in that gleaming white-on-white clean room. I wish I had one. It looks like heaven. I wonder how many other catalogers watch, smile, relate. Are we all, like me, a little bit like Monk?

Users and Pushers

I don't want to over-generalize and offend anyone, but of the other catalogers I've met, it might be said that we as a group can tend toward the, ummm . . . *persnickety*. It comes with the job; we put things in order, and it's all so that you, the masses (and yes, some of you are unwashed, but I'm not commenting on that now), can find what you're looking for. I found myself recently telling a stranger on a plane, trying to describe briefly what I do: "I'm a librarian, but not the kind who helps people." That's not exactly true. I do help people; I just don't do it while they're there, and they just might not ever know that they've been helped, or who did it. In fact, if we as catalogers do our job best, it's seamless and essentially invisible. We're not quite Batman, but we catalogers are *those* people. We are the behind-the-scenes librarians, and we like it that way.[1]

Catalogers obsess over punctuation and coding, true. (This is our version of having to touch the lamppost and the antennae . . . that colon is in the wrong place; that field needs a space there; that indicator is wrong: OCD!) But we also obsess over subject access and keywords: we always have the users sitting on our shoulders. What are you thinking of when you're looking for *this book*? How would you *want* to find it? How would you *not expect* to find it, but be delighted that you did? Most of all, how can I help push this into your greedy little paws, without you having the slightest clue that I was ever back here? I'm the guy behind the curtain. I'm your information pusher-man.

Monk's method is similar in that he comes at his investigations from a different angle than Stottlemeyer or Disher. In "Mr. Monk and the Bad Girlfriend," Monk reasons, illogically to most (and most alarmingly to Stottlemeyer, who is trying desperately to prove that his girlfriend isn't a murderer), that the suspect with *no* alibi *cannot* be guilty, based upon the way the killer hid in the victim's bathroom before striking. Why would someone take the time to hide, unless an alibi were *already* established for a *certain* time frame? The suspect *without* the alibi, in any other case usually the

---

[1] *Editor's Note*: in "Mr. Monk Meets Dr. House," Marc Zaffran argues that both Monk and House are 'fixers', of different sorts, who are much more interested in the problems than the people with the problems. His discussion fits well with the catalog librarian as an information provider who'd rather help by working with the books than with the people looking for them.

guilty one, therefore had to be innocent. Monk doesn't follow the straight-line path that the clues may present, but uses reasoning based on people's actions: what they would do and why. He is user-oriented, only his users happen to be criminals, and we fervently hope ours aren't.

No One Will Thank You Later

Monk's recurring insistence of "You'll thank me later" is particularly resonant with catalogers. We, like Monk, are result-driven. Monk has his detecting, crime-solving process, and he might be the only one to understand it, or he might just have a few people he lets into his inner circle to work with him. That's okay—he's going to get the job done his way, and we as an audience trust that; the SFPD must trust that at some level given how much leeway he has (even though he carries an empty badge holder, still, after all these years). Catalogers operate in much the same way: others might not understand exactly what it is that we do, or how we come to accomplish the things we do, but they trust that we'll do it, and they rely on the end result.

While Monk is satisfying his need for order within chaos, he's constantly searching for justice for someone else. He's delightfully (sometimes annoyingly, yes) selfish, but he does care about others . . . on his cases. He can be blind to the needs of those closest to him (most regularly Natalie's financial woes: directly his fault), but astutely observant of his case victims' needs. Cataloging can be a similarly altruistic and selfish dichotomy. It can be an amazingly fulfilling personal success to finish with a particularly harrowing bibliographic record, or a wrenching struggle to deal with one that becomes a known and hated entity (seriously). When we've sent it off, though, we know that it will either serve well to attract users to it, or it will sit unused, because we failed in certain ways. Or because it's just a crappy book that no one wants to check out. Either way.

We, with Monk, will get made fun of along the way. We're the nerds of the library world. (*I know*! You don't have to point out the irony in that one). Monk works independently without the locker-room camaraderie of the station house. We'd rather be left alone to do our work with a truck full of books than have to interact with *people*, even if we sometimes envy the easy interactions reference librarians can pull off. Some of us have been known to shy away from applying for positions that mentioned an hour or two of sitting at the reference desk. The horror! (Can you imagine Monk in a customer-service position? Try. Try harder. Absolute freaking meltdown.) It doesn't mean that we don't value making a contribution; just that we love our work in our own way. We'd love to be thanked later. Just maybe not in person. Send a card, maybe. We'll put it in a file. Alphabetized. Cross-referenced, with subject access. I'm only kidding. Kind of.

I'm Down with OCD, Yeah UBC!

In library school, our beloved silver fox of a reference professor (and you know who I'm talking about, Simmons GSLIS '98ers)[2] gave us a charge—that our goal as librarians (cue the *Mission Impossible* music) should be to strive for **Universal Bibliographic Control**. Ooooooooooh, I thought. YES. And then: Crap. Sisyphus.

If you take a look at Monk's apartment, you can't help but notice how well ordered everything is. I love the umbrellas hanging on his entranceway wall. He *collocates*—an underlying tenet of cataloging: put like with like. Simple, clean, brilliant in its efficacy: we want people to find things together. If you were browsing for umbrellas, you would expect to find another umbrella right next door. Even better if it's another *black* umbrella, facing exactly the same way. Monk has perfected the art of collocation in his apartment: take a look at his wall art. He has boxes on his wall, and a row of photographs on another. They are identical, and perfectly spaced. You don't find the boxes interspersed *with* the photographs; that would be madness! What kind of fool would do such a thing? Boxes go with boxes, photographs lined up with the photographs. It's even better if the subject matter is the same (Trudy, Trudy, Trudy, Trudy, Trudy). Monk has a very well-classified system of décor.

It's when Monk leaves his apartment and seeks to expand his control over the world that he runs into problems. In "Mr. Monk Makes the Playoffs," when he arrives at a football game tailgate, he asks Stottlemeyer, "Who are all of these people and where are their parents?" I can relate, though I've luckily learned to keep (most of) those questions inside my head to keep the dirty looks at bay.

---

[2] Prof. Allen Smith, of course, RIP.

Score one for me. He's clearly out of his comfort zone and would like to impose some order. He finds pleasure, or at least not-anxiety, only when he can exercise control over a situation, create order out of disorder, and analyze a crime scene.

For an example in the library world, take the Online Computer Library Center's WorldCat or the attempts of Google Books to scan millions of books the world over to make them accessible online. These are larger forays into Universal Bibliographic Control, but the truth is that we'll never push Sisyphus's rock all the way up that hill and keep it from toppling back down. It's far too huge a task. We would never agree on one universal standard for description; one controlled vocabulary (people try to use *different words* to describe *the same thing!* Totally unreasonable. It's a nightmare.); a single authorized database of names. These things are constantly evolving; they exist in other places—libraries use them the world over, make their own choices and share resources, but as the world gets in on the bibliographic game, the rules change and theories for cataloging practices are anyone's guess. Monk would have a heart attack in our shoes. Mostly because he found himself wearing someone else's shoes.

I don't mean to be a naysayer about valiant attempts at universal bibliographic control—I feel like I just told a million budding catalogers that I shot the MARC fairy,[3] but I can't even comprehend the idea of a single database with records (and I mean *good* records, ahem) for *every work of intellectual property ever created.* Because that's really what we mean, right? Or do we narrow it down? To everything ever published? Where is that line drawn? Published by whom? Does self-published count? Vanity presses are more ubiquitous than Starbucks now; do they have the same heft as an established publishing house? Who decides? And so I dive into the bushes on my path to let the boulder rumble by on its way back down the hill.

This is where the problems with universal bibliographic control and Monk become one. Within the apartment, or within a single

---

[3] The MARC fairy is like the tooth fairy, except that she deals with MAchine-Readable Cataloging code instead of lost teeth, and gives you progress towards universal bibliographic control instead of quarters. She's less sparkly, wears über-hip glasses, and is more data-entry intensive and detail-oriented, but there's also no way she's your mom. So that's a plus. She also may or may not be a vegan; rumors have yet to be confirmed, for she is a wily little fairy.

library, we're both okay. We can function, and breathe freely, without our OCD phobias eating our souls. I have a handle on what cataloging comes to me in small doses; Monk can order his world within his walls. Once the picture expands to include the world at large, we both become Sisyphus, and that rock is just too big to handle. Plus, it's *really* dirty. Wipe, please?

Adrian Monk and Charles Cutter: Separated at Birth?

Everyone knows Adrian Monk, while at the same time he's invisible. How is that? He's such a quiet person, but his OCD can be overbearing and dominate a room. He's methodical and prefers to deal with facts rather than emotions, but can get worked up rather quickly over something others consider utterly commonplace. He reminds me in certain ways of my favorite (okay, maybe obsessively favorite) cataloging figure, Charles Ammi Cutter.

They're both brilliantly observant—everyone knows that Monk is the greatest detective the SFPD has ever had, and even though he's officially off the force because of his nervous breakdown, it seems that they can't solve a single serious case without his input. Charles Cutter was the first librarian to decide that library catalogs should be written on index cards instead of in *volumes of written books* so that acquisitions and withdrawals could be easily entered and deleted. *Genius*, right? It's the sort of thing that would seem to be ridiculously obvious these days. Who would create any kind of record-keeping system of a changing entity that was bound, static, and impossible to change without starting from scratch every time? Now we joke about card catalogs and how archaic they are; we buy furniture created to resemble this outdated (therefore fashionably chic for your living room!) mode of information retrieval. Who on earth would have thought that there was a time when the creation of that system was revolutionary? In those days, it absolutely was!

Cutter also wrote about the future of libraries and envisioned the need for environmental controls, including moisture, lighting, and temperature regulation, down to the degree—he even differentiated between the heating levels allowed for the reading room and for the stacks. He went on to specify measurements of stack height for ease of reaching books, and *numerous* other visions for the future in "The Buffalo Public Library in 1983," a speech he delivered to the opening of the Sixth General Meeting of the American Library Association at Buffalo in *18*83. While he was a great advocate for opening the doors and expanding the use of libraries to educational outreach, our Monk of the 1880s let his OCD hang out a tad when he wrote about how he envisioned this library's use:

> Every one must be admitted into the delivery-room, but from the read-ing-rooms the great unwashed are shut out altogether or put in rooms by themselves. Luckily public opinion sustains us thoroughly in their exclusion or seclusion.[4]

Don't you think Monk would *love* to envision a future in which he could exclude the unwashed? I'm sure he does, daily. But to write and publish such a vision for his professional life, along with a list of demands including strict space measurements and precise cal-culations for temperature, air quality (Cutter mentions "evil dust," I'm not joking), and the exact layout of subject material of his dream space, with assigned professionals to handle everything in each area, and then to have it all well-received and *applauded?* I think that's an entire dream session with his therapist, in a nutshell. And Cutter lived in that shining limelight.

Briefly.

Harold Krenshaw Is . . . Melvil Dewey?

You might notice that no one talks much about Charles Cutter or makes Cutter librarian jokes like they do about Dewey. If you're not a librarian, or even if you are, you might not even have heard of him before. The way I see it, Cutter's *the man* in the way Monk is *the man*. Dewey, on the other hand, is Harold Fricking Krenshaw. Some biographical accounts gloss it all over and have Cutter and Dewey as friends. I imagine some random football play-ers would think Adrian and Harold were friends. We know better. Yes, they are contemporaries. Yes, they share traits and some inter-ests or . . . commonalities. Dewey and Cutter founded the American Library Association (ALA), together with another hundred or so

---

[4] Charles Ammi Cutter, "The Buffalo Public Library in 1983," in *Papers and Proceedings of the Sixth General Meeting of the American Library Association, held at Buffalo, August 14 to 17.* American Library Association, 1883. (pp. 49–55).

people. This doesn't make them buddies. I doubt anyone ever saw them going out for a beer together.

Cutter and Dewey devised two completely different sets of classification systems. Cutter's was alpha-numeric, called the "Expansive Classification Scheme," and intended to be completed in seven distinct stages, in increasing complexity and highly customizable according to the size of the library using it. It was left incomplete, open on his desk to the seventh stage at the time of his death, much like Monk's one historic, glaring, as-yet-unsolved case of Trudy's murder as we enter the last season. Dewey's classification was numeric only, finished quickly, and less complex. Many would say it was more suited to public and smaller libraries as opposed to larger academic or research libraries, and it was widely adopted soon after its completion. Dewey got famous; Cutter didn't.

While both men were certainly dedicated to their profession, I feel that Monk-like tug toward Cutter. He's got that quiet, tireless OCD feel to him while Dewey is a little bit . . . flashy and icky. What kind of OCD cataloger-type detective-ish guy would be committed to actively deconstructing the English language? As one of the founding members of the Simplified Spelling Board, Dewey nearly changed his own name to "Melvil Dui." Seriously. It was bad enough to chop down Melville to Melvil. Can you imagine Monk trying to decode one of Dewey's "simpler spelin" notes? I want to see that episode.

Dewey founded a club in Lake Placid that denied membership to Jews and he may have been one of the first to take advantage of the annual American Library Association conference to get overly friendly with women librarians, something that eventually got him in a bit of trouble and limited his professional ALA involvement. Good reason to start up a national association, Dewey! I wouldn't denigrate Harold so far as to say that he resembles Dewey in these respects; I just mean to highlight the differences between Dewey and Cutter (and because no one really talks about the *dark side of Dewey*).

In any case, Adrian v. Harold and Cutter v. Dewey offer a few parallels, even if Harold isn't a racist slut. (Are they saving that for the last season? Twist!) Monk is always working away when he feels that Harold comes swooping in to steal his thunder. Remember when Harold was briefly the Frisco Fly in "Mr. Monk and the Daredevil"? It drove Monk *nuts* when he couldn't prove to the public that Harold wasn't this superstar death-defying dare-devil—not just because it brought Harold fame and adoration, but because it meant that Harold had finally overcome all of his paralyzing phobias while Monk was still painfully in the grip of his and had never made any real progress. As long as they remained in lockstep and didn't make progress *together*, Monk could cope. But if Harold had really been cured and left Monk in the dust, it would truly have crushed him.

I really don't know if Cutter felt that way about Dewey, but it seems to me that he must have. Cutter's classification system was much more intricate than Dewey's, and yet Dewey's was widespread before Cutter could finish his. Unless you go looking for the history, no one today really acknowledges the fact that the Library of Congress Classification system is based in part on Cutter's scheme, and that our "Cutter number," a part of the larger class number, is a direct result of his work. We talk about him a little bit in library school, and move on, when he's one of the really major figures in our history. While Dewey's classification system is certainly still in wide use today, mostly by public and smaller libraries, the Library of Congress system is a widespread standard in the United States at least, and is constantly being built upon and expanded, thanks to the initial framework laid out by Cutter's system. Sigh. Poor, poor Cutter. So tossed aside. I think Monk worries that this is going to be his fate whenever Harold Krenshaw steps into the picture. Even when Monk has shown conclusively that Harold is *not* the Frisco Fly, Harold manages to fall off another building, opening his parachute and accidentally letting the public believe once again that he is, indeed. Or, as in "Mr. Monk Fights City Hall," Harold tricks Natalie into finally spilling the beans on the name of Monk's new shrink. Adrian had managed to keep it a closely guarded secret for nearly a season! Aaargh, Harold Krenshaw! Flashy, thunder-stealing, Melvil *Dui*-like Harold Krenshaw. Go spell something wrong, why don't you!

Disorder and Confusion Everywhere

Monk and Cutter both contribute an incredible amount that we don't ever notice. Monk's detection skills are renowned, and those closest to him grow accustomed to his work style and his . . . habits. We get to know him and start anticipating what he's going to see, how he's going to solve this case. We think we might know how he thinks. We're probably wrong, but we try our best to get into his head.

Cutter wrote *Rules for a Dictionary Catalog* in 1876, laying out some basic ideas that came to form some of the major theoretical framework of cataloging as we know it today. The book was really the first to address the idea of adding subject access and addressing the primary goal of cataloging: *access. We want these things to be found.* In Monk's case, *he needs to find these things.* The theory of access and of keeping the user in mind is revolutionary for the time. I've added an excerpt from the fourth edition of Cutter's *Rules,* including his Objects, Means, and Reasons for Choice.

The theory of access drives cataloging, but Cutter was the one to really highlight subject access, and this is what orders our world, and Monk's. When we make a decision to assign particular subject headings to a book's bibliographic record, or to classify it in a particular place so that it sits on the shelf near others with the same primary subject heading, we are exercising control over how that book is best going to be found. We're collocating and ordering, by broader subjects or narrower, sorting and sifting, and we're doing our best to make it seamless. If all goes as planned, you'll walk into a library and never know we were there. We want you, the washed and unwashed masses, to see the world as Monk sees it, with our help but without knowing you've had our help. Monk would find his umbrellas in perfect order just where he'd expect to, and maybe even discover some new ones—he might find out he likes a different color, or maybe a new style. One with a pattern, or automatic opening, or an ornately carved handle. He just wouldn't know that we'd put them there for his discovery.

Cutter's Reasons for Choice are the most illuminating and interesting, particularly the first one—to "choose that entry that will probably be first looked under by the class of people who use the library."[5] This is the sort of profoundly difficult yet obvious statement I can hear Monk making in an investigation, while Stottlemeyer mumbles around and Randy stands in the corner trying to have a

---

[5] Charles Ammi Cutter, *Rules for a Dictionary Catalog*. Government Printing Office, 1904. (I also *love* this the note to the second edition: "This Statement of Objects and Means has been criticized; but as it has also been frequently quoted, usually without change or credit, in the prefaces of catalogs and elsewhere, I suppose it has on the whole been approved." If that isn't an 1880s Adrian Monk, I'm not sure what is.)

OBJECTS.*

1. To enable a person to find a book of which either
   (A) the author ⎫
   (B) the title ⎬ is known.
   (C) the subject ⎭

2. To show the library has
   (D) by a given author
   (E) on a given subject
   (F) in a given kind of literature

3. To assist in the choice of a book
   (G) as to its edition (bibliography).
   (H) as to its character (literary or topical).

MEANS.

1. Author-entry with the necessary references (for A and D).
2. Title-entry or title-reference (for B).
3. Subject-entry, cross references, and classed subject-table (for C and E).
4. Form-entry and language-entry (for F).
5. Giving edition and imprint, with notes where necessary (for G).
6. Notes (for H).

REASONS FOR CHOICE

Among the several possible methods of attainng the OBJECTS, other things being equal, schoose that entry

(1) That will probably be first looked under by the class of people who use the library;
(2) That is consistent with other entries, so that one principle can cover all;
(3) That will mass entries least in places where it is difficult to so arrange them that they can be readily found, as under names of nations or cities.

This applies very slightly to enties under first words, because it is easy and sufficient to arrange them by the alphabet.

Note to second edition. This statement of Objects and Means has been criticized; but as it has also been frequently quoted, usually without change or credit, in the prefaces of catalogs and elsewhere, I suppose it has on the whole been approved.

conversation with a robot. Of *course* you'd want to choose the terms that your users would choose, right? Why not? But how are you going to determine that? Who are your users? What do they think? How do they search? See Monk start to wiggle his fingers?

This is what Monk does best, and where Cutter shines. The others kind of fade into the background, scuffing their feet on the ground looking for clues, taking pictures, talking to witnesses. The most variable, and arguably most difficult part of any cataloging record is providing *subject access*—the first thing, Cutter posits, is that we need to know *our users*. They're constantly evolving. How they search today isn't even close to how they searched in Cutter's time, or even ten years ago. These days they evolve at the speed of light. Our vocabularies don't keep up and our databases certainly don't. There are constantly new trends in cataloging interfaces to help keep up with what users expect from technology and searching. Some will overlay a database to help pull out our data and allow user tagging to share thoughts and keywords when our subject headings are inadequate or outdated. Tagging by users can only go so far, though—if someone has decided that their personal preference for a keyword is better applied to a book, do we as catalogers have an obligation to take that keyword and apply it to every other book that carries the same subject headings? How much more would that serve our users? Where would they expect to find that keyword? That's what makes Cutter's vision so profound, so stark, and so timeless. And so unbelievably difficult to accomplish. Sometimes we catalogers could really use Monk's help.

Here's What Happened

I don't so much mind being called Monk. My psychologist friend laughs at me but she also asks me for help: one day she asked me to come over to help "sort her files." I arrived to find boxes full of mail, receipts, paid bills, life-related detritus. I happily dug in, creating a system and organizing her life. I find great pleasure in being useful, as I suspect other catalogers, organizers, and vaguely (or distinctly) OCD enjoyers of *Monk* do. Sure, it still bothers me that there are empty coffee cups on TV, but as long as I'm free to yell about it every time I see it, I'm okay.

Monk wraps up each case with a happily pronounced "here's what happened" to an ostensibly perplexed audience, usually including his fellow investigators. No one cares if I expound on how I came to a particular classification number after a long wrestle with it, and if I tried to explain, I might be written up with some kind of restraining order. Once in a great while I get to share the joy—this summer I had a cataloging intern, and I got to explain in rapturous fits and starts the wonders of MARC coding and the reasons for cataloging vagaries. If only life were like Monk and I could do it regularly, with a captive audience, every week. Sigh. Would that be my white room in my hazmat suit? Maybe temporarily, but luckily for me, and for Monk, there's always another case to solve.

I'm delighted that Monk is echoed in cataloging, and cataloging is echoed in Monk. We catalogers like to stay in the back rooms and out of view, but it's nice to see a part of what we do dramatized, recognized, and appreciated! I take great pleasure in watching him detect using his style that mimics some of what we do in cataloging: we organize, we categorize, we help; we think of the user's needs, and from their perspectives; he thinks of the victim's needs, and from the criminal's point of view. If Monk retires at the end of the show, he has a new career path perfectly laid out ahead of him: cataloger. He would *love* it!

He's a Real Character

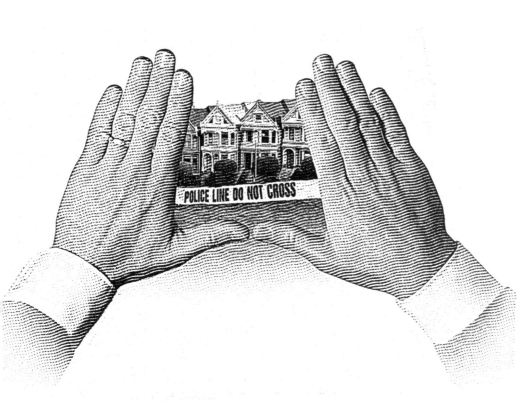

POLICE LINE DO NOT CROSS

Monk's Competition

10

Mr. Monk Meets Dr. House

MARC ZAFFRAN

Dr. Gregory House is a bachelor and womanizer who enjoys sleeping with prostitutes. He lives in a not-too-ordered three-room apartment in an East-Coast American city. He plays the guitar and the piano, and pops numerous tablets of Vicodin each day. He never shaves—or at least always looks unshaven without ever growing a beard, which is a feat in itself—and he wears sneakers, jeans, a worn-out shirt and a shaggy jacket and sometimes rides a motorbike. He has been walking with a cane since a doctor misdiagnosed an infarction which led to the subsequent destruction of a large muscle in his thigh.

The irony is that Dr. House is an Internal Medicine Physician in the very same hospital that made him a cripple (the fictitious Princeton-Plainsboro Teaching Hospital). He works only one impossible medical case at a time (incompatible symptoms, unheard-of syndromes, and such), aided by a team of physicians: the feminine and lovely Allison Cameron and Remy Hadley; and the diversely male Robert Chase, Eric Foreman, Lawrence Kutner, and Chris Taub. House's best friend, James Wilson, and Dr. Lisa Cuddy, the Hospital's Chief of Medicine, are the other main characters in his life. He makes all of them miserable but they endure because Gregory House is a living paradox: he's misanthropic, foulmouthed and disrespectful to everyone including the patients *and* he's the greatest diagnostician of all times—at least in his television universe.

Mr. Adrian Monk is a widower and lonely soul, living in a three-room apartment in San Francisco. He's no Steve McQueen of *Bullitt* fame: he won't drive, seldom wishes to leave his house, spends hours cleaning and wiping and ordering his interior and buys bottles of one specific brand of water by dozens (although he'd prefer to buy them by the tens). He wears only a very specific set of clothes (grey pants, white shirt, brown jacket, no tie) of which he has a hundred copies.[1] And "copies" is the right word for them: they are all hung together in the same cabinet, on hangers separated by exactly the same distance. When he eats, he separates foods in his plates. He has an assistant who helps him for almost everything, including passing out wipes.

A former police officer dismissed after the mental breakdown following his wife Trudy's murder, he works as a consultant for the very same police department that dismissed him and helps investigate impossible crimes—locked-room murders, vanishing killers, and such. He is helped in his investigations by Natalie Teeger, his assistant and two police officers: grumpy Captain Stottlemeyer and inept Detective Randy Disher. He makes all of them miserable, but they all endure because Adrian Monk is a living paradox: he suffers from obsessive compulsive disorder assorted with a number of phobias, *and* he is the greatest detective of all time—at least in his television universe.

Arguably, one couldn't find more different characters and personalities than those two. Still, Monk and House have a common forebear: as their names ("Adrian" is Sir Arthur Conan Doyle's son's first name; "House" is a play on words with "Ho[l]mes") clearly indicate, they were both inspired by Sir Arthur's Sherlock Holmes.

Monk and House share many common traits with The Great Detective. They both have—just like the man Holmes was based on, Dr. Joseph Bell, Conan Doyle's mentor from medical school—extraordinary powers of observation and deduction. They are confronted with puzzling mysteries of a very uncommon kind: impossible crimes (Monk) and unrecorded diseases (House). But although they have to deal with other people, Monk fears others and House despises them, and the two of them usually avoid any social interaction. Their uncommon gift of deduction is therefore hampered by a very unpleasant habit of keeping "normal" people away. While Monk won't shake hands or handle evidence (or anything else) bare-handed, House sends his own "Plainsboro

---

[1] Or at least, according to "Mr. Monk Makes a Friend," he has a hundred identical shirts.

Irregulars" to do bloodwork—or bloody work—on the patient whom he's in charge of. The two sleuths make their entourage very uncomfortable by enforcing absurd, self-imposed rules (Monk) or breaking the law and every point in the medical code of professional conduct (House).

Of the two characters, Gregory House seems to be the one most at odds with his professional ethics. If we look at both carefully, we will see that Adrian Monk's ethics are very similar to House's; that these two characters, in spite of their sometimes insufferable behavior, are very human; and that their apparent "uncivilized" behavior is closely related to their gift.

Origin

For many historians of Crime Fiction, the oldest recorded and maybe the *first* crime mystery is the myth of Oedipus, as recorded in Sophocles's *Oedipus Rex*.

A plague of infertility strikes the city of Thebes. Wishing to end the plague, Oedipus the King learns from the Oracle at Delphi that the murderer of the former King—Laius—must be found and either be killed or exiled. Oedipus is warned by the prophet Tiresias that he should not search for the killer, but Oedipus is unmoved. Solving the cold case is the only way he can remove the plague from his city.

Oedipus was already a famous investigator. He had, in fact, become King of Thebes by solving the riddle of the Sphinx. The Sphinx was a large and ferocious creature that had placed a one-monster embargo on Thebes, eating anyone who approached the city and was unable to answer her riddle, "What walks on four feet in the morning, two in the afternoon and three at night?" Oedipus had defeated her by finding the answer: man himself, for he crawls in infancy (the morning of life), walks as an adult, and carries a cane in the waning hours of his life. Oedipus, having saved the city, was made its king, and married the widowed queen, Jocasta. And so, when Oedipus the famous investigator takes on the case of the murder of his wife's first husband, the former king, there is every expectation that he will solve the riddle again, and save the city again. And he does.

Oedipus discovers that Laius and Jocasta had had a child, and a prophecy had claimed that the child would murder his father. But that child was supposed to have been killed, in order to prevent the prophecy from coming true. Oedipus discovers, though, that after the child had been left on the hillside to die, a passing shepherd decided to put it up for adoption instead. The child was brought to the city of Corinth; where Oedipus himself was from. Worse yet, Laius had bound the infant's feet together with a large pin—and the word "oedipus," in Greek, means "swollen-foot." Oedipus then remembers an incident in which he had, after an incident of ancient road-rage, killed a stranger at a crossroads, and puts all the pieces together.

The prophecy had come true. Oedipus himself must have been that infant, and Laius must have been the stranger at the crossroads. Worse yet . . . if Laius, the former king, was his father, then the widow queen Jocasta, his wife, must also be his mother. And his children with her must be his half-siblings as well as his children. Upon this awful discovery, Jocasta hangs herself, and Oedipus, overcome with grief, blinds himself with her dress-pins. And Oedipus, having solved the case, goes into exile, freeing the city from its plague, now that the king has solved the murder of the former king, and punished the murderer.

In a way, all crime fiction symbolically refers to the myth of Oedipus and, as the man searching for the truth and finding out that he, himself, is both responsible *and* one of the victims of a crime, Oedipus stands not only as the first figure of the crime investigator, but also as the most tragic one. In a way, his story is a warning: seeking the truth can both be a gift and a curse. The mystery-solver (the private eye, the investigator, the sleuth) is not a mere puzzle-solver. Uncovering the truth and catching a criminal is a worthy goal; but it has unforeseeable consequences on the victims and their families, society, and the sleuth himself. In Crime and 'Noir' Literature, many, if not all crime investigators are somehow 'marked by destiny' and carry the weight—the guilt— of an earlier, often untold, 'crime' they feel, or in fact are responsible for.

Because of their personalities and professional orientations, Adrian Monk and Greg House are both tragically marked. Monk fell deep into obsessive compulsive disorder after his wife Trudy was killed, as he feels this may have been in retaliation against him; House became a misanthropist and a drug addict after being abused as a child—and all abused children feel guilty. For these reasons, the myth of Oedipus is of particular relevance for both characters.

Nature

Being a crime-solver is no picnic. And though in reality it's a full-time job for members of the police, crime detection in fiction is not restricted to institutional police specialists. In fact, crime investigators in literature or on screen are often private investigators or amateur sleuths; most of them are gifted with specific skills or psychological traits that make their investigation progress faster than the institutional crime forces'. Just like Sherlock Holmes, who enjoyed making fun of Scotland Yard's Inspector Lestrade, most private investigators are presented as an inevitable and welcome alternative to unsuccessful police work *and* as a pain in the neck for public officials. In most situations, independent investigators are mavericks. One of Holmes's most successful heirs, Frederic Dannay and Manfred B. Lee's All-American sleuth, Ellery Queen, investigated impossible crimes and locked-room mysteries that baffled his own father, Police Inspector Queen. Another illustrious crime-fighting figure to which both House and Monk are closely related is Rex Stout's armchair detective Nero Wolfe. An obese, secluded Orchid-lover and brilliant mind, Wolfe investigates baffling mysteries by sending his assistant Archie Goodwin out on the field, while he, himself, never leaves his West 35th Street, New York brownstone.

When fiction crime investigators do belong to the police, they somehow differ from their colleagues in ways that make them stand apart. Literary characters such as P.D. James's Detective Inspector Adam Dalgliesh and Edward D. Hoch's Captain Leopold are lonely men whose investigative skills seem to be a side-effect of their particular view of mankind—a very pessimistic, if compassionate, view. On television, Richard Levinson and William Link's unsinkable Inspector Columbo is—notwithstanding recurring mentions of his invisible wife—a very lonely and, to say the least, invasive character. A very recent television cop, Graham Yost's deranged Detective Michael Raines (played by Jeff Goldblum in NBC's short-lived 2007 drama *Raines*) talks to hallucinatory figures of dead victims and through these conversations reflects on their personality and past life to identify their killer. All "cop sleuths" are misfits in the police force, usually because their minds just don't work the "police way."

Most recently, written and filmed fiction have seen the rise of a new kind of crime investigators: the forensic experts. In many ways, this trend also derives from Conan Doyle's stories. The Holmesian canon presents us with a character gifted with a sharp sense of observation and deductive skills, but also with a deliberate—albeit primitive to our twenty-first century eyes—scientific approach to evidence. When Watson first meets the man whose apartment he will eventually share (in *A Study in Scarlet*), he finds Holmes experimenting on a brand-new bloodstain identification technique. Later, he learns that the eccentric scientist studies tobacco ash under his microscope and beats corpses with his cane to determine if post-mortem bruises differ from those made while alive. In this century's criminal novels and television shows, the progress of biology, ballistics, physics and chemistry have made forensics even more present and important for investigative teams than they were in the Conan Doyle stories.

As a former cop contracted by the police "to solve sixteen crimes a year" ("Mr. Monk and the Big Reward"), Adrian Monk appears very much related to figures of 'cerebral' sleuths such as Holmes, Queen, Wolfe, and Columbo. He seldom relies on forensics but mostly uses his personal observation skills as well as logic and deduction to solve improbable or impossible crimes. In fact, in several episodes, he goes up against more 'scientific' investigators (for example, "Mr. Monk and the Really, Really Dead Guy"); in "Mr. Monk and the Wrong Man," he even allows himself to be taken in by forensic evidence and to distrust his own judgment, so much that a murderer almost goes free because of it.

On the other hand, Greg House seems to be more closely related to the forensic investigators of shows such as *CSI: Crime Scene Investigation* (CBS) or *Bones* (FOX). Just like *CSI*'s expert entomologist Gil Grissom or *Bones*'s forensic anthropologist Temperance Brennan, Gregory House is a trained scientist. He heavily draws on biological and physical evidence to identify medical culprits. But unlike them, and even though he works in an important hospital, he openly rejects authority and behaves very much like Holmes would, using many a deception to obtain the information he wants, sending his assistants on errands like Holmes would his Baker Street Irregulars, and openly breaching hospital policies on every single occasion—all of which make him a true Sherlock Holmes figure.

On top of that, Monk and House share one very important trait. They're both *sick*.

Issues

Monk and House avoid all kind of social interaction: the latter won't stand at his patients' bedside and he loathes to hear them talk; the former won't even shake hands with the victim's family. In every episode, each one of them inflicts what appears to be sadistic behavior on their close associates—Monk on his former fellow cops and on Natalie (much more so than he did on his former assistant Sharona, who used to have the upper hand on him); House on his team, his colleagues, the patients and their families. Both sleuths find themselves often distracted from the problem at hand for pathetic reasons. In Monk's case, it might well be a misplaced pillow on his therapist's couch, or a spilled glass of wine in a still life on the wall. In House's case, it might be seeing his colleague and friend James Wilson leaving his oncology office early, or his suspicion that two members of his team have been sleeping together.

Monk is an egoistic miser; House is a selfish egoist. They have little sympathy for other people's sufferings (Natalie's financial situation, Wilson's love life). They are prompt to reject cases on the ground that they are disturbing (Monk) or boring (House). They are very suspicious of women, an attitude that probably has something to do with the fact their 'ideal woman', whom they once lived with, is forever lost. They can decide to retire from work on a whim, with no respect for what remains to be done. They are both addicted (Monk to cleanliness, order, and Sierra Springs; House to gossip and drugs). They often don't follow protocol. They bear out accusations without a shred of proof (Monk points right away at someone being the culprit; House invariably accuses the patient or the family of lying), and justify this unethical behavior with their own inner conviction. ("It's him. I don't know how he did it, but he did it.") But here's the thing: *they can always tell that something is wrong.*

Last but not least, the two characters stand as symmetrical figures medically. Mr. Monk is a hypochondriac, whereas Dr. House is in denial—that is, Monk suffers from and is impaired by problems, fears, and diseases that are not real; while Dr. House is constantly in denial of the very real problems that ail him and impair his cognitive skills.

Now, as far as the shows are concerned, one might also point out that in each episode, *Monk*'s writers find a new way of putting

Adrian in some kind of new physical or moral discomfort (which, in general, involves immersing him in a situation or *milieu* he would never have entered by his own will) while giving him a new impossible crime to solve. Similarly, *House*'s producers find a new way of letting their medical genius find new ways to harass his entourage and make himself even more despicable than before while giving him a new case to crack. Monk is an intriguing figure investigating disturbing cases. House is a disturbing character investigating intriguing cases. Or is it the other way around?

The two characters also seem more interested in overcoming the current intellectual challenge they are facing than in addressing the moral issues involved in solving a crime or curing a patient, or weighing the ethical dilemmas arising from the case.

The sixteenth-century French physician-writer François Rabelais once wrote, "Science without conscience is a waste of the soul." Since crime solving and healthcare both heavily rely on the sciences to right wrongs and cure diseases, is it really possible, as it might appear, that Adrian Monk and Greg House lack any kind of moral conscience or personal ethics while working for what appears to be the greater good?

At first, the two characters seem very much different and remote from any real personality we might know. Their exceptional minds make them look alien to any "normal" human being. At first Monk's and House's love of puzzles appears to be purely intellectual and to raise no moral dilemma in their mind. After all, in true Sherlock Holmes tradition, they are superior intellects who get easily repelled or bored by the everyday and by much of what makes up a 'normal' life. But in that very sense, solving mysteries is not only their one and almost only occupation, it's also their only remedy against boredom (House) and anxiety (Monk).

Although it may seem to keep them apart from 'ordinary' people, this ongoing struggle against boredom and anxiety is actually one of the features that make them most resemble the audience: in order to capture their (our) attention, they (we) have to be presented with an *outstanding* situation, one they have never met before, one that has never been shown to us before, one very disturbing situation that we wish made sense. Even though Monk's and House's intelligence is much greater than ours, their wish to be entertained and to explain the unexplainable makes them our equals.

Heredity

The audience may have difficulties relating to Monk's and House's troubled and (respectively) irreparably phobic and intrinsically cynical personalities. But again, these are features that make them more endearing to us than Holmes is in Conan Doyle's stories. In the Holmesian canon, we learn little about Holmes' feelings and faults, but much more about Watson's inner life, beliefs, and past, and his inferiority complex towards his roommate. In *Monk* and *House, M.D.*, conversely, we learn much about the character's past and inner life, and especially their relationships with their parents.

At first, one might say that Monk has "mother issues" (he always wants to be pampered and taken care of) while House has "father issues" (he constantly rebels against authority and established codes). But this would be a gross oversimplification.

In an early episode of *House, M.D.* ("Three Stories," Season One) we learn that Greg House was misdiagnosed as a patient and that this medical mistake made him a cripple. He has lived many years with Stacy, the woman he loved (and still loves, as episodes 122 to 211 illustrate). We learn (in the Season 6 finale) that he has had a relationship a long time ago with Dr. Cuddy, the Hospital administrator who once was his doctor. That affair must have taken place *after* he was misdiagnosed, after Cuddy took care of House, and after House broke with Stacy (while House was sedated, Stacy, as his legal proxy, had taken a decision he didn't agree with). Ever since that triply symbolic event (the crippling, Stacy's treason, Cuddy's care), House has worked in Princeton-Plainsboro under Dr. Cuddy's moral authority. In the Season 6 finale, we learn he still has deep feelings for her. In the meantime he has shown compassion for a number of patients, even though he may have been rude and sarcastic with them. As early as the Pilot episode, he showed respect for a patient who refused further care. In "One Day, One Room" (Season 3), a rape victim demanded to talk only with him because she sensed that he had gone through the same kind of abuse when he was a child. In "Frozen" (Season 4), House misdiagnosed a female doctor stuck at the South Pole because he cared for her: he wanted her to undress in order for him to examine her naked body through their video connection. She complied but refused to take off her socks, arguing that to show her naked feet would be too 'intimate'. Had House insisted, he would have diagnosed her earlier: her symptoms were provoked by a fractured toe.

What of Monk, then? In "Monk and Little Monk," we learned Adrian was pretty much raised and trained to be phobic by his abusively phobic mother. We met his brother Ambrose ("Mr. Monk Goes Home Again"), only to find that he also is very deeply disturbed and socially impaired, presumably also by their mother's behavior.[2] In Season 5, we met his father ("Mr. Monk Meets His Dad") and found that Monk looks as strange to him as he is estranged from him. Knowing a bit about Mrs. Monk, there is no real question why Adrian's father decided to go away and abandon his family. Finally, when we meet Monk's other brother in Season 6 ("Mr. Monk's Other Brother"), a two-bit crook named Jack Jr., Monk has to decide whether he will help him or just send him back to jail. He has to position himself as someone who abides by the law or who chooses to stand by his sibling, however alien he may seem.

These clues and many others show that neither Monk nor House are deprived of feelings or moral values. House finds moral guidance in Wilson's friendship and Stacy and Cuddy's stance against his numerous childish and egotistic decisions; Monk finds psychological support in Stottlemeyer's, Dr. Kroger's and Natalie's presence, and moral guidance in the memory of his late wife Trudy.

From this deeper perspective, Adrian Monk and Greg House appear as boy-geniuses that abusive parents (Monk's mother, House's father-figures) kept from maturing, and whose positive male and female figures of the present help to function in spite of their difficult behaviors. House and Monk may be socially and ethically impaired, but they have not always been so. Once, House was not yet a cripple. Once, Monk was not as phobic and obsessive-compulsive. They were children once, life and specific influences changed them, and they know it. As adults, they may lack the clarity of mind (or the maturity) to make healthy, ethical and moral choices, but they certainly choose to function under the influence of a number of people who can—and do—question their misconducts and push them in the right direction. They may be sick, but they don't totally reject their friends' help. And for these very same reasons, again, they are very much like us.

---

[2] Ambrose is very much reminiscent of Mycroft, Sherlock Holmes's brother. An even more brilliant mind than his brother, Mycroft is "omniscient," serves as a government advisor, and virtually never leaves the Diogenes Club, which he co-founded. He's the first "armchair detective."

Teachings

One undisputable value of shows such as *Monk* and *House, M.D.* is their capacity to entertain the audience while enlightening them. You always *learn* something while watching *Monk* or *House, M.D.*—although it's more an emotional truth than a factual or logical one—just by the diversity of intriguing situations and the variety of disturbing cases. Both shows are obviously aimed to entertain and to stimulate the mind. At the beginning of each show, while the case-of-the-week is laid out to the team and the viewers, House and Monk often behave at first like children impatient to play with their new toy, and they pester everyone around them.

But as the story unfolds, they get more deeply involved with the case and the persons related to it. They sometimes may seem to do so because Natalie of Wilson or Stottlemeyer or Cuddy *told* them to. But one cannot say they simply *obey* their friends and partners since, in many occasions, they are shown rejecting their advice or request and acting as they see fit. Complying with an outside request can either mean that Cuddy or Natalie are right (but *really,* how can they be?) or that House or Monk understand *this is the right thing to do.* In many shows, Monk and House admit they have been wrong—even though they put the blame on someone else, instead of invoking some logical error on their own part. But, more often than not, they show they can learn from their own mistakes and from their friends' opinions and teachings.

By the end of each show, House and Monk enjoy giving the explanation of the case, the solution of the mystery to their friends and colleagues. Especially when these are cases which baffled everyone, including themselves, for days or weeks. Solving the mystery and giving out the answer to all assembled is dramatic and enjoyable. It is a moment of recognition and vindication for the characters. Still, more than once, Monk and House subsequently pretend to be unaffected by words of gratitude or admiration. This is not the sign of real indifference; their apparent remoteness is a symptom of a darker, deeper feeling.

Motives

Monk and House are damaged.

Trudy's unsolved murder has left Monk a social misfit and a phobic wreck. During the course of the show, Monk meets with several women who remind him of Trudy—including one who looks like her ("Mr. Monk and the Other Woman"). He connects with them, but always goes back to his celibacy in memory of his late wife. He would rather live alone with his obsessive behavior than live with anyone else.

On *House, M.D.,* Stacy's decision to authorize surgery on House's leg has turned the physician into a physical cripple and a misanthropic nuisance. During several episodes of the first two seasons, Greg House reconnects with his former companion, Stacy, now married, and we see him operate under her benevolent, forgiving, stimulating and then increasingly caring presence. Finally, he comes to terms with their relationship and they part. House can live without Stacy, even as a cripple.

Even though both characters refuse to be 'healed' by women who seem to care for them, they are not desperate to the point of giving up their way of life. Week after week, they tackle cases that are always more puzzling. Solving puzzles is what they like, but dealing with people is the one thing they dislike most. So why do they do it? Risking interaction to solve enigmas cannot be the result of some masochistic trait, as they show no pleasure in being reminded how *antisocial* they are. They mostly find pleasure in confronting someone or something challenging. Smart people—especially geniuses—crave for intellectual challenge, from fear of boredom. This is, in a way, the 'standard' model for detectives, again established by Sir Arthur Conan Doyle. And even Holmes had his 'lost woman': the mysterious Irene Adler, whom he met in the very first short story of the Holmes canon, "A Scandal in Bohemia," never to see her again.

Now, if the quest for the loved and lost woman is not what makes Holmes and Monk and House tick (and keep on investigating the impossible), what does? The answer lies in the characters' dynamics and relationship *with the audience.*

The single moment when House and Monk show pleasure is when they explain what they have understood and play with other people's curiosity and puzzlement. House's description of antibodies floating in the patient's bloodstream jump at us, while figures re-enact a murder in black-and-white just after Monk says 'Here's what happened'. Monk and House relish in *storytelling.* And this behavior indicates that in this continuing game of hide-and-seek that House and Monk play with us, the *real* culprits are the show's writers.

Authority

House, M.D.'s creator, David Shore once said in an interview:

> In many ways I don't consider this a medical show . . . The things that interest me in the show are the philosophical things . . . I think good shows always deal with ethical dilemmas and ethical questions. Good dramas are usually about throwing your characters into situations where, do you turn right or do you turn left? And something bad will happen if you turn right and something bad will happen if you turn left—which one's worse? This show has a lot of these moments, which is a great opportunity, but it also has chances for my personal perspective on the world.[3]

According to Andy Breckman's statements in the writers' interviews in the Season 1 DVD box set, all of *Monk*'s writers like to put each of their own personal phobias in the character's life. They like to make his life miserable and use their own phobias as something they can satirize, and somehow overcome, with laughter. On the other hand, we can guess that the twisted crimes Breckman and his team make him investigate—from the killer who arranges to be in a coma when his victim dies ("Mr. Monk and the Sleeping Suspect") to the man who vandalizes a painting in order for his ex-wife to reconnect with an old flame and remarry ("Mr. Monk and Little Monk")—are so many opportunities to explore the minds of individuals who usually have very primitive reasons to kill: jealousy, greed, power lust, revenge. This, too, is very familiar to the viewer. Which one of us hasn't, at least once, dreamed to kill his obnoxious or insufferable next-door neighbor or abusive great-granduncle using a contorted method that would make it the perfect crime?

　With their exceptional power of insight and their flaws, Monk and House are hypothetical selves, put in situations the writers want to explore in ways that echo in the audience's psyche. As exciting and fascinating as these two figures may be, their behaviors are not the actions of a *real* obsessive-compulsive investigator and a *real* misanthropic diagnostician, but what writers gave actors to play in front of (and *with*) an audience. Therefore the characters themselves cannot be adequately qualified as behaving in an "eth-

---

[3] See Stacey Gibson's article "The House that Dave Built," *U of T Magazine* (Winter 2008) <www.magazine.utoronto.ca>.

ical" or "unethical" manner. For, much more than mere representations of real human beings, they stand like the impersonation of a "moral imperative" at work in both shows: the writers'—and our—relentless quest for understanding contorted psychological and pathological processes through role-playing.

To identify the ethical motives that drive Adrian Monk's and Gregory House's *stories*, let us then go back the oldest philosophical and theatrical stage known to Western Culture: Greek Mythology.

Ethics

As continuing fictional characters, both Monk and House seem to be driven by the same goal: the relentless search for the truth. As soon as he meets a murderer, Monk can tell he's lying, even though he doesn't yet know how the crime was perpetrated. Each time he is presented with a new case study, House's motto states that 'Everybody lies'—including patients, who, by hiding the truth, are at the least accomplices to their own disease. But when you look at it more closely, you can see that Monk's and House's interest goes beyond finding the simpler answer: when they are presented with a puzzle, whether criminal or medical, their purpose is not so much to discover *who* the guilty party is (Monk almost always identifies the culprit at once; House always knows the answer lies somewhere in the patient's untold story), but *how* the murder was committed or the symptoms appeared. Their goal is not to put a murderer in jail or cure a patient; they do not act in the name of Justice, or of Medical Ethics. They aim to shed light on the obscure *process* which led to the murder or the illness. From that perspective, they are related to another mythological figure, that of Prometheus.

According to *Prometheus Bound,* an ancient Greek tragedy attributed to Aeschylus, Prometheus, himself a Titan, helped Zeus overcome the Titans, the former gods. Subsequently, Prometheus stole fire from Zeus to give it to mankind. He also taught mankind writing, mathematics, medicine, and astronomy, and he opposed Zeus's plan to destroy the human race. In punishment, Zeus had Prometheus bound to a mountain. Each day, an eagle sent by Zeus went to feed on Prometheus's liver, tearing it from him; and each night his flesh and organs would heal, preserving his life for the next day's torture. In French philosopher Gaston Bachelard's words, Prometheus symbolizes the will of human to learn "as much as our fathers, as much as and more than our teachers". For Bachelard, "the 'Prometheus complex' is the 'Oedipus complex' of intellectual life" (*The Psychoanalysis of Fire*, 1938), and in both, pain follows from knowledge.

Adrian Monk and Gregory House are both bright and literate but from a strict medical point of view, they should not be allowed to work on cases. Monk is a very troubled OCD patient, still undergoing three-times-a-week therapy sessions, and his anxiety very often interferes with his judgment. The recent demise of his long-time therapist, Dr. Kroger, has put a supplementary toll on his sanity. Is it wise to let him investigate crimes? The same question stands for Dr. House: in reality, his attitude towards patients, fellow doctors, hospital policy and medical resources would make any administrator throw him out of the hospital in a second. Is it wise to let him *treat* anybody? Why do Captain Stottlemeyer and Dr Cuddy even *stand* those jerks?

Well, the answer is simple, and it doesn't have anything to do with tolerance, it has to do with *the drama that life is*. Just like the audience, writers are individuals deeply flawed and doomed to die; through their powers of imagination they elaborate complex narratives in order to distract themselves—and us—from mankind's tragic fate, and to find answers to fundamental questions. Each in its own way, *Monk* and *House, M.D.* thus exemplify the Prometheus complex in televised narrative form. The writers' and characters' quest is one that seeks to disclose mechanisms—the hidden scheme of a murder, the hidden course of a pathological process—to free mankind (the audience) from the darkness in which they are kept. Both characters are metaphorically punished for their insights and kept in chains—Monk by his OCD; House by his addiction and his crippled leg. But even though they are cursed and punished and bound, they rebel against the gods, or the rules of man, whenever they are presented with another mystery to solve. Such is their function, whatever the consequences may be for themselves.

Identity

Who is Gregory House? Not quite the 'doctor we love to hate' but, above all, the physician each of us (writers and viewers, doctors and non-doctors) would love to *be*. A doctor who always knows there's something wrong, which is definitely *not* what other doctors believe (when House hears hoof-beats in the doorway, he can always tell it's *not* a horse . . .); a doctor who has no qualms in finding out which disease it is whatever the cost; a doctor who will never give up on his patient. House allows each of us to become the ultimate physician: one who experiments and harasses and straightforwardly tells truths nobody wants to hear; one who always speaks his mind, without any respect for social etiquette; one who always has a good reason to break the rules; one who can dismiss pain with analgesics and sorrow with scorn. He is the ultimate *transgressor.* "The better the villain, the better the film," Alfred Hitchcock said. Better still if hero and villain come all wrapped into one, and act as evil twins, very much the way Batman and The Joker do in *The Dark Knight.* House is the doctor who deliberately acts wrongly for the greater good. House is the dark-sided superhero doctor everyone would love to be, and one who carries his own villain inside. One for whom the end always justifies the means *because he understands the secrets of life and death.* And when he seeks for the truth, we know he'll not only end up finding it out, but that he'll *share it with us.*

Who is Adrian Monk? Not simply the brilliant sleuth we find so endearing because of his phobias, but the super-gifted child every one of us—writers and viewers—once wished (and sometimes still wishes) to be: one who can show his disgust when a stranger wants to touch him; one who can say 'No' to his mother when she wants him to do what he won't; one who can touch every single object he pleases to put it where *he* thinks it belongs in true godlike childishly innocent self-centered disregard. He is the boy-wonder who can open secret vaults with a simple, elegant, formula. And above all, he is the innocent child who *knows* all the wrongdoings of adults and who, even though he was spared the blemish of painful experience, is always *aware of what is right and what is wrong.* And we know that when he understands how the wrongdoing was done, *he'll tell us.*

In his recent and brilliant book *On the Origin of Stories: Evolution, Cognition and Fiction,* Bryan Boyd shows that fiction is a powerful evolutionary adaptation central to human culture. He writes that fiction provides us with "situations with enough emotional and ethical similarities" to our lives and experience "to provide a basis for our thinking." "Fiction," he claims, "can *design* events and characters to provoke us to reflect on, say, generosity, or threat, or deception and counter-deception. And it efficiently evokes our intense emotional engagement without requiring our belief." [4]

With different means but similar goals, *Monk* and *House, M.D.* thus exemplify the ethical qualities of the best TV narratives: under the guise of 'sheer' entertainment, both shows and their characters confront us with logical riddles, scientific and psychological insight, moral choices, life dilemmas and clinical ethics, while addressing love and friendship, anger and grief, the fear of death and the quest for justice. They appease our fear of boredom by designing elaborate questions in order to satisfy our craving for answers, one hour at the time.

Naturally, one episode is never enough. We come back for more, hoping it won't end, and knowing it will: the show will eventually be canceled; we might even *die* before the next episode is aired. To us, the audience, *Monk* and *House, M.D.* are very much like their characters' personality traits. They are a gift *and* a curse. And we love these two figures (and their hidden puppet masters, the writers), because they aim to find light and share its comforting warmth with us.

---

[4] Brian Boyd, *On the Origin of Stories* (Belknap, 2009), p. 193.

11

Mr. Monk and the Emotion-Reason Dilemma

E. DEIDRE PRIBRAM

Adrian Monk (Tony Shalhoub) belongs to a tradition of brilliant but personally flawed detectives. Like others in this tradition, including his television colleague, Dr. Gregory House (Hugh Laurie), Monk's genius resides in his exceptional, even excessive, rationality. Both Monk and House embody near-perfect detection or diagnostic skills. And, in both cases, the cause of their damaged personalities is excessive emotionality, represented by their respective emotional disorders. In their internal dynamics, emotion is almost always the 'problem,' and both shows suggest that troubled emotionality is the price Monk and House must pay for their intense brilliance.

Monk and *House, M.D.* explore the issue further by providing each lead with a male best-friend whose personality also encompasses aspects of emotion and reason, but in differing configurations than the main characters. In contrast to the series' leads, Police Captain Leland Stottlemeyer (Ted Levine) and Dr. James Wilson (Robert Sean Leonard) achieve a more successful integration of the emotional and rational dimensions of their lives. The trade-off, however, is that neither can reach the level of intellectual genius that Monk and House exhibit on a weekly basis. Yet they function as important alternative models of how emotion and reason might be conceived.

The Rational Detective

Toby Miller notes that, within the framework of the classic television detective drama, "detection has meant the identification and defeat of wrongdoers, by applying reason to explain events that are irregular and socially undesirable."[1] Further, detective shows as rational genres have typically *bracketed out* emotions. Emotional detachment and stoicism are among the greatest personal achievements in traditional masculine and rational codes of behavior.

Jason Mittell describes the 1950s series, *Dragnet,* as ideologically conservative but foundational to the development of the police drama.[2] Among its specific techniques, the flat and monotone acting style filtered out "most emotional nuances and dramatic pauses," prioritizing "*systemic* over *emotional* realism" (p. 137). Here, emotional detachment is equated with the successful operation of the criminal justice system, in that chaos, crime, and emotions are identified with one another, and placed outside the realm of reason, justice, and correct police procedure. Lead detective Joe Friday (Jack Webb), is "detached, objective, reliable" with "no visible flaws, biases, or even emotions," again equating elements like flaws and biases with emotions (pp. 141, 140).

In an article on the 1990s British detective series *Cracker*, Glen Creeber argues that lead character, Fitz (Robbie Coltrane), is a compelling incorporation of the traditional or "old sleuth" and the "new man." As old sleuth, Fitz fits the "masculine archetype" of the hard-boiled detective, one component of which is his unemotional professional style.[3] He is "rugged, quick-witted and the embodiment of cool masculine power," "relying almost wholly on reason to understand and decode the world around him" (pp. 171, 173). In his considerable professional skills, if not in his more disastrous personal life, Fitz is a controlled individual, driven by reason, not emotionality.

What Mittell and Creeber describe are two traditions in the 'rational detective' formula. Joe Friday is meant to represent reason in its purity, with no emotions exhibited by the character or supposedly included in the narrative, as signaled by the show's catchphrase, "Just the facts, Ma'am." Being wholly professional in this formula means, first, that emotions do not intrude upon the

---

[1] "The Action Series." In *The Television Genre Book*, edited by G. Creeber (BFI, 2001), p. 18.

[2] *Genre and Television: From Cop Shows to Cartoons in American Culture* (Routledge, 2004), pp. 124, 127.

[3] Glen Creeber, "Old Sleuth or New Man? Investigations into Rape, Murder, and Masculinity in *Cracker* (1993–1996)," *Continuum: Journal of Media and Cultural Studies* 16.2 (2002), p. 171.

business of crime-solving and, second, that the detective is represented as having no, or the most minimal, personal life. Personality, in the sense of feelings, quirks, desires, and aversions are largely absent, because they are perceived, like emotionality, as flaws and biases.

The second, more contemporary tradition in the rational detective formula is exemplified by *Cracker*. Here, a personal life and personality are a crucial part of the narrative.[4] Fitz is a forensic psychologist who provides criminal profiles for the Manchester Police Force and, in the process, solves cases through the intense psychological interrogation of suspects. He's a detective who uses "his own dark turmoil to 'crack' the mind of a murderer" (Creeber, p. 169). Along with "a deep-rooted moral compassion, a razor-sharp wit and a prodigious intellect" that he applies to his professional life, the show also explores "the troubled terrain of his personal life" (pp. 171, 169). Cracker is an alcoholic, chain-smoking, compulsive gambler. During the course of the series, he has an affair with a colleague causing his wife, Judith (Barbara Flynn), to leave him. When Fitz enters his own domestic arena, which involves a significant component of the program, he is "compelled to acknowledge the *personal* problems in his life and address areas of *private* experience not usually associated with his generic territory" (p. 176). The series' originality and appeal is located in its purposeful exploration of the contrast between Fitz's consummate professional skills and his disastrous social relationships, both professional and personal. As the brilliant forensic psychologist tells his wife, "My life's a mess. I've fouled up. Emotionally, I'm incompetent" (quoted in Creeber, p. 176).

This second tradition represented by *Cracker*—the tradition of the professionally brilliant but emotionally plagued detective—can be applied to Adrian Monk and Gregory House. Like *Cracker*, *Monk* and *House* deliberately explore the contradictions and conflicts between the main characters' rational genius and their disordered emotionality. Indeed, both shows are premised on this central character conflict, which is at least as important to the

---

[4] There are also rationally brilliant but unfailingly warm, compassionate detectives. Examples are Jessica Fletcher (Angela Lansbury) of *Murder, She Wrote* and Mark Sloan (Dick Van Dyke) of *Diagnosis Murder*. And, of course, there are also emotional dynamics in otherwise rationally-motivated buddy-cop characters or ensemble casts.

meanings and pleasures generated by the two series as any of the cases they solve.

As Creeber describes it, there's a clear-cut distinction between Fitz's professional actions and his personal and emotional behavior. This structures the narrative in an opposition in which the "flaws, biases, and emotions," in Mittell's terms, reside almost entirely in the character's personal realm—if 'personal' is understood to include both workplace and domestic *relationships*—but do not seem to affect his professional virtue: his brilliant rationality.

Emotion and reason are represented in *Monk* and *House* as distinctly separate tendencies within the lead characters. It is the struggle between emotion and reason that makes these characters both complex and fascinating; the source of their turmoil lies in their apparent inability to reconcile their rational and emotive selves. This aspect of their characters has much to tell us about how we, as a culture, currently understand emotion and reason.

Mr. Monk

Adrian Monk is an exceedingly brilliant detective with encyclopedic knowledge, unparalleled observational skills, and an ability to see patterns—or breaks in patterns—in crime scenes and other people's behavior. He also suffers from obsessive-compulsive disorder as well as numerous phobias; according to Monk, in the following order of magnitude: "germs, needles, milk, death, snakes, mushrooms, heights, crowds, elevators" ("Mr Monk and the Very, Very Old Man").

In the words of series creator and executive producer Andy Breckman, "Monk can barely function in the world. He's a walking bundle of fears and neuroses and obsessive rituals."[5] Breckman points to the debilitating nature of severe OCD: the intense anxiety and fear it causes, the time and energy required for OCD-related activities, and the inability to function successfully in professional, social, and personal capacities.

Obsessive-compulsive disorder, classified in the DSM-IV under emotional pathologies as an anxiety disorder, displays symptoms that have been grouped into the following four categories: obsessions and checking; symmetry and ordering; cleanliness and washing; and

---

[5] Terry Erdmann and Paula Block, *Monk: The Official Episode Guide* (St. Martin's, 2006), pp. 5–6.

hoarding.[6] Monk exhibits the first three of these classes of symptoms, and his agoraphobic brother Ambrose exhibits the fourth.

The various mood and anxiety disturbances are emotional disorders, not illnesses of reason. They are not, in themselves, accompanied by visual or auditory hallucinations, or other symptoms that we associate with disconnection from a commonly-shared 'reality'. Indeed, one of the more interesting aspects of those who suffer from OCD is that they are aware their behavior is abnormal or excessive but the accompanying anxiety compels them, nonetheless, to perform their OCD-related activities.

Monk's OCD produces fear, paranoia, isolation from others, and selfishness. Not only does he have an emotional disorder but it creates emotional disorder in his relationships with other people. The series repeatedly stresses Monk's genius and his illness, *simultaneously*. His brilliance and the resulting fame and admiration he receives are immediately linked with his 'problem'. Near the beginning of "Mr. Monk Goes to the Circus," a number of officials are gathered at a crime scene. An Officer Myers explains to Lieutenant Disher (Jason Gray-Stanford) his delight in watching the celebrated Monk at work:

> We really lucked out. That's Adrian Monk . . . He's the best crime scene investigator in the department. We studied all his cases at the Academy . . . I can't believe he's here. It's like meeting Mick Jagger.

Inevitably, moments later Captain Stottlemeyer, Monk's boss and friend, approaches Myers to inform him that he must leave the crime scene because his socks, although both black, aren't an identical match, and are interfering with Monk's ability to concentrate.

The two-hour series pilot depicts at least twenty instances of compulsions and phobias.[7] What is significant about these depictions, unlike the mismatched socks incident, is that many of them

---

[6] David Watson, "Rethinking the Mood and Anxiety Disorders: A Quantitative Hierarchical Model for DSM-V." *Journal of Abnormal Psychology* 114:4 (November, 2005), pp. 521–532.

[7] When out, he is anxious that he left his gas stove on; at home he counts strokes as he brushes his teeth and reaches into his closet of identical clothing; straightens objects (pillows, flowers) in his therapist's office; panics when Sharona, his nurse-assistant, drives; cleans his hand with a sanitizing wipe immediately after shaking Stottlemeyer's hand; twice indicates his fear of heights; avoids being touched; moves mixed-colored push pins on a map to solid blocks of color, then

are anxieties and fears with which audience members can understand and sympathize. Early on, Monk's compulsions and phobias
were intended to evoke empathy as much as humor, although, as
the series progresses OCD-related behaviors are increasingly
played for their comedic value. Initially, however, the series represented a strikingly original development for American television by
placing the audience in the position of someone who lives with
such fears. For instance, we share in Monk's horror when he must
descend into the city sewers in order to rescue Sharona (Bitty
Schram) in the series pilot. We understand his terror and how difficult this must be for him.

At the end of the first scene of the pilot ("Mr. Monk and the
Candidate"), three police officers, having just witnessed Monk's for-
midable abilities in analyzing a crime scene interspersed with his
gnawing anxiety that he has left the gas stove on at home, sum up
the situation:

FIRST OFFICER: So that's the famous Adrian Monk?

SECOND OFFICER: Yeah, the living legend.

THIRD OFFICER: If you call that living.[8]

In three brief lines of dialogue, the officers summarize both the
central conflict in Monk's character and the premise of the series.

---

puts them all back as they were by memory; panics that he has lost his keys; is terrified by a classroom full of coughing schoolchildren; won't go down the hill to a
crime scene because it involves stepping in mud; eats the same food on specific
days; counts each pea that goes into his chicken potpie; straightens the objects on
a restaurant table; uses the TV remote only when inside a baggie; throws away a
can of food because it has an imperceptible dent; counts and touches each parking meter as he walks along the street; takes shredded documents out of the
garbage and resequences the strips of paper; is immobilized on a fire escape ladder due to his fear of heights; wraps his walkie-talkie in plastic; and is understandably horrified when he must descend into a sewer filled with human waste
and rats.

[8] *Editor's Note:* An old joke, used very well in this scene. Sigmund Freud wrote
of this joke almost a hundred years earlier, in his 1905 book, *Jokes and Their
Relation to the Unconscious.* The version he wrote of featured a young man angry
at a matchmaker. Confronting the matchmaker about the woman he had been set
up with, and was now engaged to, he says "You said her father was no longer living! But now I have found out he's serving a prison term!" The matchmaker replies,
"You call that living?"

Although we realize that Monk's genius and disorder are linked, how that actually occurs is never fully explored. The series builds on a long-standing tradition in Western culture that links genius (most commonly, artistic) to emotional disorders or other forms of mental illness. Yet, precisely how his emotional disorder might enhance his rational brilliance is more presumed than explained in *Monk*. The OCD-related attribute that comes closest to achieving such a link is the concern with symmetry and ordering. Monk's striking ability to see patterns, or breaks in patterns, in crime scenes or in other people's behavior is enhanced, perhaps, by his compulsion for symmetry and order, allowing him to meticulously and rapidly assess what has been added, what is missing, or what is out of place—his keen observation of the incongruous. However, it is less clear how obsessions and checking, cleanliness and washing, or any of his specific phobias (heights, crowds, physical contact) might enhance rather than diminish his intellectual acumen.

The USA Network website indicates that Monk's professional expertise exists *in spite of* his disorder: "Yet despite his condition, Monk remains a brilliant detective."[9] More often, however, series episodes link the two aspects of Monk's personality as if they were *necessary corollaries*, in which he cannot have one (intellectual genius) without the other (emotional torment). We see this link in his simultaneous performance of crime scene analysis and personal obsession, a recurring element of the show, as displayed in the opening scene of the pilot when Monk juggles his acute insight of the evidence with the acute anxiety that he has left his gas stove on.

In "Mr. Monk and the Very, Very Old Man," Stottlemeyer tells Monk, "I don't mind living in your shadow, Monk. You're a freak of nature." Stottlemeyer suggests that he must live in Monk's shadow because of the latter's crime-solving virtuosity but that Monk's abilities, in turn, are tied directly to his emotional oddities. In "Mr. Monk Takes His Medicine," Stottlemeyer's premise is borne out when Monk takes a medication that alleviates his OCD but also eliminates both his desire and aptitude for crime-solving.

The *Monk* series indicates repeatedly that Monk's OCD fuels or somehow purifies his intellectual powers of reason. His excessive rationality is matched by his excessive emotionality, represented by his OCD. Monk's extreme emotionality is essential to his exquisite

---

[9] USA Network, <www.usanetwork.com/series/monk/theshow/characterprofiles>.

powers of reason, in a relationship in which emotion serves as a kind of punishment for the reward of intellectual brilliance.

Dr. House

Gregory House is an exceedingly brilliant diagnostician with ency-clopedic medical knowledge, the ability to provoke ideas and debate among collaborators beyond any single individual's poten-tial, and a dogged determination to analyze clue-like symptoms until the pieces fall into place and the truth is revealed. Echoing Monk, a fan website describes the doctor "as an observational genius with the ability to see a pattern in small things and draw conclusions from that," providing a definition of both House and the rational process.[10]

House also has an unspecified mood or personality disorder. Additionally, he is addicted to Vicodin. Substance abuse is considered an externalizing dimension of a psychopathological condition, accompanying the emotional, internalizing dimension of mood or personality disorders (Watson, pp. 529–530).

House's disorder results in cruelty to others, social isolation, and extreme self-absorption. As Wilson, his colleague and best friend, tells House, "They could build monuments to your self-centered-ness" ("House vs. God"). He is disdainful and misanthropic, seeing virtually no good in people. Socially and interpersonally immature, House is either coldly indifferent or overtly hurtful to his patients. He is a miserable person in both senses of the term—how he treats others and what his existence is like.

House's one redeeming quality is his intellectual brilliance. A patient's family member observes, "I assume House is a great doc-tor." Chase (Jesse Spencer), a member of House's medical team, asks, "Why would you assume that?" The family member answers, "Because when you're that big a jerk, you're either great or unem-ployed" ("Sex Kills").

Deborah Kirklin notes, "Fear and pity are not emotions that Dr. Gregory House acknowledges or accommodates in either his pro-fessional or personal life. He is arrogant, rude and considers all patients lying idiots."[11] At the same time, "He will do anything, ille-

---

[10] House M.D. Guide, <www.housemd-guide.com>.
[11] Deborah Kirklin, "Lessons in Pity and Caring from Dickens to Melville," *Medical Humanities* 34 (2008), p. 57.

gal or otherwise, to ensure that his patients—passive objects of his expert attentions—get the investigations and treatments he knows they need" (p. 57).

In "The Afterbirth of the Clinic: A Foucauldian Perspective on *House*," the authors focus on the notion of House treating patients "as passive objects of his expert attentions."[12] They argue that House represents a modernist approach to medicine that emerged in the US in the nineteenth and early twentieth centuries, and which coincides with Foucault's analysis in *Birth of the Clinic*. Like Foucault's modern clinician, House "subtracts" the patient as "deceptive background noise" in order to deal directly with the disease (pp. 2-3). The patient becomes interference in the physician's "distanced, authoritarian scientific style" (p. 7).

While I agree with the authors' description of House's central character conflict, the show's premise is based precisely in exploring and critiquing House's lack of 'humanity'; another signature modernist concept. When Foreman (Omar Epps), another member of House's medical team, poses the question, "Isn't treating patients why we became doctors?", House asserts: "No, treating illnesses is why we became doctors, treating patients is what makes most doctors miserable . . . If you don't talk to them they can't lie to us, and we can't lie to them. Humanity is overrated" ("Pilot").

While this may be a fair representation of House's position, the series itself repeatedly questions modernity's scientific, rational approach by evaluating it against modern humanism, with its emphasis on the rights and uniqueness of the individual. The contradiction between the goals of science and the values of humanism is exactly where House's (and perhaps modernity's) deficiencies and internal conflict reside.

The Emotion-Reason Dilemma in Western Thought

A common Western motif is to position emotionality against rationality, thereby structuring emotion and reason as oppositional

---

[12] Leigh Rich, Jack Simmons, David Adams, Scott Thorp, and Michael Mink. "The Afterbirth of the Clinic: A Foucauldian Perspective on *House, M.D.* and American Medicine in the 21st Century," *Perspectives in Biology and Medicine* 51:2 (Spring 2008), pp. 1–12, <muse.jhu.edu/journals/perspectives_in_biology_and_medicine>.

categories. Contemporary theorists, including feminist scholars, have challenged the idea that modern Western thought and practice is dispassionate and wholly rational. In this view, reason has been regarded as the faculty most essential to the production of objective, reliable, and universal understandings of reality. Philosopher Alison Jaggar has argued that, while a distinction between reason and emotion has a long history in Western thought, the extreme polarization of the two developed only with the rise of modern science in the seventeenth and eighteenth centuries.[13] As part of this development, emotion became accepted as the inverse of reason, dangerous because it subverted scientific inquiry.

The logic of this approach rests on a series of conceptual dichotomies—culture-nature, mind-body, reason-emotion—in which culture, mind, and reason dominate the inferior categories of nature, body, and emotion.[14] While scientific and rational thought have been understood as largely masculine, emotions have been associated with the feminine, nature, the body, and the private. Women have been one of the main social groups aligned with emotions and, as such, inevitably regarded as more 'subjective', biased, and irrational (Jaggar, p. 158).

Medical historian Fay Bound Alberti, describes how "men of science" sought to master their emotions "in order to convey an image of detached investigation in the scientific process," because it was believed, from the eighteenth century on, that medical practice required being unemotional "as a necessary precondition for an objective diagnosis."[15] Instead, she claims that medical diagnoses are "culturally situated," and that the emotions of the investigator are key to understanding how diagnoses are "socially and politically generated" (p. xiv). We can take as examples the widespread nineteenth-century phenomenon of hysteria, diagnosed almost solely in women, or twentieth-century beliefs that the mood shifts associated with female menstrual hormones made women unsuit-

---

[13] Alison Jaggar, "Love and Knowledge: Emotion in Feminist Epistemology," in *Gender/Body/Knowledge: Feminist Reconstructions of Being and Knowing*, edited by A.M. Jaggar and S.R. Bordo (Rutgers University Press, 1989), p. 145.

[14] Harding, Sandra, *The Science Question in Feminism* (Open University, 1986), p. 23.

[15] Fay Bound Alberti, "Introduction: Medical History and Emotion Theory," in *Medicine, Emotion, and Disease, 1700–1950*, edited by F.B. Alberti (Palgrave Macmillan, 2006), pp. xxi, xiii.

able for top political positions. In Alberti's argument, these illnesses tell us more about the gendered values and attitudes of the medical professionals making the diagnoses, the result of the cultural contexts in which they existed, than in describing the illness or condition itself.

Emotions, because they have been perceived as occurring predominantly at the level of private, individual experience, have been dismissed as a disturbance: irrational and unreliable. The attribution of emotions as 'personal' evokes models in which emotions originate within and leak or burst out to affect the external social world. They overtake the individual, "rather as a storm sweeps over the land" (Jaggar, p. 146), posing a threat to both the feeling individual and the social world he or she occupies. Emotions are firmly located in a private sphere, their 'control' left to the individual, while reason is public, understood to be shared collectively. In contrast, this chapter considers emotions as social practices that infuse cultural discourses, institutions, and activities with meanings.[16]

Conflicted Characters

In keeping with the traditional Western view, both *Monk* and *House* treat emotion and reason in their main characters as incompatible categories. Although both characters are unusual for US television in their combining of heroic and anti-heroic elements, House is substantially the darker of the two. Where Monk is irritating and insensitive, House is deliberately cruel and unapologetic. Monk is in therapy, attempting recovery. House is in denial.

By playing Monk's OCD for its comedic opportunities, rather than for shock value as is more often the case with *House*, the former series achieves a lighter tone. This may explain the program's motivation in shifting increasingly to comedy. The move has softened the edges of the show's hero-antihero, making Monk a more likable character, tending toward the endearingly eccentric rather than the insufferable. The hero-antihero mix is based on each character's potential for redemption. Redemption for Monk appears distantly possible; the prognosis for House is hopeless. In the hero to anti-hero equation, the two characters are different in degree, if not in kind.

---

[16] For more on this, see Jennifer Harding and E. Deidre Pribram, "Introduction," *Emotions: A Cultural Studies Reader* (Routledge, 2009), pp. 12–47.

Additionally, although both series are built around a similar premise—how the lead characters manage the emotion-reason dichotomy—*House* more overtly acknowledges this subject matter. Perhaps nowhere is this made more explicit than in an episode titled, "One Day, One Room," written by series creator and executive producer, David Shore. Based entirely on clinic duty rounds, House's usual justification for his behavior is absent in this episode: the solving of a life-threatening medical mystery. Instead, his attention is occupied with a rape victim whose physical condition, an STD, is easily solved with a simple prescription. Far less easily resolved, however, is her emotional and psychological state.

For no rational reason, Eve (Katheryn Winnick) insists that she will talk only with House. At the same time, she adamantly refuses to discuss her 'condition' or 'problem': the rape. When she demands that they talk about other subjects, like the weather, House responds in frustration:

HOUSE: That's not rational!

EVE: Nothing's rational.

HOUSE: Everything is rational.

EVE: I was raped. Explain how that makes sense.

Eve forces House to deal with her as a person, not as an illness, disease, or pathological condition.

It is evident that Eve understands the logical arguments House makes to her (the rape wasn't her fault, it doesn't have to destroy her life) but that is not what she is looking for from him. For his part, House can't come to terms with what she wants or needs. To others, he admits that he's "useless at this."

House seeks advice from his hospital colleagues on the best way to interact with Eve. Yet when Chase tells him, "There is no wrong answer because there is no right answer," House denies the possibility that there are no objective certainties. House: "Wrong. We just don't know what the right answer is." Similarly, when House frames his discussion with Eve as a dialectic debate, she adamantly stops him: "I don't want to chat about philosophy." House responds, "This is the type of conversation I do well."

EVE: But the other type? The personal stuff?

HOUSE: There are no answers. If there are no answers, why talk about it?

In House's logic, if there are no clear, scientific answers to the "personal stuff" it must be, in effect, non-existent. He is not simply arguing for the pointlessness of such a discussion. Taking it one step further, in order to believe that the terms of his world make sense, the rationally inexplicable, of necessity, must be *absent*. House's emotional difficulties, particularly his anti-social behaviors, permit him to work, think, and exist in an illusory world of rational purity.

Emotion and reason must be portrayed as irreconcilable. Not because, as Monk maintains in the mismatched socks incident, the emotional poses a distraction. On the contrary, for both Monk and House, their emotional disorders, which represent an extreme or excessive form of emotionality, are important assets that somehow enable their exceptional powers of reason.

As we saw, *Cracker's* Fitz moves between two separate realms: the world of his successful professional performance, and the arena of his disastrous social and personal life. Monk and House, too, exist in dual fantasy-domains, in which their emotional disorders do not diminish or undermine their rational brilliance. In the first rational detective formula, represented by *Dragnet*, emotion is purportedly absent in the main character and in the narrative. In the second formula, exemplified by *Cracker, Monk,* and *House*, both emotion and reason are embedded within the person of the lead detective, but only as contradictory, ever-warring parts of the self. In the narrative model represented by *Cracker, Monk,* and *House*, the detectives represent a desire for an imagined uncorrupted rationality, attainable only in opposition to a creative but dangerous emotionality.

Best Friends

In "The Man of Passion: Emotion, Philosophy and Sexual Difference," Christine Battersby argues that the Western philosophical tradition of an extreme opposition between reason and emotion is not the whole story.[17] Although reason has been associated with

---

[17] Christine Battersby, "The Man of Passion: Emotion, Philosophy, and Sexual Difference," in *Representing Emotions: New Connections in the Histories of Art, Music, and Medicine*, edited by Penelope Gouk and Helen Hills (Ashgate, 2005), pp. 139–153.

the masculine, "emotions that have been deemed philosophically useful or valuable have also been assigned to the male sex" (p. 140).

In the work of Hume, Nietzsche, Spinoza, and others, Battersby points out that pivotal emotions, such as sympathy, courage, and joy, are defined as masculine attributes. Instead of a polarized opposition between male reason and female emotion, Battersby finds a gendered hierarchy of emotions, in which those deemed useful are likely to be associated with men while those considered less productive become linked to women.

Despite their disorders, Monk and House are surrounded by a cadre of co-workers who also serve as friends. Although they are often mistreated by the series' leads, the supporting characters' loyalty appears to be based on their deep admiration of his consummate powers of reason and, perhaps more importantly, on their *own* superior *emotional* skills, particularly their compassion.

One of the interesting aspects about *Monk* and *House* is that in their efforts to represent the oppositional nature of emotion and reason in their main characters, and to critique emotion as their 'problem', both shows also have alternative models in which emotion and reason are more successfully integrated. And in both programs, the alternative models are embodied by the main characters' best friends: Captain Leland Stottlemeyer and Dr. James Wilson. In keeping with Battersby's arguments, the friends allow us to see emotions represented in male characters when they are useful.

Stottlemeyer is more reasonable, more focused on the task at hand, and much more aware of others' feelings than his employee, Monk. Where House is brash, childish, and vindictive, Wilson is kind, sensitive and emotionally ethical. Usually, it is left to Stottlemeyer and Wilson to point out the hurtful effects of his respective colleague's mistreatment of others.

Both Stottlemeyer's and Wilson's professions and personalities require that they operate as highly rational individuals which, unlike Monk and House, they manage to do while maintaining a measure of emotional steadiness. Crucially, the friendships exist in both realms. Monk and Stottlemeyer are connected through a mutual interest in crime-solving; they also share an emotional bond developed over a long, complex history of interaction. House and Wilson are linked through elaborate rational debates on medical issues, other people's motivations, and each other's self-justifications. They also share an emotional bond developed over a long, complex history.

The defining attribute that makes Stottlemeyer and Wilson such good friends is their impeccable loyalty. Both, on occasion, have placed their professional careers on the line because of their unshakable belief in their colleague's rational capacities. The responsibility for reining in their friend's worst social and personal missteps also most often falls to them.

However, loyalty does not mean being naive, foolhardy, or dishonest. Stottlemeyer is the person who originally suspends Monk from the police force and then refuses to support his reinstatement appeal because he believes Monk's disorder makes him unreliable in a dangerous situation ("Mr. Monk and the Candidate," "Mr. Monk Goes to the Carnival"). Stottlemeyer points out other forms of damage caused by Monk's condition. For instance, in "Mr. Monk on Wheels," Stottlemeyer warns Monk that his selfish mistreatment of his assistant, Natalie (Traylor Howard), will cause Monk to lose her. Stottlemeyer says he knows this because he lost his wife through a similar taking for granted. In this sense, Stottlemeyer is capable of learning from emotional experience, while Monk is not.

Like Stottlemeyer, Wilson is the person most capable of speaking bluntly and directly, with the highest chance among those who surround House of being listened to. And like Stottlemeyer, Wilson's version of loyalty is not based on infinite kindness and concession. Essential to the maintenance of Wilson's relationship with House, for instance, is their ongoing game of one-upmanship in which Wilson gives almost as good as he gets. These competitions can take the form of intellectually-driven debates ('the type of conversation' House 'does well') or cleverly-planned pranks, as long as they involve one friend attempting to outmaneuver the other. This is the only type of relationship House can sustain or enjoy, an insight that Wilson grasps. Towards the end of "Safe," following a succession of House-generated stunts with Wilson as the recipient, House's cane breaks in half and he topples to the ground. Wilson filed through the cane that House depends on, setting up the accident. While some viewers may have found this to be a cruel action on Wilson's part,[18] the important point is that House does not. We realize this when, still humiliatingly slumped on the floor, a smile spreads across House's face—an indication that he continues to be engaged by the friendship.

---

[18] Barbara Barnett, "*House, MD's* House and Wilson: A Fine Bromance" (September 3rd, 2008), <www.blogcritics.org/video/article/house-mds-house-and-wilson>.

At the same time, Stottlemeyer's and Wilson's emotional capacities are far from idealized. Stottlemeyer is depicted as unsuccessful in some of his personal relationships, particularly in the story arc concerning his separation and divorce. He can be gruff, impatient, and demanding. Similarly, Wilson can be sanctimonious, overly-protective, and too acquiescent. During Season 2, his third marriage fails.[19] Rather than a perfectly resolved solution to the emotion-reason dilemma, Stottlemeyer and Wilson simply represent a more workable, less miserable arrangement. In doing so, they offer a model that moves towards the integration of emotion and reason. The attribute of integration, instead of opposition, is precisely what enables them to tolerate their colleague's irritating or offensive behavior. By combining comprehension with compassion, they go one step further: they occasionally succeed in bringing out the best their flawed best friends can summon.

The Emotion-Reason Dilemma, Part II

Stottlemeyer and Wilson serve an important narrative function in offering a way of imagining a more balanced version of the emotion-reason impasse embodied by Monk and House. Much of their social and interpersonal practices are productive rather than destructive, to themselves and to others. While the leads depict brilliant rationality joined to damaging emotionality, their best friends indicate more successful ways of incorporating emotion and reason. In keeping with Battersby's argument, Stottlemeyer and Wilson personify certain emotions, such as loyalty and compassion, in a manner that is not equated with flaws or disorder.

Of course, there is a price to pay for their abilities of integration. The USA Network website makes clear Stottlemeyer's limitations: "although it can drive Stottlemeyer crazy to know that he'll never be quite as brilliant a detective as Monk, the divorced father of two remains a loyal friend." Stottlemeyer is repeatedly faced with evidence that he is not, and never will be, as superior a detective as Monk. To his credit, although Stottlemeyer frequently feels envious of Monk and doubtful of his own abilities, he is never petty enough to let his jealousies or self-doubts stop the better detective

---

[19] We learn much about Stottlemeyer's and Wilson's personal limitations in parallel subplots when, due to marital difficulties, they each temporarily move in with their ordinarily more troubled friend ("Mr. Monk and the Very, Very Old Man"; "Safe").

from solving a crime or allowing his feelings to hurt their friendship. As series creator Breckman notes, Stottlemeyer is "a smart cop, but not *the* smartest cop. He has to feel a little embarrassed that he always has to call in Monk. He still has to have his pride" (Erdmann and Block, p. 10).

Wilson's relationship to rationality is somewhat more bewildering. We are frequently reminded that House is the more brilliant doctor. Dr. Cuddy (Lisa Edelstein), the Dean of Medicine, repeatedly (and implausibly) refuses to fire House because of his outstanding diagnostic skills, voicing some version of: "the son of a bitch is the best doctor we have" ("Pilot"). Yet, as head of the hospital's Oncology Department, Wilson clearly holds considerable medical credibility. House often calls on Wilson's medical knowledge when working on a case, and we occasionally see Wilson with one of his cancer patients, whom he invariably treats with both reason and empathy (for instance, "House vs. God"). Still, as far as brilliant physicians go, Wilson remains in the background. The series assumes House's greater intellectual and medical genius without raising the possibility that Wilson's balance of knowledge and empathy may make him more ideally suited and, therefore, more successful a doctor than someone like House for the particular medical field in which Wilson practices.

Paradoxically, Stottlemeyer and Wilson offer a more successful integration of the emotion-reason dynamic, but a less successful rational outcome. The penalty they pay is the sacrifice of glory. Both Stottlemeyer and Wilson quietly toil away at their respective professions with little fanfare or acknowledgement. Despite their significant service to others, they are not exceptional but merely ordinary.

In this common although questionable equation, polarization equals greatness while integration signals the mundane. For Monk and House, their reason is exceptional, their emotions dysfunctional, and integration impossible. But they achieve a level of virtuosity. For Stottlemeyer and Wilson, their intellectual skills are as strong as their loyalty and compassion, they succeed at a productive integration of emotion and reason, but they remain ordinary. This understanding of the relationship between emotion and reason is historically specific but culturally widespread. In outlining these dilemmas, *Monk* and *House* activate the question of whether it is possible to conceive of the emotion-reason dynamic in less limited terms.[20]

---

[20] My thanks to Danielle Holewa for her insightful assistance on this chapter.

12

Mr. Monk and the Reestablished Harmony

ZERRIN ORAL KAVAS

Years and years ago, I read a good critic seriously reprimanding an author (don't ask for names or references; that was in another country, and besides, both are long dead) who had a disabled character in one of his novels: "Why on earth is this girl lame?" the critic asked, "You just can't disable people as you wish! So what if you're her author?"

The critic was clearly appealing to Anton Chekhov's famous principle for storytelling and drama: If you say in the first act (or chapter) that there is a rifle hanging on the wall, it must have gone off by the end of the play (or story). Otherwise, why should it be there? Everything has to make sense, and to play a role in the plot. No, I'm not going to argue that the producers must have been loyal to Adrian Monk's obsession by ending the series with Episode 100; that's another point (and a silly one). Still, we all have the basic fans' right to ask: Why is Trudy dead in the first place? Still more pressing: Why is there evil? And for that matter: Why is there something rather than nothing? (Okay, that's like a record-breaking triple jump, but I can explain that the questions are interrelated.)

Why Things Happen, Especially to Mr. Monk

Chekhov's principle is just a version of what philosophers call "the principle of sufficient reason," which states that nothing happens without there being sufficient reason for its happening and that nothing happens as it does happen without there being sufficient reason for its happening as it does rather than otherwise. In accordance with this principle, we must believe that, for any case that

Adrian Monk is dealing with (including Trudy's death), there is sufficient reason that the incident had to be and had to be as it has
been. Otherwise, why should anything happen? Why should Mr.
Monk "get stuck in traffic," seemingly because of an accident,
which turns out to be anything but accidental? Why should there
be six toothpicks in a vault and why should one of them be shorter
than the other? ("Mr. Monk Goes to the Bank") There must be
something wrong with all these incidents and accidents, a wrong
that must be corrected or at least justified.

Just how often does Mr. Monk *get* and *go* and *visit* and *meet*
people! Just how often do things *happen* to the poor Mr. Monk!
What an abundance of incidents! As if "the time is out of joint"
(Shakespeare), as if "things fall apart; the centre cannot hold"
(William Butler Yeats). Then, suddenly, everything falls back into
pattern, for what accounts for the incident is the detective's account
of the case itself. For Monk, an incident makes sense only if it can
be narrated, accounted for as part of a coherent story. Here's Mr.
Monk's version of Chekhov's principle: First, if there's something,
there must be a pattern or order in which the thing, person or event
is a constituent. Secondly, if there's a particular order, it must be
exposed and verified. Thirdly, that particular order of things must
fit into the overall order of everything else. For Monk, it's a matter
of course that any particular pattern is there just because it's part of
the complete order of his world.

An excess of encounters, an excess of incidents causes disturbance and Mr. Monk, like Herman Melville's Bartleby, the
scrivener, "would prefer not to" be disturbed. Unlike Bartleby
and his brother Ambrose, however, Mr. Monk can't just retreat.
A regular and dutiful copyist of documents in the attorney's
office, Bartleby just declines, all of a sudden, when the attorney
asks him to proofread two clerks' copies. Then he continues
refraining from doing whatever he's asked to do until he reaches
to the point of doing nothing at all. He isn't there to correct the
world, but to leave it as it is. Mr. Monk's attitude is the opposite.
He's an *orderly* man or, more precisely, a man of *patterns* (given
his photographic memory and his obsession with frames of
images), loyal to the harmony of the present world, this given
order of things. He's ready to leave the world as it is, but only
after confirming the order already inherent in the world. That's
also what distinguishes Monk from all other detectives: his
method and attitude.

Method and Mr. Monk

All detective fiction is about the problem of evil, but each detective work is limited to a particular evil and the question of explaining it or eliminating it. Unlike our Monk, detectives are committed to correcting a given, particular wrong, not to reestablishing the order of the world as a whole after an incidental disorder. What do the detectives detect, exactly? What do they look at? However obsessive an interest in entomology Gil Grissom might have, CSI detectives (in Las Vegas, New York or Miami) trace the evidence of the most minuscule kind. Grissom resembles Adrian only insofar as he attempts to reconstruct the crime scene (although he does so actually, not mentally as our Adrian does) in order to replace the evidence and reinstall the event in miniature. Then the case is closed and Gil goes back to his insects. CSI teams just collect evidence, discover the causes and catch the people who have committed the crimes (two cases per episode) and go home. Allison Dubois's method in *Medium* is the opposite: She's asleep at home, has an insight, through dream knowledge, into what has happened or what will soon happen and then goes out to verify her intuitive cognition. The FBI team in *Criminal Minds* starts from a series of cases, constructs them as a single story pointing at a certain pattern of behavior, which then reveals the profile of the person who must have committed the crimes and who will most probably take the easily conjecturable next step. *Criminal Intent*'s Robert Goren follows similar lines in getting into the minds of people: he reads the symptoms, browses through possible and probable causes and (especially) motives of the prominent or ignored suspect, reconstructs her train of thoughts in his mind, corners her and helps her confess that she has actually gone through that particular process. Enter Gregory House (yes, diagnostic medicine is also detective work): Given a set of symptoms, what is the best explanation? Suppose that it's true and eliminate the causal element. You have a new or additional set of symptoms. Go through the algorithm with the new data. The case becomes worse and hopeless. Eliminate, eliminate, and yes, eliminate! Then a seemingly irrelevant remark about an irrelevant matter in House's affairs, and that's it, by analogy or revelation.

    I've saved the group of good old fellows for the last row: Remember Lieutenant Columbo, Agatha Christie's Hercule Poirot, Sherlock Holmes and Edgar Allan Poe's C. Auguste Dupin. Even

Andy Breckman, the creator, says that Monk is some combination of Columbo and Holmes. That may be true insofar as some manners are concerned, but as regards their methods, there's nothing of the fake ignorance of Columbo or of the deductive reasoning of Holmes in our Monk. Holmes traces clues, brings them together and puts them into a form the logicians call *modus ponens*: if it's the fact that *bla bla*, then it's the fact that *pla pla*; but it's the fact that *bla bla*; therefore it's the fact that *pla pla*. In that way "from a drop of water a logician could infer the possibility of an Atlantic or a Niagara."[1] Holmes's follower, Hercule Poirot, approaches Mr. Monk just a little bit. In addition to observing material and behavioral clues, he collects the accounts of the people involved in the affair. Using his "little grey cells" by "order and method," he then eliminates whatever is impossible and reconstructs the course of events. Both Holmes and Poirot are partly following their French master C. Auguste Dupin, whose method, however, was purely rational (that's why Edgar Allan Poe calls it "ratiocination") as opposed to their empirical research. Dupin basically derives a whole train of thought from some initial or elementary statements by someone and detects whatever is reasonably the case.

How different is Mr. Monk's mind! No evidence, no insight or intuition, no inferential walk, no discovery of causes, no explanation, no revealed intent, no set of symptoms, no discursive reasoning, no argument at all, no elimination of possible, probable causes counts as such by itself, unless they fit into the only possible (not merely plausible) narrative account. Any incidental deviance in the course of Monk's world must be restored to the place where it would cohere with the overall narrative order. "What might have been?" is the question: What might have been, so that once the story is told, everything else remains intact, the world is left as it is? "What might have been" so that the world's harmony may be reestablished as Adrian Monk knows it and Mr. Monk can survive the incident? The answer is not a form of inference (of whatever sort), but a plausible narrative account. When Mr. Monk introduces the ultimate story ("Here's what happened"), he's not only prepared to tell the particular tale about the case at hand, but also to retell the whole story of the order of the world. When a particular

---

[1] Sir Arthur Conan Doyle, *A Study in Scarlet and The Sign of the Four* (Wordsworth, 2001), p. 14.

piece fits into the pattern, the whole puzzle is solved, unless other defects are recognized.

Mr. Monk Tells Tales

What does Adrian Monk exactly do while telling everybody what has happened? What kind of a narrative does he give? Rick Altman distinguishes between "some" narrative and "a" narrative.[2] In a sense, his distinction could also be defined as the difference between "potential narrative" and "actual narrative." Daily life in Monk's world, as well as in our own, is full of narrative material: it's populated with characters, contains series of events and actions, which display the potential of "some" narrative only when an element of "following" is added. When Adrian chases Maria Cordova in the episode "Mr. Monk Stays Up All Night," without knowing why, the act of following constitutes a potential narrative. However, until the truth that Maria Cordova had received Trudy's corneas is revealed, that is, until the complete tale is told, Mr. Monk doesn't have "an" actual narrative. What is required for the recognition of a narrative is "framing"—cutting life into meaningful slices that make implicit narratives explicit.

Obviously, all episodes of all serials are based on framing, but these frames are for an external eye, the gaze of the viewer. Within the episodes, the attention of the detectives is usually limited to other frames: those of the microscope, camera and the computer screen matching the fingerprints. Even Holmes's forward bend of his head with his magnifying glass and Robert Goren's sideward bend of his head with his penetrating eyes are elements of following, not framing. Mr. Monk's narrative method, however, works with frames from the beginning to the end. Consider his initial and final use of his hands, first cutting out the whole frame of the crime scene where only the actual event is missing ("Here it was that . . ."), then putting the whole frame filled with "what must have been" back into its proper place ("Here's what happened there.").

A prompt objection to this argument would be what Tony Shalhoub told to Susan Stewart: "I'm looking between the fingers, because it actually isolates and cuts the room into slices, looking at

---

[2] Rick Altman, *A Theory of Narrative* (Columbia University Press, 2008), pp. 15–21.

parts instead of the whole."[3] Can actors be mistaken about what the characters they're playing really do? Well, they can, but that's not the case here, because what Shalhoub says isn't incompatible with my argument; to the contrary, they're quite consistent. Everything depends on what kind of "parts" Mr. Monk is looking at, and what their relationship with the whole is.

Wittgenstein Helps Mr. Monk

A particular overall theory of the world will help us here: the version Ludwig Wittgenstein defended in his *Tractatus Logico-Philosophicus*. One of the most curious claims in this book is the statement that any item in the world can be the case or not the case—and the rest of the world can remain the same (1.21). Come on, Ludwig! Do you mean that Sharona Fleming can relocate to New Jersey and Natalie Teeger can stab an intruder, while everything else remains the same? Yes, that's what he means from a logical point of view, for this is a composite claim, which puts two distinct ideas together.

The first argument is that the constituents of the world are not things, but facts. Wittgenstein really holds that the world divides into facts, not into things or persons. The world doesn't consist of items like parking slot machines, but of facts, like a certain number of parking machines being in a row with regular distances between them. Mr. Monk is fond of regularly checking and verifying such facts usually ignored by others. Wittgenstein's second argument is that the truths about the facts of the world are independent of each other and contingent by themselves. To call a fact or truth "contingent" is to say that it's not necessary, but might have been otherwise. The fact that Sharona relocates to New Jersey is contingent, for she might have stayed in San Francisco. This particular fact is independent of the fact that Natalie stabbed an intruder, for it might well have been the case that Sharona didn't relocate and Natalie did stab the intruder (or not).

For Wittgenstein, a fact is an existing state of affairs and a state of affairs is a potential fact (*Tractatus* 2). What makes up the world is the *totality* of actual states of affairs or "the facts in logical space" (*Tractatus* 1.13). The "logical space" encompasses all

---

[3] Susan Stewart, "Happy to Be Neurotic, at Least Once a Week," *New York Times* (16th September, 2007).

possible states of affairs, only some of which exist, that is, only some of which are facts constituting the world. What Mr. Monk does is to picture to himself a possible case in the logical space. If it's a logical, consistent picture corresponding to what is a case in the world, it's a true thought. Wittgenstein tell us that "The totality of true thoughts is a picture of the world" (*Tractatus* 3.01). That's what Mr. Monk is trying to achieve: a well-ordered total picture frame encompassing all actual states of affairs, together with all their sufficient reasons, and true to the facts.

The way Mr. Monk solves the case in the episode "Mr. Monk and the Genius" is the paradigm of Monk's strategy. Consider the chessboard as the universe or the logical space, and each of the different chessboards, together with the particular games played on them, as a possible world or a complete state of affairs. A complete account of the facts in any of these worlds will be a narrative describing all of the moves and states of all pieces on the board in consecutive order. Revealing Patrick Kloster's strategy in the Poisoned Pawn variation isn't a sufficient description of the game by itself. What Mr. Monk needs is the totality of Kloster's moves displaying a coherent account of all the acts committed. For the sake of the completeness of the world, he's even prepared to plant evidence—or rather install a fact, because that particular fact *must be* among the constituents of the world, if the world is to be a coherent whole. Then he recognizes the pattern of "castling": it isn't just a matter of two pieces (on the chessboard or in the cemetery) switching places, but rather a question of switching the facts. The move changes the complete state of affairs by shifting the pattern of the facts in the world, which thus becomes another world, because "The world is determined by the facts, and by their being *all* the facts" (*Tractatus*, 1.11).

Mr. Monk has to consider all possible states of affairs and think through the whole logical space. The ideal state would be a descriptive account of all facts within a total frame, but until the primary defect (Trudy's death—or was it his father's abandonment?) is eliminated, the narrative won't be complete and coherent. Thus Adrian is still stuck in the "following," tracing all evidence towards the ultimate tale of the world. What if it turns out to be a fact about the world that it ultimately lacks order? Unlikely, for Adrian Monk will invent the order anyway, for there must be an order.

Herr Leibniz Consoles Mr. Monk

Wittgenstein's theory of the world supplies a ground for Adrian Monk's method of handling the cases one by one and as a totality of facts, but what does it say about Trudy's death? Simply that *it's* the case among all possible states of affairs, and nothing else. Trudy is dead, because the world is as it is. Take it *and* leave it as it is. If Mr. Monk is to follow Wittgenstein's suggestion, he has to accept what every other detective takes for granted: There's evil and a particular evil in each case. Even if Wittgenstein condoles with Mt. Monk, he can't console him, because he can't explain why there is evil at all.

The consolation comes from Gottfried Wilhelm Leibniz. He was a very optimistic man who believed that the world we live in is the best of all possible worlds, governed by a preestablished harmony, and based on "the principle of sufficient reason." He would argue that there is something rather than nothing because there is sufficient reason for that—and what's more, the world is better like that; just ask God, who knows everything! Then, Trudy's dead because there was sufficient reason for the fact that she was killed—and the world Adrian Monk lives in becomes better with that fact; just ask the writers and producers! The argument sounds as absurd as any initial conjecture by Mr. Monk does to Captain Stottlemeyer, or as Randy Disher's "name and catch" theory about the "Lipstick Assassin" ("Mr. Monk's 100th Case"), but once the whole story is told, it may turn out to be quite plausible.

Underlying Leibniz's argument is the claim that God had a couple of options. First, God might have chosen another world to create from among an infinite variety of possible worlds conceivable by God. Before proceeding ahead, let's clarify the idea of a "possible world." The actual world, the world we (or Mr. Monk and company) live in is a totality of contingent facts. The facts in (or truths about) our world are contingent in the sense that none of them is necessary, but might have been otherwise than it actually is. Since the actual world consists only of contingent facts, the world itself is totally contingent, which means that it isn't necessary as a whole. In other words, the world could have been totally different than it actually is. Therefore, worlds other than the actual one are not only imaginable, but also possible.

Still, God *couldn't* create *any* other world basically because of two divine perfections: rationality and benevolence. On the one hand, the principle of sufficient reason doesn't allow the perfectly rational God to choose at random; on the other hand, God's supreme goodness doesn't leave any choice but opting for the best possible choice. So, therefore, the actual world must be the best of all possible worlds:

> It follows from the supreme perfection of God that he chose the best possible plan in producing the universe, a plan in which there is the greatest possible variety together with the greatest possible order. The most carefully used plot of ground, place, and time; the greatest effect produced by the simplest means; the most power, knowledge, happiness, and goodness in created things that the universe could allow.[4]

Now let's consider Mr. Monk as a pessimistic Leibniz. The optimistic Leibniz was strange enough, but the pessimistic one is certainly stranger. The world Adrian Monk survives in, from his point of view, must be the worst of all possible worlds, not simply because Trudy is killed, but also because he can't make sense of her death. As long as Mr. Monk believed that the bomb missed its real target (himself), the world was still meaningful, although uncaring and sorrowful. *That*, at least, was an explanation, an unbearable but understandable account of what happened. Once he learns that the bomb was meant for Trudy, in "Mr. Monk Goes to Jail," the world as a whole lacks any sense: The question "Why her, rather than me?" is replaced by the painfully simple question "Why her?" Translated into Wittgensteinian terms, the question becomes: "Why this fact among all possible states of affairs?" Translated into Leibnizian terms, it becomes: "Why this actual world among all possible worlds?"

Given the present state of affairs, Mr. Monk has very limited alternatives: First, he can wait for a *deus ex machina* to solve everything, which is unlikely to come down, unless the creator sends it in. This brings us to the second option: The intervention of Andy Breckman and the team. (Some fictional worlds are certainly polytheistic, as you see.) Still unlikely, because the world Monk lives in (which is *fictional* from *our* point of view, but *actual* from *his* point of view) would lack perfection, if any divine (or creative) intervention is needed there. This is the ground on which Leibniz

---

[4] "Principles of Nature and Grace, Based on Reason," paragraph 10, in G.W. Leibniz, *Philosophical Essays* (Hackett, 1989), p. 210.

defends the idea of a *preestablished harmony*, which guarantees the greatest possible variety and richness of facts that the greatest possible order would allow. With a whole population of individual substances (which Leibniz calls "monads", but you can imagine them as ordinary individuals, for the sake of the argument) and all possible states and actions of those individual substances, God chooses to create the best possible world, organized in such a way that all states and actions of each individual are in conformity with all states and actions of every other individual. That overall conformity of all facts in the world is what Leibniz calls "the preestablished harmony."

Now, Mr. Monk probably doesn't know anything about Leibniz's theory or about his creators, but he seems to believe a theory about the world which is similar to Leibniz's: The world must have a preestablished harmony. Within his limited viewpoint and with his strict commitment to the given order of his world, Monk has no access to the will and deeds of Andy Breckman and the team. That leaves Adrian on his own: Unless we're wrong (which, you know, we're not), and unless he's wrong (which, we know, he's not), his world must be perfect and there has to be a reason why Trudy is dead. This particular fact needs explanation in the particular way Monk explains facts.

Leibniz may be right in suggesting that the presence of evil is inevitable in any possible world just because it's among the possible actions of individuals. The writers and producers may be right in filling in Monk's world with evil for the obvious fact that there can't be a detective without there being crimes. Still, our poor Mr. Monk, even though he's quite aware that there's disorder and that it can be accounted for, is at an impasse when it comes to Trudy's case. "He can't die until he knows" ("Mr. Monk's 100th Case") and as the Greeks said, "Nobody should be called happy before he dies," or, to generalize, no world should be deemed best of all possible worlds before it ends.

He's...Not Like Everyone Else

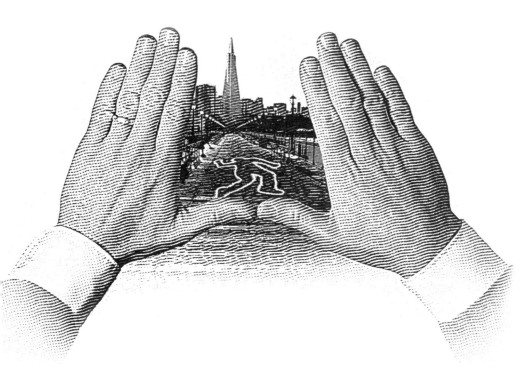

The Spiritual Side of
Adrian Monk

13

Mr. Monk and the Medieval Monks

ANDREW B.R. ELLIOTT

It's a familiar scene, usually around halfway through an episode of Monk. The murder investigation gets to a point where the team becomes divided into two seemingly irreconcilable parties, leaving them at something of an impasse.

On one side stand the pragmatists, Stottlemeyer and Disher, who have done the leg work, collected and collated the evidence and are closing in on their primary suspect. They have motive, they have opportunity, there's no alibi and (in the words of Stottlemeyer) "that's how you spell 'primary suspect'" ("Mr. Monk Goes to the Circus").

On the other side stands Monk, alone, hung up on the one piece of evidence which doesn't fit the puzzle. He endlessly turns it over in his head, unable to leave the riddle incomplete—incapable of letting the imperfections slide. It is, in fact, reassuringly familiar; when an exasperated Stottlemeyer once asks him "does *everything* have to make sense, Monk?", we already know what his response will be: "Yeah . . . yeah, it kinda does" ("Mr. Monk and the Other Woman").

This stalemate is not only familiar to us as *Monk* fans, but is recognizable throughout the Middle Ages in a conflict between theology and philosophy which raged both in the universities and on the pages of thick books. The medieval theologians were, like Monk, engaged on a quest to make sense of the chaos of the world, and carve out a space for Truth using arguments which "*had to* make sense.*" In an inquiry similar to Monk's investigation into his wife's death, the medieval monk was engaged in a fundamental and perhaps ultimately impossible quest to prove the existence of

169

God, against which the trivial questions of the world (like fashion or money) paled into insignificance.

Furthermore, their concentration on this one great question forced them to adopt an increasingly rigorous and painstaking attention to detail, treating each fact, each tiny shred of evidence, as a critical piece in a giant mosaic. For both Monk and the monks, one piece of evidence (like, as we will see, a rock) can lead back through a chain of logic to answer a fundamentally important question. For both the medieval monastic and the modern obsessive-compulsive, the primary focus of their quests led them to reject all that was not immediately relevant to their central aim, causing them to lead the life of an ascetic—something like a hermit—rejecting societal norms, values and bonds in a fruitless but insistent quest to restore order to the world around them.

Anatomy of a Murder Investigation

Let's look at this familiar scene in action. In "Mr. Monk Goes to the Circus," a circus ringmaster is shot in public, from thirty feet away, by a masked acrobatic assassin who promptly somersaults off the scene and disappears. Around halfway through the episode we reach the point at which the team have collectively lined up a series of clues, followed the leads and exhausted the evidence taken from the scene. There is, in short, no more information to be gleaned. They are left with just two primary suspects from the circus-folk: an animal wrangler and the victim's ex-wife.

The first suspect is a potential love rival, having been romantically linked to the victim's date, and as a lion-tamer he has access to—and is trained in the use of—powerful firearms. The captain learns later that he is training to become a trapeze artist, thus matching the profile of the killer to the letter.

The second suspect, the victim's ex-wife, is an accomplished trapeze-artist who *also* happens to be an award-winning sharp-shooter. She is known to be jealous, has attacked her ex-spouse in the past and makes no attempt to conceal her pleasure at his demise. Thus *both* suspects have motives, *both* match the profile and *neither* is able to furnish the police with a concrete alibi for the night of the killing.

If those are the pros, then we must take into account the cons, of which there are several. Though Stottlemeyer claims that all circus performers are ambidextrous, Monk notices that the wrangler is dominantly left-handed, a making him a poor suspect for a right-handed shooting witnessed by a small crowd. However, the evidence indicating the ex-wife's innocence is even more hurtful to the case; having broken her foot, the trapeze-artist is wheelchair-bound with her leg in a cast, making such an acrobatic escape impossible. The choice between the two thus comes down to 'gut instinct', a solution which has no basis in empirical, rational proof. There's no logic, it's messy and, as such, is of course deeply unsatisfactory for Monk.

God, Proof, and *Clue*

The whole situation, however, is eventually resolved by Monk when he reverts to a system of deductive thinking. Instead of looking at the clues and gathering suspects, Monk solves the case by looking at the proof and then reasoning backwards. A nice—and appropriate—analogy can be found in the game of *Clue* (called *Cluedo* in the UK). We can imagine a point in the game at which we have a certain profile, we know certain facts, and we have certain gut feelings. If we combine all of these, then the correct answer could be one of potentially two or three combinations: it's either, say, Col. Mustard with the lead piping in the Dining Room, or Professor Plum's kitchen assault with the rope.

But the problem here is this: although several of them *could have* done it, *only one* of them *actually did*. There are only three cards in that envelope: the question is, of course, which ones! And this is what Monk must establish by working backwards, starting with the perpetrator (as his catchphrase goes, "I don't know *how* he did it, but he did it") and working back to see what clues would point to *that* person, and crucially taking nothing for granted as he goes along.

This problem bears a similarity to a logical problem which raged throughout the thirteenth century and which was ultimately to be addressed in the same way by one of the sharpest medieval theologians, Saint Thomas Aquinas, in the late 1260s. The problem he was trying to solve was not homicide, but no less than how to prove that God exists. The trick here, of course was not to actually prove beyond doubt the existence of God (which was, and still is, an article of faith), but to provide a concrete logical means by which we could go about demonstrating his existence. Sounds like the same thing? Think of it like Monk would after he's decided that some suspect or another is "the guy:" the outcome is not in doubt, only whether it can be proved, and how. For Aquinas and the other medieval theologians, the question wasn't whether God actually did exist, but whether we could ever prove it, and how.

Let's imagine our *Clue* murder case once it reaches court. The accused Colonel Mustard *could* have done it (otherwise he wouldn't have ever been brought up on the charge). The prosecutor doesn't have to prove that the colonel *actually* committed the crime: what they're trying to prove is that the *evidence* is valid. The defense, on the other hand, can't prove he didn't do it, but what they're trying to do is prove the evidence is *wrong* or flawed (Colonel Mustard has a rare allergy to lead piping, or had no key to the dining room, for example).

So if we relate this back to the problem of the circus murder, we can see that we do not doubt the existence of a killer (with thirty witnesses, it's obvious that someone has been murdered), but we doubt the proofs which are supposed to implicate their guilt. It's perfectly reasonable that there might be two suspects (two *potential* killers) but there's only one *actual* killer. Thus Stottlemeyer and Disher (who favor the lion-tamer as the killer) are working using a very different process to Monk (who points the finger at the ex-wife), because they're using the facts which their senses have provided, and which go unchallenged, and reasoning forwards from there. For them, the lion-tamer's left-handedness makes it *improbable* that he was the killer, but the ex-wife's broken foot makes it *impossible*. And as Holmes famously tells Watson in *The Sign of the Four*: "When you eliminate the impossible, whatever remains, however improbable, is the truth." But we've already seen in Chapter 2 of this volume that Monk does not always or only follow Holmes's method.

How Can They Both Be True?

The same criticisms of the process of reasoning were at the heart of the medieval monastic debate. Why? Because it was at around this time that the medieval thinkers had stumbled across some revolutionary new material: copies of the ancient philosophical texts translated from the Greek. For the first time, thinkers like Aristotle, whom we take for granted, were being passed back into the hands of professors and scholars. Now, this was a problem, because these Christian philosophers and theologians had been using certain assumptions about the nature of God to answer new questions. As soon as they were beginning to find some answers, they were confronted with a new way of thinking which *was not based on* the indubitable existence of God. It's like Randy's "crazy ideas"—on the surface they can sometimes seem to make sense, and sometimes even Stottlemeyer gets taken in for a while. Even so, when Monk comes onto the scene and applies his ruthless deduction, we find out that they just don't stand up to his new way of thinking; and so too were various important arguments and theories called into question when Aristotle appeared on the medieval scene.

It would be misleading, however, to imagine that the existence of two different ways of thinking makes them necessarily mutually exclusive. Aquinas writes as much in his major work, the *Summa*, saying that "there is nothing to prevent another science from treating in the light of divine revelation what the philosophical disciplines treat as knowable in the light of human reason." In other words, even if two thinkers might agree on the same outcome, they might all the same be fundamentally at odds about how we arrive at that point. (*Summa theologiae*, Ia, q. 1, a., ad 2).

Before the rediscovery of Aristotle, then, Christian thinkers might have thought in the same way as Stottlemeyer and Disher have done in the circus case: they had a hunch (God exists/the lion-tamer did it), and therefore they followed the evidence which pointed to it (evidence of God's work is everywhere/all the evidence points to him). In the eleventh century, for example, a brilliant logician, St. Anselm of Canterbury, came up with a celebrated proof of the existence of God. In the following argument (see the chart on page 174), he imagines that someone has made the claim that "God does not exist," and uses logic to prove its impossibility.

Monk and Aquinas's Approach

Despite the neatness of Anselm's approach, it has its problems. For Stottlemeyer, these problems begin when Monk introduces question marks; in the same way, for Anselm these problems really start to emerge when Aquinas introduces the thoughts of Aristotle into the equation (for instance, is a *real* ice cream better than an imaginary *God?*). Instead of a direct line of problems, propositions and solutions, what Aquinas reveals is a complex system of deduction and intuition, which comes as a result of his fusion of different kinds of thought with a range of other ways of thinking (as Monk

PROBLEM	Someone understands the statement that "God exists," but claims that it is not true.
POSSIBLE OUTCOMES	EITHER God does not exist in reality, but exists in the mind (because we understand the statement "God exists" and can imagine Him); OR God exists *in both mind and reality.*
PROPOSITION 1	"God" is the name we give to the greatest thing we can imagine.
PROPOSITION 2	It is greater to exist in the mind AND reality than only in the mind (or put differently, a real ice cream is better than an imaginary one, no matter how good we imagine the imaginary one to be).
SUMMATION	If God existed only in the mind, it would be possible to imagine something in reality *which was greater, but which was not God.*
CONCLUSION	Therefore, in order to be the greatest thing possible, God *must exist in reality.*

Neat, isn't it?

We can, therefore, put Stottlemeyer and Disher's theory into this same pattern:

PROBLEM OUTCOMES	A man was shot in front of witnesses; *therefore* someone did it. The killer was good at shooting *and* could do a somersault.
POSSIBLE	There are two suspects. Each has motive, evidence and no alibi: EITHER the wrangler did it, OR the acrobat did.
PROPOSITION 1	It is impossible to do acrobatics with a broken foot.
PROPOSITION 2	It is improbable that a left-handed man could shoot accurately with his right hand from 30 feet away.
SUMMATION	one is *impossible*, the other is *only improbable*
CONCLUSION	Therefore, the improbable suspect *must have done it*

uses mathematics, logic, science, taste, observation, and art to arrive at his conclusions). Much of both approaches, that of both Monk and Aquinas, has to do with deduction, and what we might call 'thinking backwards', as we shall see.

We remember how Monk is plagued by the one piece of the puzzle that doesn't seem to fit? Well, that's a kind of deduction in itself, in exactly the same way as Aquinas understood it; rather than looking at the incomplete puzzle and wondering why that piece doesn't fit, they look at it from the other way around. They realize that this piece which doesn't fit must belong to a different puzzle. So instead of looking at the puzzle, they then look at that piece and use deduction to work out what kind of puzzle should fit around it. For Aquinas the piece which doesn't fit is Anselm's first proposition, since it assumes that God is unsurpassed in his greatness. This may be true, he concedes, but it is a starting position which cannot be verified by the senses or by things found in the world. As the captain would say, "Where's your evidence, Monk?" The whole argument relies on logic, but at some point you have to make a leap to *assume* that God is greater than all things. This leap, Aquinas objects, is not verifiable by anything you can touch or smell (like in "Mr. Monk and the Psychic," when he says "I don't believe in anything that's not in front of me"). You can't 'see' the causality, and there are no obvious reasons for it.

Anselm's problem, according to Aquinas, was that *it was all in his head*! Aquinas's object was to start off by looking at the things he could see around him, and here he used Aristotle's arguments about a First Cause. In this argument, Aristotle talked about everything in the universe, the mundane, tangible things, and he observed that if you push something, like a rock, then it moves. If that rock then hits something else, then it moves too. And so he showed that each moving thing had to have been *first moved* by something else, which in turn had to be moved, and so on. This could almost go back to infinity, he said, but not quite: *at some point* there had to be something which started it all, something which moves something else but which is not itself moved (it's a bit like the chicken and egg debate). To put this into Aristotle's terms, there must be a *Primus Motor*, an "Unmoved Mover." Aquinas therefore fused the two arguments together (remember he said that two arguments can *both* be valid at the same time), and suggested that we might as well call this Mover "God."

So when Aquinas introduces pagan philosophy to the logic of Anselm (designed to prove God's existence), it's like the demolition of Randy's crazy theory—he exposes the holes. What he actually does, then, is to approach the problem from a different starting position, one which can be proved in the world, and then *later* apply it to the same problem. Rather than assume that God is the greatest thing imaginable, Aquinas like Monk, used things observable in the real world—clues—to lead to answers based on deduction. Even though logically *both are true*, only Aquinas can prove it using tangible evidence.

Never Assume Anything

The critical difference between the two, therefore, is that Anselm works by assuming that God exists, and that he is perfect, and then proves it based on this assumption. Stottlemeyer similarly *works forwards* in a chain of logic, following a hunch. He assumes that the killer cannot have been the trapeze artist with a broken leg, and so he arrives at only one possibility: if the suspect has a motive, access to a firearm, acrobatic ability and opportunity, *he must have done it*. He's not a bad detective (just as Anselm was by no means a bad thinker); but this kind of thinking can only go so far.

Aquinas, however, starts off by using everyday occurrences, things that are verifiable immediately by anyone, believers and non-believers, before using those to prove what no one else could be sure of. Aquinas and Monk look at the problem by *working backwards* from the solution to the cause using irrefutable deductions and assuming nothing beforehand: if the victim was shot by an acrobatic assassin, then the perp must be acrobatic and have access to a gun; *anyone* who has a motive, access to firearms and acrobatic ability is therefore a suspect, regardless of their alibi.

It is, in fact, this reasoning which causes Monk to solve the case, proving that Stottlemeyer's assessment is unfounded—curiously, the assessment is not *wrong,* it just *isn't right.* Remember the cards in the envelope in the game of *Clue?* We said that although several people *could have* done it, only one *actually did;* by using assumptions, it's as though Stottlemeyer had guessed the other one.

So how exactly does Monk solve the case? Well, like Aquinas, he takes nothing for granted, and looks at all the evidence for anything out of the ordinary (by chance, this also resembles another favorite exercise of the medieval monk: Scholasticism, in which they would read and re-read texts looking for an anomaly, and then spend the rest of the time trying to fix it. If this sounds like a curious notion of fun, then just consider what you're doing next time you do a Sudoku . . .). When Monk looks at the scene over and over again (doing his "Zen thing"), he realizes that what Stottlemeyer and Disher had assumed was a *lead* was actually a *clue*: the somersault.

An Illogical Leap?

Just as Aquinas asked why the stone moved, Monk begins to ask *why* the assassin did a somersault. If the acrobatic display wasn't *necessary* to help the perpetrator to escape from the murder scene, then why was it done? While for 'forward thinking' Stottlemeyer, the somersault is significant because it means he can restrict his search to anyone who fits the description and who is capable of doing the acrobatics, it is Monk's more important question which separates out the two suspects. By demonstrating acrobatic ability, *both* of the trapeze artists must have known that they would draw attention to themselves. But why would anyone knowingly draw attention to themselves when it comes to first-degree murder? If the lion-tamer had done the somersault, it would have been totally illogical, because he would deliberately be telling everyone he did it.

The only logical answer we have therefore is that the assailant was deliberately drawing attention to the fact that they were *capable* of such acrobatics. The only person who would want to draw attention to this is someone who would later rely on this as an alibi—by claiming that it was impossible. So it must have been the acrobat!

Thus Monk sets off finding out a different logical question, asking how it might be possible for someone with a broken foot to carry out the acrobatic murder and, for those who might not have seen this particular episode, I won't give away the whole of the ending.

Contemptus Mundi

So we have seen that Aquinas and Monk were both able to solve their cases because they were able to reject the 'forward-logic' of the world around them and concentrate on the details. But how, one might ask, can Monk do this, and what makes him so special? And how, one might also ask, does it happen that medieval monks got to sit around all day, pushing rocks and wondering who moved them? Didn't they have work to do?

It is at this point which we need to consider one final similarity between Monk and the medieval monks—the fact that the world doesn't get in their way, because they have quite simply rejected it. This rejection of the world was what was commonly termed *contemptus mundi*, contempt for the world, and its object was not so much a negative sense of dropping out, but rather a more positive, ascetic 'retreat'. Much like a modern spiritual retreat, the medieval monks of certain orders would withdraw themselves from the world in order to devote their lives to a higher purpose, in the belief that the world was corrupt, just like nature is 'dirty' for Monk ("Mr. Monk and the Kid"). The world is chaotic and disordered, and could only serve to stain their souls, leaving a mark that no amount of wipes and baggies would erase.

So is Monk an ascetic? He does certainly display many of the same characteristics of purity (a rejection of dirt, smut, and baseness), chastity (devotion to only one, spiritual woman, be it the Virgin Mary or the spirit of Trudy) and poverty (a total disregard for finances, for flashy clothes and material wealth, together with an uncanny ability to forget to pay his staff). But does he withdraw from the world to pursue truth? Well, although his OCD is clearly involuntary, there are innumerable cases in which Monk's withdrawal from the world is precisely that which enables him to either solve the case, or at least enables him to gather the evidence. You know; gift . . . curse . . .

In "Mr. Monk and the Big Game," for example, Monk is called in to examine the suspicious death of a basketball coach in a locker room, a crime scene which triggers painful memories of high school (in much the same way as "Mr. Monk Goes Back to School") and serves to forcibly distance him yet again from the material world. In fact, we can see that states of nervous tension thrust him even more forcefully back into his own rejection of the world, and his most obvious symptoms tend to become exaggerated (touching lamps, avoiding cracks, or language dysfunction during the earthquake).

Thus, where other investigators have found traces only of a tragic accident, Monk's entrance to the crime scene sees him already in a state of tension, marking the detachment which will allow him to focus on the imperfections of the scene. Despite the general cleanliness of the locker room, dirt is unsurprisingly one of the first things which Monk notices on the window-frames and on the electrical socket. Where all others accept the world for what it is, they might be impressed by its cleanliness (considering what we might expect had it been the *boys'* locker room!). Forward thinking thus works on a 'standard' of the world, and we are impressed when it rises above it. Instead, Monk's desire to see a perfect world leads him to notice where it falls short of the ideal, just as Aquinas wanted to see a perfect heaven, and knew that the earth could never measure up. Consequently, it's only by focusing so directly on the *imperfections* of the scene, which are those seemingly trivial details, that Monk is able to identify the signs of sabotage which reveal the accidental death to be, in fact, a homicide.

Does the Habit Make the Monk?

So he thinks like Aquinas, he withdraws from the world, and devotes himself to an ideal of truth and order. But does this make Mr. Monk a monk? Well, not necessarily. He's certainly no tonsure-wearing, humorless friar, relentlessly cloistered in the monastery and prevented from engaging with the wickedness of the world. We've seen occasional glimpses of his childish joy which endear him to us and we would hate to lose him to that austere world.

But does he *reject the world* like a monk? Absolutely. By seeking out a greater truth in the world, by devoting his life to solving one ultimate question, he is able to help others out in their own quests for truth. And it is his state of withdrawal from the world which very often allows him to see it from a rational, detached standpoint—which means in turn that he is not bound, like us, to think forwards. Like Aquinas, he is able to reason backwards.

Umberto Eco, one of the great authorities on Aquinas's thought, tells a wonderful story about the young Thomas, about how his family were determined to dissuade him from joining the monastery. They tried everything from bribes to threats, but all to no avail: the boy had clearly set his mind on the pursuit of Truth and the denial of all earthly pleasures. His brothers, exasperated by his obstinacy and less sensitive than his fraught parents, eventually conspired to corrupt him by pushing a naked young girl into his rooms in the dead of night. A silence followed, in which they thought they might have finally succeeded. But a moment later, they watched their plan backfire as a very fat, very naked, and terrified Aquinas chased the girl from his room and out into the night, in mortal fear of the supposed 'temptress' sent by the Devil himself![1]

And when I think about that story, I'm not sure that Adrian Monk's reaction would have been fundamentally different. In "Mr. Monk and the Bad Girlfriend", we see a very similar scene, and one which leaves him too fleeing the house in a state of fear. Perhaps there *is* sometimes more to a name than meets the eye.

---

[1] "In Praise of St. Thomas," in *Travels in Hyperreality* (1989).

14

Mr. Monk Does a Ritual Dance

JENNIFER CULVER

> **MONK:** I don't know what happened. At some point, I just got stuck. The world kept turning and changing. Microchips, cell phones, TV screen blackboards . . . and I didn't. I didn't change.
>
> **DR. KROGER:** You know, Adrian, I think that this is your way of keeping your mind clear . . . so that you can focus on what's really important.
>
> —"Mr. Monk and the Really, Really Dead Guy"

How does he do it? Time after time, viewers and characters alike ask that question of Adrian Monk, former police officer turned private investigator. How can someone who struggles to negotiate through daily life solve such complex crimes? Throughout the years, I've always been intrigued by Monk's methods: the way he holds his hands, his grin when he has solved the case, and the inevitable "here's what happened." One explanation of Monk's behaviors and successes stems from the idea that he functions as a shamanic figure, performing a ritual, complete with ritualized gestures and utterances, to solve each case. Because he refuses to stop mourning the death of his wife Trudy, in part because he cannot successfully solve her murder, Monk, like many shamans, remains in a transitional state that is, as Monk so often says, "a blessing and a curse." This explains why Monk's attempts at "moving on," which he is often encouraged to do, often causes Monk's investigative skills to diminish, if not disappear altogether, until he returns to his usual state: within society, but not a part of it; in time, but not moving forward; filled with humanity, but committed to the dead.

Monk as Shaman

Monk: When I was on the force, I used to hate cashing my pay-check. I still do. To me, police work is—it's like a higher calling, like the priesthood.

Dr. Kroger: But Adrian, even priests have to get paid.

—"Mr. Monk and the Big Reward"

From the perspective of ritual, life is a series of passages from one stage to another, each marked with a ritual occasion to separate the individual from one portion of society and incorporate him into another. This is how a boy becomes a man, or, in this case, how a cadet becomes a police officer. In between those stages lies the stage Arnold Van Gennep called the "transitional" stage[1] and which Victor Turner would later label the "liminal" stage.[2] In this liminal stage, the individual exists in an undefined state between social categories, not one thing anymore, but not yet something else. This is where the shaman resides. He is an observer of life while living on the margins of it. Other detectives prior to Monk lived a marginalized existence as well, such as Conan Doyle's Sherlock Holmes or Christie's Hercule Poirot. All three detectives are able to see what the officials cannot see, largely because the officials are part of a larger system that comes with assumptions and limited points of view. Because these shamanic figures are not a part of the world, they all require assistance. Holmes has Watson, Poirot has Colonel Hastings, and Monk has Natalie. In each case the assistant helps the detective negotiate through the world, past compulsions, letting him focus intently on the problem at hand.[3]

Working in the margins of society, the shaman functions to provide healing and to restore balance to the community. The Native American shaman proposes a rain dance to restore the tribe's connection to the earth and provide much needed water. In the same way a statesman can propose a monument, such as the Vietnam Memorial, to provide healing for the whole country. Mircea Eliade argues that shamanic elements can be found in isolation and within

---

[1] *Rites of Passage* (University of Chicago Press, 1960).

[2] *The Ritual Process* (Aldine, 2007).

[3] The DVD extras from Season One show that producers and writers were using Holmes as a model, making Stottlemeyer or Disher a type of Lestrade figure for Monk.

other forms of magical or religious practice.[4] This means that sometimes a shaman needs to create and enact a ritual to heal or serve his society, but other times the shaman may only need to employ certain gestures or phrases to achieve his end, just like sometimes Sherlock Holmes had to compulsively play his violin to help him think but other times it was not needed. Working in a trance-like state, the shaman "sees" the source of disorder and how it can be remedied. With this understanding of shaman as a figure who seeks out disorder to remedy and restore society, let's return to Adrian Monk.

During Season 1 of *Monk*, the first image as the theme song began was an image of Monk cleaning a smudge off his window—a very telling image for the man who has asked for hundreds of wipes throughout the seasons. Almost-nemesis Dale "the Whale" Biederbeck once taunted Monk saying, "One hand washes the other. Now there's a metaphor I know you can relate to" ("Mr. Monk Goes to Jail"). Monk's avoidance of dirt also makes him a good candidate for a shaman. According to anthropologist Mary Douglas, in her 1966 book *Purity and Danger*, dirt represents defilement and disorder. Rituals create boundaries and reinforce societal structure, making something that is labeled "dirty," a disruptive force.

Monk's role as a police officer is symbolically equivalent to his personal quest to remove dirt and smudges from everything he comes near—both Monk the detective and shamans believe they are invested with a sacred duty, and there is no doubt from above that Adrian sees his police work in a similar light as performing a spiritual function for society. When talking about his function as an officer, Monk said he wanted to fix the world "one little piece at a time" so that he could "put things back together" ("Mr. Monk Gets Fired"). Seeing crime as "dirt," Monk believes he is cleaning up and reordering society; something he does well.

While married, Monk may have been an unorthodox and impeccably neat officer, but he was well respected. Former partner Joe Christie said in "Mr. Monk and the Employee of the Month," "I learned more from Adrian Monk in two days than I learned in two years at the academy." We know from the first episode of the series that the mayor calls Adrian to be a consultant on difficult cases.

---

[4] *Shamanism* (Princeton University Press, 2004).

Adrian's problem is that he cannot work as a police officer until cleared from his psychological hurdles that intensified after his wife Trudy's death. Since being a liminal figure also defines the work of the shaman, this aspect deserves more consideration.

Remaining Liminal—Remaining in Limbo

CAPTAIN: You should think about your future.

MONK: What future?

CAPTAIN: Your future.

MONK: I don't have one.

—"Mr. Monk and the Captain's Wife"

Mourning Trudy is not the only experience that keeps Monk marginalized, which is why, to some degree, Monk has always been Monk, even before his breakdown. We learn this in the episode "Mr. Monk and Little Monk," where we see Adrian as a child using his hands to frame the scene and say "here's what happened." Glimpses of his childhood with brother Ambrose and periodic flashbacks confirm that Monk never really fit in. Sharona said in "Mr. Monk and the Three Pies" that Monk's childhood bedroom was the "saddest" thing she'd seen because he'd clearly put up posters of bands he did not even know, just to fit in. But unlike his brother Ambrose, who refuses to leave the home and continues to save newspapers in case their father returns, Monk did manage to venture out into the normal world far enough to find someone special who was already a functional part of society: Trudy.

Before Trudy, Monk was used to living on the fringes of society with his phobias and compulsions. Marriage to Trudy incorporated Monk directly into the world he typically separated himself from, one of the few times in his life when he was in the world and not only on the margin. Flashbacks show Trudy gently redirecting Monk when a compulsion would interfere with a social occasion, or times when Monk's compulsions seem to disappear when Monk was sharing an intimate moment with Trudy on a park bench. His love for her overpowered his phobias, his compulsions, and even amnesia in "Mr. Monk Bumps His Head," when a woman pretending to be Monk's wife tried to kiss him and Monk whispered Trudy's name. Losing Trudy caused a downward spiral for Adrian Monk.

Often, in and out of therapy sessions, Monk refers to Trudy as someone he was lucky to marry. It is not unusual to find Monk encountering a stranger and, soon after, finding a way to discuss Trudy, as happened in "Mr. Monk Meets the Playboy," as well as many other episodes. In "Mr. Monk and the Marathon Man," Monk shows how Trudy's death has left him in some kind of stasis, saying she is "always with me," which is borne out by the visions he has of Trudy, visions that are more prevalent in earlier seasons. In the same episode, Monk says that she is "always thirty-four" and "always in the same dress" he saw her wearing the day she was murdered. He even continued to pay for her office downtown for nine years after her death ("Mr. Monk vs. the Cobra"). Monk's decision to continue to mourn Trudy has cost him his job and keeps him static in a dynamic world, but it also may give him the advantage of a unique perspective; something a true shaman possesses.

Adrian also remains in a transitional state because others around him consistently encourage his hopes that someday he will be reinstated as an officer, which inhibits Adrian from fully developing his new life and new role as a private detective. When obstacles to reinstatement emerge, such as the physical in "Mr. Monk Takes a Punch," or a hiring freeze in "Mr. Monk Is at Your Service," the captain and others work to keep Adrian's possible reinstatement viable. Monk often refers to himself as a "cop" first, usually followed after a pause with a modification such as "or I used to be a cop."

One reason they may continue to encourage his hopes for reinstatement is because of their desire to see Monk in a more defined role. Figures between roles in society make us uncomfortable, because they show us that the roles we have are not absolute. Aside from Monk, another example would be people suffering from chronic health conditions, such as rheumatoid arthritis or fibromyalgia, which are invisible ailments that attack normal, young individuals, making them need more care than they should for their age or appearance. Those who are no longer children but not yet adults similarly suffer from their inability to fit into established and stable categories, and also hold a kind of danger and power, as explored in Nabokov's *Lolita*, or in *American Beauty*.

Without a truly defined role, Monk remains in limbo. Not a cop, but not a not-cop and unable to solve the only murder that truly matters to him, Trudy's, Monk cannot move forward. The "dirt" caused by her murder must be wiped away for Monk to feel he has performed his sacred duty and restored balance to his corner of the world. Until then he is a self- proclaimed "broken machine" ("Mr. Monk Takes His Medicine"), trapped and only with his "system" of ritual gestures and utterances—his shamanic skills—to propel him from one case to another.

The Hand Thing

MONK: You look between your fingers. You just let your mind go blank . . . You let the room wash over you. I mean, you could go up, or you could go down . . . or you could lean. Lean. You're just making connections. Just looking for . . . inconsistencies.

—"Mr. Monk and the Actor"

Here Monk explains to an actor how he forms a frame with his hands to help him focus on the crime scene. According to Mary Douglas, social rituals must contain ritual and symbolic actions. These actions provide focus and help the shaman delineate time and place. For example, a marriage ceremony is marked with specific actions and rituals: vows must be said, witnesses must be present, and typically an exchange of a ring serves as a concrete reminder of this ritual event. The viewer knows Monk is on the case when he begins to frame the scene with his hands.

For Monk, the act of framing in a ritual setting helps him alter his perspective. The action is instinctual, as even when Monk has amnesia in "Mr. Monk Bumps His Head" he tells people that he needs to use his hands as a frame to "see things." The moment his hands begin to frame the surroundings, Monk enters what Sharona called his "Zen, Sherlock Holmes thing" and others have called his "magic," or "trance." To the untrained eye, it can appear that Monk is performing a "parlor trick" or acting "drunk," but for knowledgeable participants, this is a sign that Monk is on the case. Captain Stottlemeyer describes the hand motion and its dance by saying "He flows. It's like he's floating. He's on a sea of motion" ("Mr. Monk and the Actor").

If Monk does not perform the ritualized gesture of framing the scene with his hands, his friends and colleagues worry that he's not taking the case seriously. During the garbage strike, Monk refuses to do "the thing" with his hands at Natalie's request because he doesn't want to solve the case, believing that the "greater good" lies in getting the mayor's office and the garbage worker's union to resume negotiations. Why? He's distracted by the trash on the streets and is willing to sacrifice anything to clean up the literal dirt. Despite Sharona's son Benjy's insistence that a murder has occurred in a hotel room in "Mr. Monk Takes a Vacation," Monk does not raise his hands to investigate the scene because the room does not look like a typical crime scene. Marci, Monk's one-time biggest fan, got "goose bumps" watching Monk frame the scene with his hands. People who understand how Monk works realize that, as Douglas asserts in her work, rituals must be performed in certain steps. The repetitive use of his hands at crime scenes make this gesture a necessary step in the perceived process Monk must undergo to solve a crime.

Monk's use of his hands allows him to "see" the scene in a unique way, but it is not his only gesture. Monk displays a subtle gesture to indicate he has solved the case: a smile. Smiling for Adrian Monk is a rare thing, and actually quite uncharacteristic. As Monk once explained, "Joy is a trick. A diversion. It doesn't last forever. It breaks your heart every time . . . Damn Joy!" ("Mr. Monk and the Man Who Shot Santa"). Monk only smiles when solving a crime or dreaming about Trudy, which makes this gesture a significant occurrence. When Monk does smile, his smile is contagious, mainly because Monk is about to reveal the solution with his famous words, "Here's what happened."

Ritual Utterances

Monk: There's no hugging during the "Here's what happened!"

—"Mr. Monk and His Biggest Fan"

Speech functions as another ritual symbol alongside gestures. During any social ritual, specific utterances are expected at their particular moment. The expected, sometimes formulaic, utterance must be exact for participants to believe the ritual will carry the needed efficacy. As a case in point, remember President Obama's inauguration. Because there was a moment of stumbling in the wording of President Obama's swearing in by the Chief Justice, the country felt unsettled and the administration repeated the swearing-in ritual to reassure the nation that Obama was rightfully installed as President of the United States. Why would this be necessary? The will of the people and a democratic election only "counts" if we say the magic words? It's because we treat inauguration as a pseudo-religious governmental ritual that these specific utterances must be exact or cause discomfort and anxiety in the audience.

Monk's phrase "Here's what happened" serves as an indicator that he has solved the case; a symbol that the world (or, in particular, the case) is about to change, and this particular bit of impurity and disorder has been overcome. Like with the use of his hands, participants wait for Monk to say "Here's what happened" and begin to reveal the solution. We wait for this expression as well, because it signifies that the revelation is coming. It's like a moment when the jury has announced they have reached a verdict. We know that resolution is coming. Monk, like the members of the jury, does not need this utterance: we do. This explains why, at times, Monk, or the situation, gets carried away and there is no "Here's what happened." Because of the power of the phrase, others vie for the chance to say it first, then revealing Monk's explanation of events on his behalf.

Another expression Monk uses as a marker in his process is "he's the guy." When Monk believes he knows the identity of the guilty party, he typically says "he's the guy" to his colleagues, marking a turn in his process, a turn towards shifting his perspective to how his suspect committed the crime. Unlike "Here's what happened," this statement appears early in Monk's process and is not always met with enthusiasm, usually because Monk's suspect is one of the more unlikely candidates. This means the search for proof will be more difficult and possibly unpopular, as in the case of "Mr. Monk and the Astronaut."

Unlike "Here's what happened," "he's the guy" may not always be accurate. Monk does not always know the solution right away. Instead, he can, like the other detectives around him, be swayed to believe in the wrong course of action. That does not mean that "Here's what happened" is infallible—as in "Mr. Monk and the Garbage Strike," when Monk, distracted by the sight and smell of mounting garbage in the streets, blamed rock star Alice Cooper for the murder (presumptively of supellectile[5] motivation) of a union leader. These moments remind us that, comparisons to

---

[5] *Supellectile*: of, or related to furniture. Congratulations, you now know a word that you will never need to know again!

Sherlock Holmes and Columbo aside, Adrian Monk has human qualities and tendencies, something that those around him forget.

Shaman, Heal Thyself

MONK: This is not the life I wanted. It's unbearable. I don't want to be an extraordinary man. I want to be the guy on the bus, coming home at five P.M., help his kids with their homework . . . I'm not even a man.

—"Mr. Monk Takes His Medicine"

If the function of a shaman is to heal and restore balance to a community, Monk's adamant refusal to heal himself seems out of place. According to Douglas, the act of removing "dirt" and repurification derives from cleansing, burying, or erasing the object representing disorder. She likens the process to annulment, which fits Monk's condition beautifully. Monk repeatedly vows never to "move on" from his marriage to Trudy. He continues to wear his wedding ring and surrounds himself with her image. By continuing to see himself as married, Monk does not allow himself to fully heal, grow, and reincorporate into society. He will not cleanse himself by taking off the ring and moving on. He will not erase his connection to Trudy, or even lessen it, by removing some of her pictures. While Monk restores balance to society at large with this talent for solving crimes, he does not even try to heal himself.

Healing Monk may lead to a diminishment in his abilities, as it would move Monk out of the liminal, transitional space he has remained in for so long. The show periodically explores this question with different scenarios. Mary Douglas comments in *Purity and Danger* that some choose to deceive themselves into believing that they attained a purified state. In each of the examples below, Monk does exactly that.

In Season 3, in "Mr. Monk Takes His Medicine," Monk decides to take a new drug called Doxinyl and he exhibits immediate changes. He appears at a crime scene with his top button unbuttoned and eats from a sandwich the captain already took a bite from, causing everyone around him to recoil. Calling himself "The Monk," he calls people "cats and kittens" and leaves ketchup on his shirt. Despite his assertion that his mind is "clear for the first time," Monk proves to be ineffective. He does not use his hands in the ritualized gesture that frames his way of seeing and does not try to focus on a possible suspect. When his friends try to take away his pills, Monk yells, "I'm well and you can't stand it, can you?"

Unfortunately, even Monk realizes over time that the drug cannot completely heal him. While trying to frolic in a pool with younger people, Monk finds himself abandoned. When he returns to his friends, dressed again in his typical clothing and style, he said that Trudy "didn't like" him as "The Monk." He even says later "I missed me" as the pills are tossed away, showing that deep down Monk realizes his sacred calling requires him to sacrifice his own happiness and belonging now that Trudy is gone.

Another pivotal episode appears in Season Five, when Monk believes he finally has a best friend, Hal, in "Mr. Monk Makes a Friend." After a chance meeting in front of a grocery store, Hal immediately starts to hang out with Monk, even taking him to a hockey game. The change in Monk again causes a distraction in his work. Instead of paying attention to an interrogation, Monk talks to Natalie about fun with Hal. Monk puts his feet on his own coffee table and seems to enjoy watching martial arts movies. Unlike many episodes, the viewer knows Hal is the murderer. Deep down, Monk realizes this as well, but intentionally pushes this knowledge aside for the chance at a real friendship.

Among other examples of Monk exhibiting temporary happiness in controlled settings, such as a clean room, office cubicle, or butler role, is Monk's short stay in a cult during "Mr. Monk Joins a Cult." Believing he can infiltrate the cult for a case, Monk enters the compound and begins to find a sense of peace in the structure and harmony presented to him. A perceptive man, Father wins Monk over with the very object he struggles with the most: dirt. Father calls the wipes a "crutch" and that for Monk to be "free," he needs to "surrender" to the dirt.

Given the symbolism of dirt throughout the series, Monk faces a critical decision in this moment. To accept the dirt on his hand means to step away from his sacred role and begin to tolerate disorder. Once Adrian lets go of the wipe the decision is made. In the next scene, Captain Stottlemeyer tells Randy and Natalie that Monk was at the airport selling flowers (although they were all flowers with exactly ten petals, illustrating that Monk's compulsions are not completely gone).

Father gives Monk another test by exposing his detective role and threatening to expel him from the compound. In order to stay, Monk renounces his former profession and begs to stay, saying "I love not thinking. I'm so tired of thinking." Douglas writes that purity can be perceived as hard or dead when finally attained, and Monk's experience supports this. He has deadened his mind to reach a purified state. As a result, a cult leader may get away with murder. But Monk fights for this sense of peace—indeed, when his friends kidnap and attempt to deprogram him, Monk remains committed to his new belief.

In the end, a picture of Trudy restores Monk to his former unhappy, liminal state, and Monk solves the case, resulting Father's arrest. The resolution of Monk's experiences with the cult illustrates the main choices for the future of Adrian Monk. For Monk to achieve purification and/or happiness, he must abandon his sacred duty, complete with ritual gestures and utterances, and attempt to move out of his transition state by embracing his role as a private citizen and widower. For Monk to remain effective in his shamanic role, a role needed by his society, he must continue to remain in mourning and isolate himself from the rest of society. Because this sacrifice keeps Trudy alive for Monk, it's a sacrifice he's willing to make.

As the final season of *Monk* progresses, we watch the parking garage where Trudy was murdered transformed into a memorial park, evidence the town has moved on. Monk remains the same, as he always has. Like the quote at the beginning of this chapter, Monk remains timeless: locked by choice in a world where everything needs to be rounded to the nearest ten, the umbrellas all need to face the same direction, and where Trudy's memories and her unsolved murder remain close at hand. Happy does not factor into what Adrian Monk needs to fulfill his sacred duty.

15

Mr. Monk and the Bodhisattva Ideal

RONALD S. GREEN

For seven seasons, he has engaged a carnivalesque cast of astronaut and acrobat; cult leader and candidate; movie star and marathon runner; playboy and paperboy; Santa Claus and sportscaster; union boss and used-car salesman. Given this cavalcade of figures from every sector of American mythic consciousness, it seems as if Monk must be something other than a mere detective; that he must be playing some larger role in addition to solving crimes.

Might Mr. Monk be a Bodhisattva as described in Buddhist literature? The Sanskrit indicates "awakening" (*bodhi*) and person or being (*sattva*). Bodhisattvas are awakening in two ways, transitive and intransitive; becoming awake and awakening others. With the same root, the title "buddha" means "awakened one."

On the surface, Adrian Monk's primary task is to solve murder mysteries in conjunction with members of the San Francisco police department. In the process, he hopes to gain control over the obsessions, compulsions, and phobias that render him dysfunctional in many ways and make him extraordinary in others. Might this be the business of an awakening being? Mr. Monk, like a Buddhist monk, also transforms the lives of some of those around him in fundamental ways quite beyond his overt work. Perhaps in this sense he is awakening others, but more interesting is the transformative potential the series possesses in awakening the viewer.

In Mahāyāna Buddhist writings, the Bodhisattva is represented as a special individual who brings others to an acceptance of Buddhist principles. These include the ultimate emptiness of our received reality, the interdependence of all constituents of that

193

reality, and the view that there is no real "self" in the sense of a soul, essence, or ego. According to Buddhist texts, the Bodhisattva has great compassion for all sentient beings and so endeavours to relieve physical and mental sufferings. The Bodhisattva accomplishes this goal not by argument but through "skilful means," through creating circumstances in day-to-day living that bring individuals material comfort and a different, Buddhist perspective on life. Typically, the subject of the Bodhisattva's efforts is unaware this is happening but is deceived for his or her own good. It's in this sense that Mr. Monk is an unintentional Bodhisattva.

Mr. Monk and the Jungle *in* There

Randy Newman's song, "It's a Jungle Out There," is fitting for *Monk* in a number of ways (Marci Maven's objections aside). Mr. Monk is afraid of germs. Outside his clean environment, the world is full of them. This is no less than the Buddhist view of defilement in the world, which, according to the theory, is so because of our defiled minds, the jungle in there. Mr. Monk is aware of these two defilements, the disorderliness of the world and his disorders. These are in some ways interrelated and in others contradictory. Likewise, to an extent the world is unsafe because Mr. Monk perceives it as unsafe. We can see that his perception of order is not absolute when he is confronted with perhaps another Bodhisattva figure, Harold J. Krenshaw (Tim Bagley), a rival who also suffers from OCD. While Mr. Monk arranges items one way, Mr. Krenshaw does so in quite a different order. It is likely that Mr. Krenshaw's version of order is as valid as Mr. Monk's and not just wrong, as the latter argues. Even though Mr. Monk can use his power of perceiving disorder where order should be, Mr. Krenshaw's role implies it is not the only logical possibility. This corresponds to the Buddhist concept that our logical constructions concerning the world allow us to survive, but are not ultimately true. As Randy Newman puts it, "I could be wrong now, but I don't think so."

Herein lies the key to Mr. Monk's extraordinary powers as a detective; powers not unlike those attributed to Bodhisattvas. Mr. Monk desires the world to be orderly. Because of his obsession with this, when the slightest thing is disorderly, he notices it, though others don't. This apparent flaw makes him invaluable to humanity. Legends of Bodhisattvas, such as those found in *Miraculous Tales of Japan* (*Nihon Ryōiki*, ninth century C.E.), tell of those who could know the thoughts of individuals in need and intuit and put a stop to the plans of malicious people. These powers supposedly come from putting one's own mind in order. According to the same writing, those called Bodhisattvas, at least in Japan's Nara period, were monks unaffiliated with institutional Buddhism. In this regard, we should note the often-used name "Mr. Monk" in the series has a combination of lay (Mr.) and monastic (Monk) qualities.

What characterizes a Bodhisattva, or "awakening being"? Buddhist literature provides various descriptions, including the famous "Ten Stages of a Bodhisattva" chapter of the fourth-century *Yogācārabhūmi-śāstra*, and the eighth-century *Guide to the Bodhisattva's Way Of Life (Bodhicaryavatara)* by the Indian Buddhist scholar Shantideva. According to these documents, the first thing that happens to an individual entering the path of the Bodhisattva is the arousal of the aspiration to become awakened. This aspirant quality is referred to as the Buddha-mind (Sanskrit, *bodhicitta*). After arousing the Buddha-mind, the Bodhisattva takes particular vows. Some of these vows are resolutions to overcome obstacles to awakening, thought of as infirmities. Some vows promise to help others arouse their own Buddha-minds and thus embark on the Bodhisattva path.

Although there are various vows taken by Bodhisattvas, perhaps the most famous are the Four Bodhisattva Vows, which give us an image of the ideal work of a Bodhisattva, and begin to show how Mr. Monk may have entered upon the path of the Bodhisattva. In East Asia, Zen monks and lay Buddhists may take these vows as follows:

1. *Blind desires are inexhaustible; I vow to overcome them all.*

2. *The Dharma gate is immeasurable; I vow to enter it.*

3. *Sentient beings are innumerable; I vow to save them all from suffering.*

4. *Nirvana is unfathomable; I vow to accomplish it.*

All Americans Have OCD

The first vow speaks of overcoming blind desires, a basic principle of Buddhism and driving force for Mr. Monk. What desire could be blinder—more meaningless and yet compelling—than the desire to touch a lamppost? And yet this can fairly represent our worldly strivings in general. What more sense does it make to strive for wealth and fame than to touch lampposts? Both are desires that amount to nothing in the end, and yet occupy and clutter up our lives and minds.

The fundamental message attributed to the Buddha from earliest times is recorded as the opening passage of the *Dhammapada* (*Verses on the Dharma*): the mind precedes all phenomena. If one acts with polluted mind, the passage continues, pain follows. Buddhists believe what we perceive as reality is filtered or created by the mind. However, considering our perceptions as objectively real, and going through life led by our untamed minds, suffering arises. In the same way that Mr. Monk is at the mercy of his compulsions, so too is all humanity. We are compulsively attracted to things and repelled by other things. Quite beyond our control, this rules our lives. Buddhist monks and Bodhisattvas resolve to take control of the impulses of their minds and thereby overcome the suffering that results. For Mr. Monk and Buddhist monks, this is no easy task.

There is a story of a thirteenth-century Chinese public official who liked to dispute philosophical points. He sought out a monk, asking to hear the abstruse teachings of the Buddha for argument's sake. The monk replied simply, "Reject evil, embrace good, purify your mind," which is recorded as the words of the Buddha in Chapter 14 of the *Dhammapada*. The official scoffed, "This is the deep message of your teacher? Even my child knows that." The monk replied, "Though every child may know this, even a silver-haired old man finds it difficult to put into practice."

While we don't ordinarily reflect on this, *Monk* makes the difficulties of controlling one's mind clear to the viewer. And we're shown that even if we are aware of the potential harm caused by the mind's activities, those activities are still not easily controlled. Think of all the times you say, "I know I shouldn't, but I just can't help myself," and the even more times you don't say it, but could. Among those who acknowledge their blind desires and seek to manage them, just as Mr. Monk does, there are aspiring Bodhisattvas who take the first vow.

Mr. Monk Is Lucky to Be Sick

What is the Dharma gate Bodhisattvas vow to enter? How is it entered and is it even remotely related to Mr. Monk? The Dharma is the teaching of the Buddha—that is, Buddhism. Another translation of the second vow would be, "The Buddha's teachings are incomprehensible, I vow to penetrate their depths." This points to the importance of simplifying life. Buddhist ascetics do this in a variety of ways, such as giving up family, social ties, extravagant foods and conventions of clothing.

Mr. Monk has lost his family in his beloved Trudy. Like the Buddha, who left his wife and son, Mr. Monk gave up a child he refers to as his son in "Mr. Monk and the Kid," and his adoptive mother in "Mr. Monk and the Lady Next Door." Mr. Monk has also lost his job on the police force. He eats only certain foods arranged in definite ways, like monastic food restrictions. He has a closet filled with only one kind of suit, like those Buddhists who wear only one type of robe. Mr. Monk's house is streamlined, neat and minimalistic, like a Zen monastery.

There is an interrelationship between his minimalism and his obsessions. While his obsessions cause him to have only one type of suit, for example, having one type of suit also serves to help overcome his obsessions. While he lost his job on the police force because of his obsession, having no job on the force allows him to get better. In Buddhism, there's a similar understanding of the interrelationship of defilement and purification. A certain ideal of what constitutes "purification of the mind" is essential to the Bodhisattva path, just as cleanliness is in Mr. Monk's life. Yet, by his involvement in crime, Mr. Monk seeks out disorder and dirtiness and makes it his job to set it straight. Like a Bodhisattva, Mr. Monk is not concerned simply with his own defilement and purification, but with the purification of defilement in the world, in terms of crime, disorder, and disease. Others may not always see that the disorder is a real problem, but, as he insists, they will thank him later.

Without the disorder, order cannot be established. In Buddhism, awakening cannot occur without the sleeping illusion, which is how ordinary consciousness is considered. In fact, there is no absolute state of one or the other, awakening or sleep. Belief in apprehension of absolute states is considered also illusion, as is a perfect system of philosophy, including logic and Buddhism itself.

The relationship of the profane and sacred is well known in other religious traditions also. One may question the relationship in Christianity of the Holy Mother Mary and the prostitute who shares her name. In Buddhism, there is a similarity in the names of *Maya*, the mother of the Buddha (and who is, by extension, that which

gives rise to awakening), and *Mara*, the personification of death
and deception. The Sanskrit name Mara is said to be related to the
English word murder. From illusion comes awakening. From murder comes order. Might the above be said of Trudy and Mr. Monk?
Trudy may represent order as Mr. Monk, who longs for order and
Trudy, is cursed by the disorder of the world and of his afflictions.
When Trudy died, so did the perceived amount of order in his
world that allowed him to function. His inability to cope with disorder is intricately connected with his inability to solve the mystery
of Trudy's murder. At the same time, one cannot exist without the
other.

Mr. Monk's desire to put things in order may be obsessive
because it causes him to be unable to function socially in an ordinary way. If so, this is true also of a Bodhisattva. According to the
Life of the Buddha (*Buddhacarita*, second century C.E.), Prince
Siddhartha, the man who became the Buddha, witnessed four
sights that aroused the desire to attain Buddhahood. On successive
occasions, he saw sickness, old age, death, and a religious renun-
ciant. Ordinarily, when one sees these, some discomfort may be
expected. However, when Siddhartha happened upon them, he
could not stop thinking about his relationship to each. As a result,
he left his family, gave up his claim to the kingship, moved to the
forest and practiced austerities. To change your life so radically,
based on these four sights, may certainly be called obsessive and
compulsive.

Mr. Monk Is a Liar

The third Bodhisattva Vow is to save all sentient beings from suffering. Suffering is viewed as externally imposed by social conditions, but ultimately self-inflicted due to ignorance of the mind's
activities. But how can a Bodhisattva help people who by and large
do not want to be "saved," and who may, in fact, never 'thank him
later'? Indeed, as in Plato's analogy of the cave, they do not think
they are ignorant, but that the Bodhisattva is. What's a Bodhisattva
to do? The scriptures are clear. A Bodhisattva must devise clever
means of trickery.

Perhaps the most famous Bodhisattva appearing in Mahāyāna
scriptures is saint Vimalakīrti. His stories, found in *The Holy
Teachings of Vimalakīrti* (*Vimalakīrti Nirdesa Sūtra*) correspond in
some ways with those of Mr. Monk. Vimalakīrti is not a monk but

a Buddhist layperson who has very special abilities he uses to help others. He pretends to be sick so that people of the town come to his bedside to pay their respects. But this is only a lure. Once in his house, Vimalakīrti confuses the visitors with various arguments aimed at making them question their assumptions about reality. In addition to his somewhat Socratic method, Vimalakīrti also causes visions to manifest, just as the makers of the television series do. Just like the television series, these visions cause the viewer to question assumptions about self-identity, such as gender and the passing of duration.

The USA Network has advertised a number of related detective dramas with the phrase "characters welcome." The protagonists in the series are unusual, yet the viewer comes to identify with these individuals. Three of these are *Monk, Law and Order Criminal Intent,* and *Psych.* In addition to having things in common that make them right for the USA Network, they also share Bodhisattva characteristics. Likewise, in recent films with overt Buddhist messages, Bodhisattvas are portrayed as detectives.

In *I ♥ Huckabees* (David O. Russell, USA, 2004), Dustin Hoffman and Lily Tomlin portray "existential detectives." They discover the specific manifestations of clients' sufferings and lead them to awakening. In the director's commentary on the DVD, David O. Russell explains that he based the detectives and their work on classes he took from the Buddhologist Robert A.F. Thurman. Similarly, in *Zen Noir* (Marc Rosenbush, USA, 2006), a film noir–like detective is "called" to a Buddhist monastery by an unknown source, likely his own aspiration for awakening. His quest to solve an apparent murder in the monastery becomes a journey of self-discovery and ultimately Buddhist rejection of the idea of self. In both films, and in the USA Network's dramas as well, the job of detective represents the search for self-discovery or a broader understanding of reality. In particular, a reoccurring theme is the impossibility of understanding reality, and the suffering caused by the quest to do so.

Like Mr. Monk, Detective Robert Goren (Vincent D'Onofrio) of *Law and Order Criminal Intent* is endowed with extraordinary abilities that could at times properly be characterized as superhuman. The comic-book or scripture-like characterizations of these abilities and the representation of the profane and the sacred are evident in the episodes involving super-villainess Nicole Wallace (Olivia d'Abo). She is like him, but has applied her abilities to crime. As in

Mr. Monk's struggle with the case of Trudy's murder, Nicole's are the only cases Goren is unable to solve satisfactorily. Also like Mr. Monk, even with Goren's brilliant and impossible display of knowledge in arts, sciences, and languages, there is a flaw, making him a USA "character." His mother is schizophrenic and the detective continually shows signs that he may be inching toward a mental disorder. While Mr. Monk's OCD may not be clearly connected with his parents in the series, we're repeatedly reminded that while Trudy was alive he was able to function as a police officer.

Mr. Monk Is Not a Liar

In the USA Network detective series *Psych*, Shawn Spencer (James Roday) pretends to possess psychic abilities so that the Santa Barbara Police Department will consult him. In fact, he does have extraordinary abilities to solve mysteries but it is not psychic. He has a photographic memory. Again, like the other USA "characters," there is comic book-like action extremely unlikely if not impossible in what we accept as ordinary reality. Such astonishing or miraculous attributes are given to Bodhisattvas in scriptures such as *The Holy Teachings of Vimalakīrti* and *The Lotus Sūtra*. In that context, we are to consider those in possession of these qualities as evolutionarily different from human beings: *Übermenschen*[1] or Buddhas. In *The Lotus Sūtra*, the Buddha relates the famous "Parable of the Burning House." The story tells of three children trapped inside a burning house. Their father calls to them to run out, but not knowing the full strength of fire, they ignore him and continue to play. So, the father calls to them again, this time promising to give them chariots pulled by three animals, a different favorite animal for each child. Thus luring them out of the house, he provides the vehicles. After the story, the Buddha explains that the father's real reason for calling the children had been the fire, not to give them carts. The carts were tricks. It wasn't a complete lie, since he provided the carts, but it was a partial lie in that he concealed his true purpose. Somewhat surprisingly, the moral of the story turns out to be that lying is good given the danger of certain circumstances.

The burning house is a metaphor for our world of suffering caused by the activities of the mind. In order to draw people out

---

[1] See Chapter 6 in this volume, "Mr. Monk Takes on the *Übermensch*."

of this condition, the Bodhisattva's task is to use any trickery necessary, basing this on each individual's personal affinities. This is known as a Bodhisattva's "skillful-means" and appears similar to Shawn Spencer's deception for the greater good in *Psych*. More importantly, it is like illusions created by the shows' producers, potentially causing a reflective state to arise in the views. It also makes us want to be like the Bodhisattva figure.

Is Mr. Monk using skillful-means deception? Is there a partial lie like that of Vimalakīrti and Shawn, concealing the fact that the show is not all about OCD, germs, and disorder, but suffering and loving kindness? At the very least, there are visible inconsistencies in his conditions. He is a germaphobe who must wipe his hands after shaking. However, in a familiar shot in the opening mix, he jumps up on his dining table with his shoes on. One does not have to be a germaphobe to find this disgustingly dirty. Bobby Flay discovered this from ongoing reactions after standing on the cutting board in Japan's original *Iron Chef* (1997). Although he demonstrates a hierarchy of phobias and compulsions, one would expect knees on the table. In "Mr. Monk goes to Las Vegas," he displays miraculous abilities to know cards not yet displayed. When asked if he is counting cards he denies it, and says he is memorizing cards. This feat goes beyond what we have previously seen concerning Mr. Monk's undoubtedly great memory. If at all possible in terms of ordinary reality, it would appear an abnormality more consistent with autism spectrum condition. In the same episode, he declares the casino owner is not in love with his wife. When asked how he knows this, Mr. Monk replies he just knows. Clearly, he has remarkable abilities. However, these are not neatly explained by OCD and phobias.

Three main possibilities come to mind concerning these inconsistencies. First, maybe within the context of the story he is lying like Vimalakīrti. Another explanation probably occurring most often to viewers is that the writers do not understand OCD and are making mistakes. This does not seem plausible since they otherwise wrote these shows fairly sensibly and must have received innumerable letters about these inconsistencies. A third possibility is that the writers are lying. They are misrepresenting OCD and otherwise using a mishmash of "symptoms" for some purpose. If so, what would be their purpose? Of course, to create a "character" that is entertaining and marketable regardless of the medical feasibility of his personality traits. Even if this is the correct explanation, other things are happening as well. Through Mr. Monk's mild manners, remarkable traits, and regard for justice, the writers are conveying and proselytizing their values to the viewing public in the same manner religious texts do. His are didactic tales of wisdom, compassion and also retribution.

Although these appear to be basic values for American and other cultures, in fact television, media, and capitalism in general bombard us with opposite values by glorifying self-interest and gratuitous violence. Basic to the Bodhisattva ideal is having "loving kindness" for others. Again, this is embodied in the third of the Four Bodhisattva Vows, to save all beings from suffering. According to the theory, taking an attitude of loving kindness, in itself arouses the Buddha-mind in the one who does so. Whether or not Mr. Monk thinks of himself as a Bodhisattva figure, whether or not the writers thought of this, and whether or not the producers know the potential affect on the audience does not matter for the designation to be valid. Even a Buddha, passing beyond discursive thought, may not be aware of Buddhahood.

Mr. Monk Murdered Trudy

Mr. Monk cannot solve the case of Trudy's murder because he accepts responsibility for it. He cannot apprehend the culprit and remain free of apprehension, apprehension as in being arrested, and as in experiencing anxiety. In fact, though someone else likely committed the murder, Mr. Monk is also the culprit in a number of ways. First, according to Buddhists, we are all inter-connected and there is no absolute self and other. Some Buddhists have argued that the murderer on death row is a part of each of us. The Vietnamese monk and Nobel Peace Prize nominee Thich Nhat Hanh calls this "Interbeing." Accordingly, we all live in relationships of mutual interdependence. This extends both to human relationships and to the environment. Harming the environment is harming oneself.

Second, on the way to becoming a Buddha, the Bodhisattva gives up blind desires one after another until all that is left is the desire to become a Buddha. At this point, one comes face to face with herself or himself and in so doing, comes face to face with the Buddha. This is related to the famous Zen saying, "If you meet the Buddha on the road, kill him." Killing the Buddha is precisely what the Bodhisattva must do to enter nirvana. Nirvana is not a heavenly paradise as imaged in yoghurt commercials. The basic meaning of the Sanskrit term is "extinction." It is extinction of the mind's activities. According to the theory, by killing that, the imagined self is finally eradicated. How does this pan out? No one knows. It is allegedly unknowable to the discriminating mind. For this reason, the fourth of the Bodhisattva Vows says, "Nirvana is unfathomable; I vow to accomplish it."

In order to solve the ultimate mystery that is at the base of the series, Mr. Monk must eradicate his self. He will face his final obstacle, himself, face the Buddha and kill him. This is not a simple matter of admitting his culpability. He has done that verbally throughout the series, but his compulsions are a kind of admission of culpability as well. His obsessions, taken as representatives of his blind desires and ours, bind him to suffering as they do us. Through obsessions, he perpetuates his own suffering and that of others; a kind of irrational and unselfconscious vindictive punishment. In one sense, Mr. Monk cannot be who he is if he overcomes his OCD, or if he solves Trudy's murder, or if he returns to the police force. To do any of these things would be the end of Mr. Monk as Mr. Monk—and, thus, the end of the series.

The other sense of Mr. Monk's inevitable self-eradication is connected to the innate relationship between desires and nirvana, the fourth of the Bodhisattva Vows necessarily returns the aspirant to the first. The vow to overcome blind desires is the vow to attain nirvana. The two vows are the same. This is one example of the "first-in-last" or "last-in-first" principle of Buddhism. Likewise, once the Buddha-mind has been aroused, the task is accomplished, the end is in the beginning. We only have to realize this.

At the same time, because each of the Bodhisattva vows is impossible to accomplish, it can be accomplished (for example: Blind desires are inexhaustible; I vow to overcome them all). This is a basic principle of the *Prajñāpāramitā Sutra* and other Mahāyāna Buddhist texts. In this way, there can only be a Bodhisattva because there cannot be a Bodhisattva. If this is incomprehensible . . . well, then the skilful means is working. A Bodhisattva is impossible. The *Prajñāpāramitā Sutra* says the Bodhisattva has no grounds to stand upon. Without grounds to stand upon is how Mr. Monk must solve Trudy's murder. Because of his involvement, the writers' involvement, the audience's involvement and the impossibility of all of it, it all must end. This will be Mr. Monk's extinction, his nirvana and the ultimate fulfillment of the Bodhisattva vows. Everything else is talk about reality from within a dream, not awakening from it.

Our Hour Isn't Over Yet, It's Only Been Fifty-Eight Minutes

Monk in Therapy

16

Mr. Mead Starts Couples Therapy

SYLVIA RANDALL

All names have been altered to protect the identity of my clients.

I have specialized in couples therapy for several decades now and a few couples stand out in my memory. One couple I recall, Patsy and Howard, entered therapy feeling they had fallen out of love. They were able, with their commitment and some therapeutic guidance, to rekindle their mutual respect and to re-experience their love for each other. Then, two years after we had completed our sessions, I received a sweet baby announcement in the mail. In the card, Patsy thanked me for our work together and wrote: "Without our therapy sessions, this precious little being, wouldn't be in the world." I wept a little.

Another couple I will always remember, Nina and Simon, basically hated each other by the time they came to therapy. Both came with the hope that I would magically transform their partner into the original fantasy person they had each created during their initial whirlwind romance and erase all the hurts and disappointments experienced in the years since then. We could have worked with the hurts and disappointments, had it not been the case that the original good feeling had now become real mutual dislike. They had little in common and they were not a good match. This work successfully ended with separation and then divorce. Interestingly, I met Simon in the grocery store years later, and heard that they had become pleasant friends who saw each other on occasion with their new partners.

And then there is Andrew Mead. I have chosen to write up two sessions of my work with Andrew because each session is an initial conjoint meeting with Andrew and his two different working assistants. Thus, it illustrates how different aspects of a person's psyche will emerge in different interactions, especially close ones.

I had heard of Andrew Mead, since his name was often mentioned in the newspaper for reasons related to his profession, which I cannot specify in order to maintain his anonymity. He had, I learned in our initial telephone consultation, lost his beloved wife, Terry, several years before, through a violent crime. That crime had never been fully solved, and Mead was still obsessed, understandably, with the details of her death. I have worked with survivors of a loved ones' murder before, so was prepared to deal with possible "survivor's guilt" and the common anhedonic reaction—the lack of experiencing joy. The survivor often feels, because his loved one can't feel anymore, he or she also should not allow those feelings of joy. It feels like a betrayal to the memory of their lost beloved.

Mead was interested in getting help in his relationship with his nurse-assistant, with whom he had been working for some time, and I was thinking that the relationship between them must be quite interesting and complicated.

It's Monday morning at 8:00 A.M., my first appointment of the day. Mead and his assistant Sheila are in my waiting room when I arrive. I notice they're sitting in chairs as far away from each other as possible. Andrew looks very rigid—sitting up as if at attention. He looks clearly uncomfortable. Sheila is in a more relaxed posture, but I see anger and impatience on her face. She's nervously tapping her right toe. When I introduce myself, Sheila perks up and smiles warmly. Andrew stands up stiffly and nods. I notice he doesn't extend his hand—I remember after a moment that he mentioned on the phone he has severe OCD.

> **Sylvia:** Good morning, please help yourself to coffee and come on in.

> (*They sit in the two chairs provided.*)

> **Sylvia:** So, what's going on that brings you here?

> (*Sheila gestures to Andrew to start. I see a look of resignation on her face.*)

> **Andrew:** I'm very uncomfortable with Sheila's feelings towards me—though, I do realize I'm not the easiest person to spend time with.

SYLVIA: Can you tell me more about those feelings and your discomfort?

ANDREW: Yes, of course. I really need to depend on her being there for me, and sometimes she is, but other times she gets critical and impatient—especially when my compulsions come up.

SYLVIA: How do you feel at those times?

ANDREW: Most of all, I feel afraid—afraid that she will leave me. I really need her.

(Andrew told me in our phone call that his wife, Terry, died violently several years ago—his fear of losing Sheila may be partly due to his loss of Terry. I also wonder if there were earlier losses in his life, maybe of a parent. It could have been a loss by death or abandonment, or a psychological rather than literal loss— such as in the case of poor parenting or neglect. I'll get back to that later.)

SYLVIA: Sheila, is there some truth in Andrew's perceptions that you feel critical and impatient at times?

SHEILA: Of course, anyone in their right mind would! I mean, he has a brilliant mind, and yet he acts like a five-year-old afraid his mommy is mad at him! And other times he can't focus on anything or anyone because he has to put objects on the mantelpiece in a perfect row. He drives me crazy!

Actually, his self-centeredness is one of my major complaints. I am his assistant, so we work closely together, but he is totally insensitive to my feelings and incapable of empathy. He is always thinking of Andrew Mead first and foremost. It's disgusting.

ANDREW: That's not always true. Especially after you point out my failings, like at the circus with your fear of elephants. I make a real effort to consider how you must be thinking and feeling.

SHEILA: Yes, at times, but I think that's mostly motivated by your desire to keep me from getting angry with you. Remember how before you tried to listen, you just said "suck it up." What a dumb-ass comment that was.

SYLVIA: Hold on a minute! Is this a familiar dynamic between you? I see you blaming each other and wanting the other to do the changing. This is about the most common cyclical pattern I see between couples. Often, the feelings underlying blaming and anger are hurt and disappointment. Does that fit for either of you?

SHEILA: Well, it sure fits for me sometimes.

SYLVIA: Do you let Andrew know when you feel that way?

SHEILA: Yes, of course. I ask him how great he would feel if I acted that way with him.

SYLVIA: It sounds as if you like to use sarcasm—is that right?

SHEILA: Well, no shit! Wouldn't you?

SYLVIA: The problem with sarcasm is it evokes either an angry response or withdrawal—fight or flight. If you want Andrew to really hear you, including when you are angry, it might work better to tell him how you're feeling. For example, you might have said "When you said 'Suck it up', I felt totally uncared about and hurt. Then I got angry, because I felt so vulnerable."

Do those feelings, or something similar, fit?

SHEILA: Yeah.

SYLVIA: Would you be willing to share, in your own words, how you felt with Andrew—please speak to him directly.

SHEILA: Okay. (*She turns towards Andrew.*) Andrew, it's true, when you said that, I felt lousy—like you couldn't care less about me and you just wanted to not be bothered with my feelings.

SYLVIA: Andrew, what is it like for you to hear that? Please answer Sheila directly.

ANDREW: Thank you for telling me that, Sheila. I don't want you to feel badly or hurt by what I say. You seem so tough, I had no idea that you would react that way. Now, I feel closer to you and will really try to think about how you might respond to things I say and do.

SHEILA: Thanks. (*Looks at me.*) Hey, you know I think he really got it this time.

SYLVIA: Yes, I felt that too. Sheila, I'd like to do a bit more work with you, if that's okay with both of you, and then get back, Andrew, to your side of this interaction.

(*They both nod.*)

SYLVIA: Sheila, I don't know anything about your early life, but often these types of reactions, while totally normal, have a root in the past, which is why different areas are particularly sensitive to different degrees in different people. Being aware of the old associations can help you understand your reactions and help to lower the charge on the old triggers. Also in a couple, this awareness can be helpful to your partner—you, Andrew—to understand Sheila better, and this makes it much easier to empathize with her.

So, Sheila, was there a time in your early life, maybe with family or friends, that you felt deeply hurt by impatience and criticism?

SHEILA: (*Tears come to her eyes.*) Well, my family was basically chaotic. Mom was probably bipolar—she was occasionally totally high and a blast to be around, but mostly she was depressed, drank too much and was just interested in herself. She just wasn't interested in my achievements at school or my disappointments if I lost a swim meet. Actually, I guess her basic message too was "suck it up."

(*Sheila begins loud sobbing and difficulty catching her breath. Andrew sits even further back in his chair and looks down at the carpet.*)

I had to grow myself up essentially, and the tougher I felt, the better I felt.

SYLVIA: So, you built a protective wall around those feelings.

SHEILA: Yes. It makes me sad to think about it.

SYLVIA: Andrew, would you look at Sheila. (*He does, stiffly turning in his chair.*) What do you see?

ANDREW: I see Sheila crying. Sheila, could you please stop doing that?

SYLVIA: Andrew, what are you feeling as you look at Sheila— look inside yourself before you answer me.

ANDREW: I feel very uncomfortable and helpless. What am I supposed to do?

SYLVIA: Would you be willing to ask Sheila that? If you really want to be there for her, she is the expert on what she needs from you right now.

ANDREW: Sheila, what should I do?

SHEILA: Just listening with concern is really all I want—what I didn't get from my mother, I guess.

ANDREW: Is that it? I think I can do that. (*He shifts his position so that he's looking directly at her.*) I'm sad that you experienced that with your mother, and I certainly don't want to give you those same feelings. Thanks for telling me. You know, I do care a lot about you.

SHEILA: Wow—thanks. (*She smiles warmly at Andrew.*)
Hey, enough about me, let's talk about Andrew. Andrew, you act like a five-year-old when I even have to leave you to go to the store—what's up with that?

ANDREW: Oh, I just get scared that something will happen to me while you're gone and I won't know what to do. Maybe, if you help me write some notes of things I can do if something goes wrong, then I can consult my list. Actually, that would make me feel a lot better.

SYLVIA: It sounds as if you feel very alone and out of control when Sheila leaves—having a list gives you a little sense of control, just as performing your compulsions do. Does that feel right?

ANDREW: I'm a psychological disaster, I know!

SYLVIA: Let's look at your past experiences, as we did with Sheila. Andrew, were you abandoned or neglected in your early years?

ANDREW: My father left our family when I was eight—and if you think I'm in bad shape, you should meet my brother, Anthony. He's still waiting for our father to return.

Sylvia: What was that like for you when your father left?

Andrew: It was terrible. At home, my mother went crazy.

Sylvia: What do you mean?

Andrew: I realize now that she suffered from OCD even before he left—everything, including Anthony and me, had to be perfect. That probably drove him crazy actually. I never thought of that before—I always thought he left because he couldn't stand me.

Sylvia: What a devastating thought for a small boy to have, to feel you were the cause of his rejection. You must have felt helpless then and out of control—both very realistic feelings in reponse to that thought.

Andrew: Yes. Maybe that's when I began feeling so anxious.

Sylvia: You said your mother went crazy—tell me more about that.

Andrew: Well, her OCD really got terrible after my father left. She paid even less attention to me, and I felt like an outsider at home as well as at school.

Sylvia: What was happening at school?

Andrew: It was awful. The kids teased me mercilessly about not having a father. They shunned me at recess and I sat alone at lunchtime. I just wanted more than anything to be part of "the gang." So, I withdrew in to my own world of ideas, scholastic achievement, and my OCD rituals.

Sheila: Oh, Andrew, that sounds really bad. Now, it makes more sense to me that when I leave it sparks off all these old patterns. But, I still can't be by your side twenty-four, seven!

Andrew: Yes, I realize that. Dr. Randall, how can I get over these old associations?

Sylvia: Actually, the word associations is one of the keys. We have just made a beginning today by bringing to awareness some of the unconscious associations between stimuli in the present and earlier stimulus-response patterns. We will need to spend much more time revealing these memories and bringing them in to consciousness. Then we can examine them with fresh, adult eyes, which will help lower the emotional charge that originally became associated with the events. When the charge is lower, you will find an array of new behaviors that become available to you.

ANDREW: Can you give me an example?

SYLVIA: Of course. Let's take your insight today that your father's leaving the family may well have been more about his dislike and intolerance of your mother's behavior than of yours or your brother's. As you allow this to sink in to your thoughts and your reality, it will create a shifting of your life-view. If you no longer feel responsible for his desertion, that also means you were not responsible for your mother's worsening condition—or your brother's for that matter. As you let this in, do you notice anything?

ANDREW: This is ridiculous—but, I must admit I feel lighter, as if I can breathe more freely. I almost feel I could tell you, Sheila, to leave early today and have a good evening!

SHEILA: Are you serious? Hey, I could go for that idea—(*She pauses.*) Now, this is weird, but I feel a little sadness in losing the Mead I know and love. Am I crazy or what?

SYLVIA: Change can be a mixed blessing sometimes. (*We all laugh. The feeling in the room is light and the sun and its warmth, seems a little brighter.*)
I'm afraid our time is up for today. Shall we meet same time next week?

I worked with Andrew and Sheila for six months. Their communication improved and Sheila softened. As she softened, Andrew was able to show more caring and empathy to her. They decided to stop their visits and I agreed that they had learned a lot and wished them all the best.

Then, about nine months after that, I received a call from Andrew. He told me Sheila had left to return to her ex-husband. It had been a difficult loss for him but he was now working with a new assistant; Naomi. New issues had come up in this relationship and they wanted to meet with me. We set up an appointment for the following week.

As I saw Andrew and Naomi in the waiting room, I noticed a rather different "vibe" in the room. Andrew looked less rigid than I remembered him to be, and he and Naomi were sitting quietly conversing with each other. I saw that Naomi is an attractive woman, probably in her mid-thirties, dressed rather conservatively and professionally.

SYLVIA: Hi Andrew, nice to see you again. And you must be Naomi—nice to meet you. Please come in.

ANDREW: It's good to see you, Dr. Randall.

SYLVIA: Maybe we can start by you both telling me a little about your relationship and the areas on which you would like to focus.

NAOMI: Well, as you know, we work together. I am Mr. Mead's assistant. We have been working together for about six months now, and I think very highly of my boss—he is amazingly astute. I just love to watch him work and also to work with him.

ANDREW: I depend quite a bit on Naomi's help.

SYLVIA: Naomi, I notice that, even though you have worked together closely for some time now, that you still address Andrew as Mr. Mead. Why is this?

NAOMI: Oh, I wouldn't feel comfortable calling him anything else! I mean, even though I love him, he is my boss and I respect our roles.

SYLVIA: Does it bother you that he calls you by your first name?

NAOMI: No, that seems appropriate since he hired me to help him.

SYLVIA: I notice a little bit of formality in this—I'm assuming this feels comfortable to both of you.

(*They both nod.*)

SYLVIA: So, what are the issues that you would each like to focus on?

NAOMI: Well, I just love and like Mr. Mead so much, and I try to give him help in every way I can both in our work and personally, when he is upset or anxious. I try to boost his spirits when he's down. I include him in family activities with Jody, my daughter. I think I give him a lot and, my issue is, that I don't get any verbal appreciation back. It's as if all that I give is expected by him and he barely notices it. It would be nice if he could tell me once in a while that he thought I did a good job and was helpful to him, or, even that he likes being around me.

SYLVIA: Andrew, can you share with Naomi your reactions to what she just said—your thoughts and your feelings?

ANDREW: (*He hesitates.*) Um, she does a good job.

SYLVIA: It looks as if that's very hard for you to say. Is that because you don't really feel it, or is it just difficult for you to give Naomi this positive feedback?

ANDREW: I feel criticized—I suppose I am just deficient.

SYLVIA: How does that feel to you, Naomi?

NAOMI: I'm very annoyed right now. This is exactly what I'm talking about. Everything gets turned around, so that it's all about Mr. Mead again, and I get nothing.

SYLVIA: Can you make a direct request of Andrew? Please speak to him.

NAOMI: Actually, that's hard for me. In my family, if we didn't get what we wanted, we were taught to accept that and move on. I grew up being very independent. I knew I was loved at home, but I didn't get a lot of praise.

SYLVIA: So, here you are feeling in a similar situation. I know it's a stretch for you to ask for what you want, but would you be willing to do so here?

NAOMI: Well, I'll try. (*She looks at Andrew—a little shyly.*) Mr. Mead, remember when you were sick in bed, and I just took over some of the work for you, did you appreciate that?

ANDREW: Yes, I did.

NAOMI: And did you think I did a good job?

ANDREW: Of course.

NAOMI: Why is it *so* hard for you to tell me?

SYLVIA: Andrew, can you look inside for a minute—how are you feeling right now?

ANDREW: Scared.

SYLVIA: Would you close your eyes for a minute—(*He does with some hesitancy.*)—if you let a memory come up from earlier in your life of a time when you felt that same fear, what comes up?

ANDREW: (*A few seconds go by.*) Well, two memories pop up, both with the thought that life only gives you disappointments and hurt when you open your heart to someone.
First, I think of my father. I loved him and he left us. And then Terry.

(*I glance at Naomi, who now has tears in her eyes.*)

SYLVIA: Are you willing to risk a new behavior that might contribute to breaking that association between love and loss?

ANDREW: It sounds impossible.

SYLVIA: One step at a time. Maybe you could look at Naomi, and tell her a few things you appreciate and like about her?

ANDREW: (*He turns to Naomi.*) Naomi, I feel very uncomfortable telling you this, but you have a very good mind and often think of things that I haven't even thought of when we are trying to figure out a case. Thank you. Also, I really love to be included in your life with Jody—I don't often feel included with people, so it does mean a lot to me. Thank you.

NAOMI: (*She still has wet eyes.*) Oh, that feels so nice to hear. I do sense it from you, but I need to hear it in words occasionally.

ANDREW: It feels good to say, surprisingly.

SYLVIA: Thank you both for the risks you just took. Andrew, I want to ask you what issues you came in with today.

ANDREW: What just happened here, actually, relates to my major issue. I realize that since Terry's death, I have been in a pretty deep depression and closed myself off from feeling joy. That's part of why I don't have the energy or motivation to give to others, including Naomi.

SYLVIA: This may sound like a crazy question, but would it be okay for you to feel joy again, even though Terry can't?

ANDREW: I've thought of that many, many times! Why did I get to survive when she, doing nothing wrong, didn't?

SYLVIA: Yes, exactly. Survivors often feel just this way. Can I ask you to close your eyes again just for a moment?

ANDREW: I don't like it. It's so dark with my eyes closed, and I can't see anything! But all right. (*He closes his eyes.*)

SYLVIA: Would you imagine Terry is here, talking with you, and would you ask her how she feels about your allowing joy back in your life? Take as much time as you like, and when you are done, please open your eyes.

ANDREW: (*There are several minutes of silence, followed by Andrew opening his eyes.*) She was sweet and tender at first and then she got a little angry with me. She *wants* me to start living again, and especially to have fun and experience joy again. I am so surprised!

(*There is a quiet pause in the room. Then, Andrew half-turns towards Naomi.*)

Naomi, could you, Jody and me go out for pizza and a movie tonight?

NAOMI: (*Naomi's eyes are wide open and she is smiling.*) I would love to!

ANDREW: And, would you start calling me Andrew?

NAOMI: (*She laughs with a little shyness.*) I'll try—Andrew.

SYLVIA: I can't believe how much you have both risked—and gained. Have a great evening. I am here, if you would like to continue with this work.

(*Both nod and say they will call for another session.*)

And this is why I love my work so much—seeing good people push through some of their self-made barriers to allow room for those feeling that, for different reasons, have been restricting the breadth of their thoughts and emotions.

In both sessions, we see clear illustrations of the therapeutic connection between making unconscious material conscious, and the resulting lowering of the charge on that usually fearful memory, fantasy, belief, or thought. This allows the client to expand the boundaries of their behavioral repertoire and to experience new feelings and take more behavioral risks—thus, feeling more alive, energetic and joyful.

In our culture, we share with others (especially women share with other women) many of our personal issues and concerns. While this is not therapy, it is very helpful and supportive. However, there is an unspoken taboo in our culture against sharing the details of our issues and concerns relating to our most intimate relationship. Therefore, couples therapy, and especially couple group therapy, offers a unique opportunity to share as a couple these most private areas of our lives, and to learn ways to work with troublesome couples issues.

The most common goal of couples who seek couples therapy is to feel more closely connected and more harmonious with their partner. Recurring conflicts may be a problem or a lack of the initial closeness that was so fulfilling at the beginning of the relationship. An important part of closeness comes from the ability to share with each other our internal worlds—our feelings and our thoughts. Since our personal feeling and thoughts are constantly changing, this is a crucial aspect in keeping the relationship interesting and alive. For many people this intimate communication comes naturally, but for others thoughts are easy to share but feelings are not.

The first task of couples therapy is usually to teach intimate communication skills. This task involves two sub-tasks: awareness and direct, clear verbal communication. (Non-verbal communication is, of course also crucial, but I will not focus on that here). We cannot communicate clearly without being aware of what we're feeling. So, the therapist will work with both partners to identify underlying feelings. They may learn to become aware of bodily sensations connected to specific feeling. For example, when I feel a tightness in my abdomen, I am often experiencing fear.

Secondly, we will practice clear and direct communication between the partners. For example: "When you forgot it was my birthday last week, I felt hurt and very sad." We often work with changing critical or blaming statements in to non-blaming "I statements." A blaming version of the previous example would sound like: "You always forget days that are important to me. You are thoughtless and uncaring." Blaming statements tend to lead to defensiveness and growing distance between the partners. The "I statements," however, increase closeness and intimacy.

These are just a few of the basics of couples therapy work. This work is endlessly fascinating and the help that couples can receive from this work is most meaningful. After all, what is more nurturing and life-affirming than a partner who is, not only the closest to you, but also your best friend![1]

---

[1] This chapter includes excerpts from "An Experiential Account of Gestalt Therapy Approaches within Platonic Couples' Relationship Counseling," reprinted by permission from *The Journal of Tenure Studies Quarterly* (Fall 2008), pp. 1024–055.

17

Mr. Monk and the Jungle Out There

MICHAEL KAGAN

> I think that taking life seriously means something such as this: that whatever man does on this planet has to be done in the lived truth of the terror of creation, of the grotesque, of the rumble of panic underneath everything. Otherwise, it is false.
>
> —ERNEST BECKER, *The Denial of Death*

Monk is right. It's a jungle out there. We know it. We don't like it. It's scary. So, we try not to think about it. We do things to make it seem less scary.

If a group of us get together and do the same things to cope with our fear and uncertainty, what we do is called "normal" and no one questions its rationality—but when someone works out his own individual set of things to do or avoid, it seems bizarre and unreasonable. When a culture avoids eating dogs, cats, or insects, and takes comfort in the belief that they are avoiding dangerous, taboo, or unclean foods, that's one thing. But, when Monk feels the same way about milk, he's phobic.

Adrian Monk and his fears are like us and our fears. Monk, though, stands far enough away that we can laugh at these fears. He and his fears are written in larger letters, so to speak, so we can see them more clearly. That's one of the reasons he appeals to us: he presents our own fears to us as if in a funhouse mirror; huge, distorted, and suddenly very hard to take seriously.

Monk was born afflicted by hyper-awareness and reason. He then had to learn to live in a world with sickness, old age, death, and the temptation of withdrawing from the world into a life of protective rituals, a temptation exacerbated by losing someone he loves. Monk's problems are very much like our problems. They are fundamental basic human problems. It's no wonder that many of us need to step away from the world and its demands from time to time. This is evidenced by the success of liquor stores and summer movie blockbusters, even in challenging economic times.

In *Hero with a Thousand Faces* (New World Library, 2008), Joseph Campbell retells mythical stories that get to the roots of human experience. One of these is a classical story of someone's first encounter with human suffering. In this story an unusual baby boy, who turns out to be the future Buddha, is born. If he is to fulfill his destiny, he needs first to wake up to the suffering present in the world. His father, the king, has been told that his son will be either a great king or a great spiritual leader. To try to ensure he will become a king, the boy is sheltered and entertained. But, later, the young man, while out for a drive, encounters four different manifestations of human suffering. The four things he sees are a sick man, an old man, a corpse, and a passing monk who has withdrawn from the world (*Hero*, pp. 46–48). These are the same challenges that face Monk, variations of the fate that looms over all of us. Monk, though terrified of death and its causes, chooses to confront the situation. He tries to bring some justice to the enemies of life who commit murder. Monk, despite multiple phobias, begins to return to the world after a three-year period of withdrawal and mourning for his beloved Trudy. As Monk returns to the jungle, he confronts it, explores it, clears new paths, and guides others through it.

Wiping the Windows

If he had tried to understand the appeal of Mr. Monk, Aristotle would have drawn upon his explanation of our strange attraction to sad, even tragic stories, and our identification with their flawed heroes. Aristotle tries to solve the puzzle of why people seem to enjoy sad or scary productions, a question that many of us have wondered about after hearing someone say they cried through a movie and that it was wonderful. Aristotle's solution is that our exposure to these productions helps us with the task of internal house cleaning, of eliminating dangerous emotions that can accumulate in our souls the way trash piles up in Monk's apartment during the garbage strike ("Mr. Monk and the Garbage Strike").

In Chapter 6 of his *Poetics*, Aristotle explains that theatrical presentations of tragedy allow us to experience a *catharsis*, a purification or cleaning out of emotions like pity, fear, terror, and disgust. We feel better because we have gotten these feeling out of our systems. The satisfaction that we get from this is like the relief Monk gets when, overwhelmed by the garbage that was piling up during the strike, he packed it up and shipped it to his psychiatrist, Dr. Kroger. When we see Monk, in hypnotic regression ("Mr. Monk Gets Hypnotized"), pick up a piece of old gum from the floor and chew it, we are grossed out. Yet, when Monk manages to go on, live his life and do his work after realizing what he has done, we share in his getting past this.

Later writers like Ernest Becker explain that each of us is born gifted with great awareness, that we start out with clear windows and doorways of perception that allow us to experience the world intensely and vividly. Normal development is learning to experience less, in order to function in the world. We learn to find ways to avoid recognizing the death and destruction around us. We realize that if we really think of the worst that can happen, we will become paralyzed, and be unable to act or decide. So when we ask about the worst that can happen (say, on a first date), we try to answer with something that is not so bad, even if far worse things have happened. Monk understands that the apparently nice guy who's interested in Sharona could really be a fraud or an accessory to murder. Those who think that the worst that can happen is not so bad have learned not to pay attention to what's happening to many people, or they have forgotten how to imagine what might happen next. According to Becker, comic and tragic art can be like window cleaning, allowing us to see more and recover the awareness we have learned to deny. Like Monk before a smudged window, the artist wants to remove the obstructions that obscure our view.

An old joke says that the optimist thinks this is the best of possible worlds, and that the pessimist agrees. Comic and tragic artists are more imaginative optimists and pessimists than the ones in the joke. They challenge the agreement that this is the best of all possible worlds. They can imagine far better and far worse, and are aware that their inability to imagine something does not prevent it from happening. They realize that there can be unpleasant surprises. They clean, even if only temporarily, the windows of our soul, allowing us to get a glimpse of the bright intensity some of us still remember from early childhood.

Monk shows us a little of what it would be like to be aware of what's going on, to know about the awful things and not be able to forget a detail. As he likes to put it, his gifts are a blessing and a curse. From the beginning of his life, even when faced with the horrible unknown, he all too often looks and remembers when others would shut their eyes and forget. His fear of nakedness begins here, because he remembers the first time he was naked (namely, the day he was born; "Mr. Monk and the Naked Man").

Monk's viewers can experience an encounter with Monk's blessing and curse of awareness and then—most of us—return to lives we appreciate all the more through learning from Adrian Monk, who entertained us earlier. According to Becker, normal people learn over time how not to see what's going on around them. According to this view, we began our lives as aware as Monk. What happened?

Learning How Not to See

Healthy, normal babies have big heads. A newborn's head is about a third the size of the baby's body. New babies' heads are too heavy for them to lift on their own. The warning, "Support the head," is often the first instruction to the inexperienced when handed a newborn to hold for the first time.

New babies are pretty helpless. They can breathe; many know how to suck on something. Placed in water, they make swimming motions. But, all in all, a baby left alone on a hillside is a baby left to die.[1]

What, then, are healthy babies good at? They are good at being aware. It's as if human evolution were an attempt at breeding creatures with giant heads limited only by their mammalian mothers' capacity to live thorough the delivery process. As a result, we're born helpless and aware. But babies can learn things. They discover their own bodies, playing with their feet for hours when they first find them. They explore the world with gusto, trying to taste everything they can, providing nervous new parents with plenty of opportunities to learn the limitations of baby-proofing when confronted with infant and toddler curiosity. As we grow, we can figure things out. Before you know it, a child can learn a game and then teach it to someone else.

---

[1] Oedipus's case to the contrary—see Chapter 10 of this volume.

As cultures evolved, our ability to learn and to teach allowed us to plan a hunt or plant for the next season. But to do all these things, we have to focus on tasks, put other concerns into the background—sometimes deny that the other concerns exist at all! We do for ourselves what Sharona and Natalie do for Monk when they remind him that he needs to pay more attention to the case than to some other disorder in the environment.

One of the most important things we learn is how *not* to be aware. Born into a confusion of light and sound and unfamiliar sensation, most of us as newborns learned to look away from the light. As we grow, we learn other ways to control the onslaught of experience. We forget, we ignore, we deny. We move certain things into the foreground and pay attention to them. We move certain things into the background and ignore them. We prioritize.[2]

As we grow, we live more and more in the symbolic world of words. We're taught that what people say is extremely important, that the words we use make a difference to the way things are. We have to ask for things we used to get by wanting them or pointing at them. Parents and caregivers tell us, "Use your words." We learn that people and other creatures have names. Some words have positive power, words like "please" and "thank you." Some have negative power, like Carlin's list of words you cannot say on television. When we grow older, most of us forget what it was like to be born helpless and live in a world before we learned how to talk. We experience infantile amnesia. Monk, however, does not. He remembers virtually everything, bad things like the first slap of birth ("Mr. Monk and the Naked Man"), the trauma of being bullied in school ("Mr. Monk and the Bully"), and good things like the first time he met his wife, Trudy ("Mr. Monk and the Class Reunion").

We learn how not to feel. We lose the infant's excruciatingly sensitive sense of touch. But Monk remains so sensitive that he feels every stroke of the pen when someone uses his back as a writing surface, and can later reconstruct what they wrote ("Mr. Monk and the Class Reunion").

We have names. We began as the center of our universe before we were born. We want to stay that way. Everything that happens is evaluated in terms of its importance to us and how it may increase or diminish our symbolic importance. When pain and suffering conflict with our feeling of importance we try not to feel

---

[2] For more on this process, see Chapter 1 in this volume.

them; we disassociate and forget. We can ignore very large scary lumps and be surprised to learn that we were hurt in accidents or sporting events. For Monk, such forgetting is rare and disturbing. When he forgets something, it's a serious problem. On one occasion, it led to his being held in a mental institution, when, without being fully aware of what he was doing, he showed up at Trudy's old house and began to prepare a special anniversary meal ("Mr. Monk Goes to the Asylum").

The frightening confidence some of us had as small children and wild adolescents often may have involved our protesting a bit too much against the possibility that we could get hurt. Then, as we get older, we may be in danger of developing into the controlled and controlling type of people that Freud taught us to describe as "anal." We can learn to tell ourselves that we won't get hurt because we are careful, we have said the right words, we have made the proper sacrifices ("I won't be sick; I take care of myself, I go to the gym. I don't smoke. . . . "). When someone dies, no matter how old or ill, many of us act as if something unnatural happened. We identify ourselves with things and then neatly arrange our lives when we neatly arrange the things. How closely some of us identify with the stuff we own can be seen not only in the marketing of new automobiles, but the new owner's dramatic reaction when that car receives its first scratch.

Traditionally, our self-esteem and desire for immortal importance were protected by religious-cultural hero systems. According to Becker, most traditional societies and their religions provide their members with significant roles, and ultimate value throughout this life and after death. In these societies, one offers the proper sacrifices to gods. Through being a member of their people and family, one is protected by the very forces that run the universe. People are guaranteed immortality through their family or clan, or, in cultures which have concepts of individual immortality, eternal life waiting for them in the world to come. People from such societies take comfort in knowing that death is but a doorway, reuniting them with friends and loved ones who have preceded them. Without some kind of shared belief system to protect us, we need to find solace in some other form of validation. Otherwise, we can meet threats to our mortality with classical Freudian ego-defense mechanisms. We may employ defenses like denial of bad things happening to us, displacement of negative feelings to targets that are weak enough for us to attack safely, projection of our destructive impulses onto others who we can then treat as bad people deserving whatever happens to them, and repression of our fears. These defenses allow us to turn away from death, to just not think about the bad things. We can protect our egos with limited attention and by focusing on ordinary efficiency. We may develop ways of turning away from the vivid and harsh encounter with life by working too much, drinking too much, shopping too much, by finding hide-outs in one place or another.

One of the advantages of limiting the field of experience is that we can do ordinary tasks more efficiently, like a daily commute that can be accomplished without thinking. This works so long as we can break out of the disassociation when necessary; otherwise, we can find ourselves automatically driving halfway to work on our day off, or, worse, over a bridge that isn't there anymore. Death-denial and constrictions of experience allow for a more pleasant life. Even the support of a modern society's consumerist ideals can offer a kind of equanimity. A well-polished climate-friendly car and a stylish set of exercise clothes may be enough to provide a certain peace of mind and confidence that sickness, old age, and death are for the other guys, but not for people like us; things like that don't happen to people who take care of themselves.

Normal Unawareness, or How Lieutenant Disher Could Get in a Cab with a Corpse for a Driver and Not Notice

Many of us learn not to pay too much attention to people who pass through our lives, like servers in restaurants, bus boys, and cab drivers. If we're on a date, like Randy Disher in "Mr. Monk Falls in Love," we're likely to be paying more attention to our date than to the driver of the cab we just hopped into. As a result of our normal narrowing of focus, we can do things like drive a car without being distracted by details on the side of the road. We can sit at a messy desk and ignore the clutter while we finish writing up a report or return a phone call. Unless the mess is important to us, like a leaking coffee pot threatening our outgoing mail, we can ignore it. In our normal way of distracting ourselves with the tasks of work and socially recognized forms of play, we learn to ignore the details that are normally considered irrelevant, to focus on task.

Monk is very poor at distracting himself; luckily, however, he has found a career where noticing what normally goes unnoticed is helpful. He doesn't ignore smells, he uses them as clues (as in "Mr. Monk and the Candidate," where he notices what kind of cigarette was smoked at a crime scene, which allows him to link it with another investigation). We normally learn to avoid paying too much attention to the constant experiential reminders of the overwhelming beauty and terror the world presents us. Monk, on the other hand, pays attention to all the little details. He uses his hyperawareness and excellent memory to cope with his loss of sight in "Mr. Monk Can't See a Thing." His memory of details and awareness of his environment allow him to accept his loss of sight more quickly than most would. He, for example, already knew how many steps it takes to go upstairs to his apartment. Once there, he already knows exactly where everything is. *Everything. Exactly.*

Normally, however, we tend to get along better by not paying too much attention and by not worrying about what we cannot see. Contrast the way a healthy small child, still perceiving the world vibrantly, can be terrified by the shadows in the closet at night. Or the way a five-year-old can focus on the dust motes floating in a sunbeam, oblivious to the parental call to carpool to kindergarten, where the children will be taught to move efficiently through the various stations of the class in order to receive their gold stars and teacher's praise.

Nowadays, those who can't—or won't—be distracted from these "distractions" are identified and treated as early as possible, to be taught organizational skills or to be medicated, if necessary.

There are drawbacks. As we learn to become adults, we learn to ignore these elements of perception which are not 'important'. Entertainment needs to be louder and brighter and more vivid. It may be necessary to block distractions with anesthetics of various kinds. Some will need drinks to get through a meeting, and then pain killers to get through the hangover. Boredom can become a problem; indeed, it is striking that the child, once able to be enthralled by playing with disposable plastic cups or an empty cardboard box, is later trained to be bored by the everyday objects and events of life. The need to keep enough perception open to survive, without letting too much in, will generate tension.

If I pay too much attention to my students, I notice the heart beating too fast in that one's neck, the precancerous mole on the next one's face, the dilated pupils on the spaced-out student who is a little too careful sitting down. I smell the beer in the tinted water bottle in the second row. I'm going to get distracted from my lecture. If I bring up what I perceive, I may be experienced as invasive. But, if I just don't notice in the first place, things go easier for all of us. On the other hand, I need to pay attention to the confusion on their faces when I'm explaining a difficult point. I have to be sensitive to body language indicating fatigue and the need to vary lecture with group work and provide an opportunity for all of us to move around. Work and daily living require a balance between perceiving too little and too much. If I smell alcohol on a fellow teacher's breath as he's arriving late to his 8:30 A.M. class, I have to think about something other than my own work. If I act like I don't notice his drinking, he might think it's not noticeable. Perceiving just enough becomes like driving down the street with frost-covered windows, trying to see what's going on through a small gap that was quickly scraped away by a driver late to work. It's tense. Necks get tight, backs go out. It's harder to sleep without a little chemical help, harder to wake up and get things done without caffeine or something a bit stronger. Harder to get all the required work and expected play done without buying, borrowing, or talking your way into some stimulants. By the time young adulthood is reached, on college campuses across the country, the drug varies with the rhythms of the semester and the days of the week. Adderall or alcohol, among others, depending on the time.

Adrian Monk, though, painful as his life is, usually resists the temptation of medications. But, on one rare occasion he tried taking drugs for his problems and, as a result, became "The Monk" ("Mr. Monk Takes His Medicine"). In doing so, he lost touch with beauty, terror, and Trudy, his one true love. He began to chat with strangers. He even bought a fancy car. And, with all that, he could no longer see what was going on around him any better than most of the other people around him.

A Clarinet at the Cemetery

In "Mr. Monk Meets the Red-Headed Stranger," Adrian Monk describes himself as Willie Nelson's second greatest fan. When Nelson asks, Monk explains that Trudy, who died about five years before, is Mr. Nelson's greatest fan. Later, Monk asks Nelson to sign an album for Trudy. As the show ends, Willie Nelson is singing and playing guitar and Adrian Monk is playing his clarinet. The song is "Blue Eyes Crying in the Rain," with lyrics about lovers parting yet meeting "up yonder . . . in the land that knows no parting." The place is by Trudy's grave.

The advantages of religious responses to the conflict between what we are and what we wish to be—cosmically important and somehow free from the threat of death—are many. From the perspective of many religious people, these responses improve the quality of life in this world while guaranteeing an even better life in the world to come. They provide the individual with a role in the divine scheme of things, giving the individual recognition by others for playing an important role in creation. They give each person cosmic and social importance as a member of the truly human, truly elect group of the enlightened or saved upon which the world depends.

The religious stance frees some people up from the ordinary constriction of experience. It allows them more freedom to perceive what's out there since what's out there is no longer threatening in an ultimate or final way. Religious solutions can fail, however. The facts about what's out there can threaten the solutions, leading to deceit and deception in the service of the religion or its leaders. For example, a religious leader who claims faith will set us free must deny that not everything makes sense, or can be fixed—remember the cult leader who was supposed to be a model of perfect health in "Mr. Monk Joins a Cult."

Sometimes though, the deceived are not self-deceiving, and may even have opportunities to gain insight even when led into these opportunities by the less than sincere. Monk gets relief from some of his compulsive symptoms as a cult member in "Mr. Monk Joins a Cult." And Captain Stottlemeyer sincerely claims to have experienced change at an existential level after drinking what he was told to be healing water in "Mr. Monk and the Miracle." In that episode, Stottlemeyer's physical relief was caused by getting appropriate medication, but the feeling he had of being reborn is characteristic of sincere religious followers—even sincere followers of insincere religious leaders. The sincerely religious people are freed up to experience and express more of the wonder and terror of the worlds they live in, often allowing close connection of religion and the arts.

The physicist Niels Bohr was once asked why he had a good luck horseshoe when it was clear he did not believe in such things. Bohr replied that the horseshoe was supposed to work even if you didn't believe in it. But, unlike a horseshoe that is supposed to work whether you believe in it or not, religious answers are less useful to the inauthentic who merely pretend to believe them and pretend to be comforted by them. When presented with someone with a sincere religious belief that goes beyond the temple or church walls, the pretenders may become quite unhappy and willing to express their unhappiness in concrete ways. It's no surprise that prophets go without honor when they try to change the way people do things in their hometown. Outwardly religious people may, for example, lock up the activists, treating the religious individuals who try to apply their religious teachings to contemporary situations as criminals or as insane. Sometimes—in low tolerance societies that present alternative religion-like solutions to these human problems—they outlaw and execute the annoying believers.

Some few can be sustained or driven by the artistic impulse. Sincere religious belief, by opening up freedom for awareness in other areas, furthers those areas of art and perception that do not threaten the religions themselves, and the overlap of religiosity and former religiosity in many great writers and artists may support this view. Artistic projects, like the solutions that seek salvation through romantic love, are fragile for the reason that the beloved and the created work so often are themselves fragile physical creatures doomed to ultimate dissolution. The work may not sustain the projections; the gap between reach and grasp may be too large. Demanding too much may leave us feeling deserted.

The One Who Dies with the Most Toys Wins?

Many people are left with the cultural heroes and role models found on prime-time TV and the covers of fan magazines. The lifestyles of the rich and famous and the physiques of the young and good-looking serve as signs of grace. In this spirit, a wealthy colleague, the one with the fanciest cars, houses, computers, and other tech toys can proudly show up at the department picnic wearing a t-shirt that states, "The one who dies with the most toys wins." Even this kind of victory is fragile, since the logic of the enterprise limits the number of alleged winners, and people may be threatened by competitors and critics. Citizens of the most modern states can end up responding like low-tolerance societies. They may end up responding to threatening perceptions with persecution and war, while at the same time, perhaps, accelerating the process of acquisition.

I remember that when my adviser died suddenly and unexpectedly, I suddenly felt an intense need to go shopping for some high tech audio equipment. When thousands died suddenly and unexpectedly as a result of the attacks of 9/11, this kind of apparently idiosyncratic personal response became a national shopping mandate issued by the highest political authority. The mandate not only stimulated the economy, but, according to Becker's analyses, it also may have helped the people following it to feel more secure.

In the absence of traditional solutions, other forms of ritual and sacrifice (both by throwing away the bad stuff and by offering up the good stuff) will develop. Changes in styles will turn once-fashionable gowns into clothing donations. People will make annual pledges not only to churches, but for designer gymnasium memberships. Becker's work indicates that religions public and private can respond to this challenge of finitude and address what he takes to be the human need for illusions to cope with an overwhelming world of experience.

The compulsions of organization, acquisition, amassing of goods, and concern with precisely keeping track, by developing and conforming to measures of human success, work well in certain contexts. In a world of spreadsheets and PowerPoint reports, of quantifiable outcomes assessment, annual evaluations, and performance reviews, the people who fill out their paperwork neatly and precisely, checking off every measure with the appropriate flourish of bullet points, will find themselves among those most likely to succeed.

Mr. Monk, Jungle Guide

The fundamental human need is to be cosmically important in the face of death and its challenge to that importance. This, with other fundamental needs like the need to eat and avoid being eaten, leads us to limit our awareness in order to concentrate on our work and rule-driven play. These limitations themselves can constitute a problem by causing us to live in a state of frustrating unawareness. To solve this, we find or are assigned roles in the scheme of things. Some of us who are not satisfied look to solutions that go further—fictional solutions may do if we believe they are or could be true—to give us the freedom for more awareness. The less terrified can take more time to look around, to listen to whatever may be humming in the distance, to smell the flowers and hear birds.

Monk's own solution was to find importance in his work and true love, Trudy. This, with his own rituals and quest for order, held him together enough to tolerate an exceptionally high degree of awareness, until Trudy was murdered. After she died, Monk could no longer function, and he lost his job. The intensity of awareness and passion for order that led to success in his work now paralyzed him. Three years later, with the help of good friends and good therapy, he was able to begin a long journey forward, working as a private investigator.

The special satisfaction we get through the art of tragedy, according to Aristotle, has to do with the feelings of pity and fear we are able to bring out and burn off through catharsis. For Becker, the comfort of art is to the artist, like (and sometimes with) religion, a source of cosmic importance, an attempt to offer something to the universe that makes a difference. The gift the artists share is their own greater awareness. When the audience accepts this gift, they are, for a time, able to see more clearly; they experience life with more awareness.

Monk offers such a gift, for he shows that someone even more afraid than we are can do great things, can, with a little help, search out truths at levels of cosmic importance, the levels of life and death and justice. With the loss of his beloved, he may suffer daily, but he goes on, seeking difficult truths behind confusing waves of misdirection. He's a private investigator on an ambiguous path. He wants to know what happened, he wants the truth, he wants justice. Amidst his fears, he seeks these things. And for at least a little while when we watch him—perhaps even longer if inspired—so do we.

18

Mr. Monk and the Death Drive

GIANCARLO TARANTINO and
D.E. WITTKOWER

We have long been familiar with dramadies, "black comedies," and the tragicomic. Richard Klein, in his fabulous book, *Eat Fat*, even argues that Hamlet—as indicated by his name—was supposed to be played by someone a little too chubby to take all that seriously. *Monk* is something different. It shares the comic elements, of course, but it's not a drama, a black comedy, or a tragedy; not even in part. In a drama, the hero strives to succeed, or at least struggles against failure. Monk strives to just make it day-to-day—solving crimes seems to be something he does almost to distract himself from his real struggles. In a black comedy, we laugh at the kind of thing we're not supposed to laugh at. We may laugh at Monk sometimes, instead of with him, but it's always a pained laughter; we identify with him even as when we laugh at his social awkwardness. And in a tragedy, the hero loses everything in the end. Whereas in *Monk*, the hero has already lost everything.

Monk is a kind of comedy about what happens *after* the tragedy—but the tragedy, for its part, is always serious. Consider "Mr. Monk Stays Up All Night." It's a goofy enough episode, overall. Throughout most of it, the viewer doesn't even know whether a crime has been committed, much less what the crime was (or wasn't). But while the viewer is moving forward in the plot, trying to figure out what has or hasn't happened, Mr. Monk is concerned with something else: finding a mysterious woman for an unknown reason. After the plot has moved forward to its conclusion, Monk solves his own mystery. Upon finding the mysterious woman, he discovers why he was looking for her. Trudy was an organ donor, and this woman had been given sight when she received Trudy's corneas. Monk had recognized the eyes of his dead wife, and had been haunted for days, unable to sleep, preoccupied with a momentary glance from beyond the grave. A glance that held a promise of what the world once was for Monk, and what it never again could be.

While we, the viewers, move forward through the plot, Monk is always moving backwards; always trying to return to his life before the show began; always trying to recover what he has lost.

Repetition

A detective story truism: The killer always returns to the scene of the crime. Why? He feels bound to it—or, as in "Mr. Monk Makes a Friend," he wishes to retrieve his sunglasses. Whichever. But mourners and victims return to the scene of their crimes as well, and this is a bit harder to explain.

Monk, of course, wants to protect the gray wall with "B-5" written on it, because it's the last thing that Trudy ever saw.[1] And, of course, he returns to her case over and over again because he wishes to solve it, and to gain some closure by making some sense of what seems like such a meaningless and incomprehensible event. In his motivation, at least, there's no mystery. Here, he has clear psychological reasons to return to those painful scenes—it's less painful for him to remember those tragic moments than it would be for him to let the memory of Trudy slip away. And so there is a kind of libidinal economy at work: it's painful to remember her death, but it would be more painful to not remember her, and so he returns.

But how can we explain his fixation with naked people? Why does he dwell on them, unable to stop thinking about how they are naked? In "Mr. Monk and the Naked Man," he looks straight in the air when talking to a nudist. Is he afraid of seeing his nudity, or is he afraid that he will *look at* his nudity? Of course, it's both. Our phobias are also our fixations; when Monk is unable to follow up on his compulsion to look at what horrifies him—as in the strange freedom he finds after being blinded[2]—he is relieved.

With Dr. Kroger, he is able to trace back this particular phobia to a traumatic event. He doesn't really remember it; he has only

---

[1] "Mr. Monk Fights City Hall."
[2] "Mr. Monk Can't See a Thing."

vague impressions. He's naked, and crying. There's a man in white, hitting him, and holding him upside-down. His mother is there, and she isn't stopping the man in white. In fact, she's *happy*. Dr. Kroger is able to put together that Adrian is remembering his own birth. Once Adrian is able to understand this *as a memory*—a collection of images that makes sense as thing in his life that *happened*—he is freed from his fear (mostly), and is able to think clearly about the case, since he's not always constantly distracted by thinking about how *naked* all those nudists are.

Why are we compelled to think about painful things like this; to return to these scenes of crimes long past? What did Monk gain from constantly thinking about how *naked* naked people are— where's the libidinal economy? Why didn't he just *stop* thinking about it, since he didn't like thinking about it?

Anxiety and Trauma

In his 1920 book, *Beyond the Pleasure Principle*, Sigmund Freud discusses the "traumatic neuroses," including "war neuroses," that we today call Post-Traumatic Stress Disorder (or PTSD). He brings up the anxiety dreams brought on by traumatic experiences, where someone who has suffered a great trauma returns, in sleep, to the "scene of the crime." This, he says "astonishes people far too little" (p. 11). If dreams usually function by giving us a fantasy in which our wishes and unconscious desires are fulfilled, why does the soldier, when back at home and asleep, return herself to the battlefield? Freud suggests that the function of repetition—constantly thinking of the thing we fear, whether awake or asleep—may be to gain a kind of mastery or control over the feared object or event. How this applies to milk we may never know,[3] but in the case of Monk's fear of nudity, we've got something to go on.

Freud uses the example of children's play. He speaks of a child he observed, who seemed to take joy in taking his toys and throwing them under and behind things. When finding them again, he would express even greater joy. While playing this game, the child—although not yet able to speak clearly—seemed to be saying "*fort*" (gone) and then "*da*" (here). Freud hypothesizes that the child is responding to his fear of his mother leaving him alone in the room. He could not control his mother's movements (although

---

[3] Although we might suppose it would have to involve Oedipus, and weaning.

surely he tried), and so he took consolation in his ability to control his toys. By throwing them away himself, he lost a toy that he liked, but he gained more back in his feeling of power and control. His mother would go away *against* his will, but he could feel less helpless by making the toy go away *according to* his will.

And Freud goes on to point out that this is a common principle in children's games. The fact that an experience is painful or frightening does not mean the child will avoid thinking of it. In fact, "if the doctor looks down a child's throat or carries out some small operation on him, we may be quite sure that these frightening experiences will be the subject of the next game" (p. 16).[4] In doing so, the *fright* of the experience is lessened, because the child is able to play an active rather than a passive role.

In anxiety dreams, such as the soldier's sleeping return to the battlefield, the dreamer is also trying to be more active, less passive, and in this way, to gain some feeling of control over what has happened to her. Freud says that one thing that characterizes traumatic events is that we are unprepared for them. Something that happens suddenly and unexpectedly is far more likely to bring about dreams in which the experience is repeated. Freud hypothesizes that the function of these dreams—in which we are anxious, we return to the scene of the crime, and we know and fear what is about to happen—is that they allow us to attempt to relive the traumatic event, but with the *foreknowledge* and *anxiety* which would have made the event less frightful, sudden, and traumatic. In anxiety dreams, we are horrified to know what's about to happen—but at least this time we know what's about to happen, and this makes us feel less helpless.

And so, as long as it's more pleasurable for us to regain control than it is painful for us to return to the trauma, we will keep thinking of it again and again, and experience a constant anxiety or phobic fixation on things associated with the trauma (be they nudity, milk, toilets, snakes, or whatever else). We can loosen or release this fixation if we are able to make the traumatic event into a memory. As long as Monk only had his vague recollection of his expe-

---

[4] In a brief scene in Terry Gilliam's *Brazil*, children are shown playing a game which seems to involve putting a bag over someone's head and interrogating them at gunpoint. It's impressive that Gilliam thought to include this detail in his dystopian world. We might wonder whether children in recent years have been playing "Guantanamo" instead of "cops and robbers."

rience at birth, he couldn't avoid his fixation with nudity. It bothered him—it was awful and painful and he couldn't stop thinking about it. As soon as this was transformed into a memory, it made sense, and he no longer needed to gain control or mastery over it. Once he understood what had happened, and had come to peace with it, nudity no longer made him feel helpless, and so he no longer needed to compel himself to keep thinking about it, so that he could retrospectively try to be anxious about it ahead of time so that his own nudity wouldn't be so traumatic. As Monk says, "One down, three hundred and twelve to go."

Dirt, Danger, and Disorder

If only all of Monk's fears and fixations could simply line up in a (very) straight line, and step forward one-by-one, perhaps Monk could work through them as well as he (more or less) did in the case of nudity. And surely we all desire this on some level. The feeling of having our fears and worries crowding in on us, threatening to overtake us, is not specific to those with Obsessive Compulsive Disorder. As in "Mr. Monk and the Garbage Strike," we occasionally get the sense that our "garbage" is piling up, with no hope of being taken out any time soon.

This episode provides a troubling moral dilemma for Monk. The city's garbage workers have gone on strike, and when their union boss is found dead of a supposed suicide, they suspect foul play. So Monk is on the case, with the knowledge that if he says that it was in fact a suicide, the garbage workers will go back to work and the garbage will go away again. But when the evidence points to a homicide, Monk must make a choice; to investigate the crime further while the garbage piles up, or lie to get his garbage taken out sooner. Of course Monk chooses to lie at first. But it doesn't take much prodding from Natalie—who, for Monk, is Freud's reality principle incarnate—before he resolves to sacrifice his own wish to see the city clean right away, and instead investigate the crime to help the city's garbage workers. In some ways, "Mr. Monk and Garbage Strike" is a clear expression of the inward battle that Monk no doubt goes through every day. And Freud would expect nothing less.

For Freud, what we deem ugly, dirty, different, or disorderly, is part and parcel to what provokes feelings of anxiety and fear in us. For someone like Monk, who associates anything less than complete sterilization with being dirty, it makes sense that he would be terrified of nearly everything he comes in contact with, including nature itself as a whole, as in "Mr. Monk Gets Cabin Fever" ("Ooh, I got nature . . . I got nature on my hand!"), or "Mr. Monk is Underwater" ("I've got ocean in my pants! Ocean in my pants!!!"). And when these things begin to pile up, the feeling of anxiety provokes the "flight or fight" response in him, and us. Monk, left to his own powers, will often choose "flight." However, Natalie, Dr. Kroger, Captain Stottlemeyer, and others know that Monk's selfless desire to help is always there waiting, just barely under the surface. Here, Freud might suggest, Monk is no different than any one of us who often struggle to do the right thing. In fact, to the extent that Monk is willing to admit that he needs help to do what he feels is really the right thing, he's got a leg up on many of us.

So what is it about dirt, garbage, and disorder that frightens Monk to the point of provoking the "flight or fight" response in him? We might say, along with Freud, that Monk feels helpless in the face of disorder, and uncleanliness. In trying to explain why people characterize certain situations as "dangerous," Freud has this to say: What someone considers dangerous "consists in the subject's estimation of his own strength compared to the magnitude of the danger and in his admission of helplessness in the face of it. In doing this he will be guided by the actual experiences he has had."[5] It is in this light that we begin to see why Monk has such low self-esteem.

Of course his cynicism and extraordinary ability to solve crimes usually masks this, but Monk often needs Natalie to help him when he believes that he cannot deal with some impending situation on his own. Monk has deemed himself helpless in the face of what appears to be so much disorder and dirt. Monk certainly does his best to keep things tidy and clean, but with very little confidence that his actions will last. But it's not just that Monk often feels unable to meet that demands of a situation that calls for getting his "hands dirty." The real question is rather, "what does Monk think will happen if he is overtaken by the dirt and disorder?"

Fear; Rational and Otherwise

As most viewers of the show can probably attest to, one of the great joys of "Monk" is Randy Newman's opening theme. "It's a

---

[5] Sigmund Freud, *Inhibitions, Symptoms and Anxiety* (Norton, 1989), p. 101.

Jungle Out There" is the first glimpse we get into the heart and mind of Monk, as well as the overall mood of the show. While the content of the song is dark, its presentation, melody, and rhythm are anything but. Truthfully, for the most concise explanation of Monk's inner turmoil, one need look no further than here:

> People think I'm crazy 'cause I worry all the time
> If you paid attention you'd be worried too.
> You better pay attention or this world we love so much
> Might just kill you.
> I could be wrong now
> But I don't think so.

We can see that right from the beginning, Monk's anxieties and worries deal with that most ancient of themes: death. Monk is convinced, to draw from Newman's song a bit more, that "disorder and confusion" in addition to "the very air we breath," and "the water that you drink" have the power to kill. Monk admits he might be wrong, but for his part, he's taking no chances. Enter hand sanitizer, wipes, labels, and the rest.

So Monk's sense of helplessness is not necessarily the problem (after all, who among us has the power to overcome death?), only his estimation in what is more likely to kill (jealous spouses, greedy business partners, vengeful ex-cons . . . or a handshake?). This is why we might classify Monk's anxiety as a pathological condition, and not simply heightened awareness or caution. Monk shows no more or less anxiety in the face of a gun pointed at him than anyone else, however, in the face of a painting of a spilled wine glass ("Mr. Monk and Little Monk") . . . well that's another story.

Freud too, wondered whether anxiety might be an expression of the fear of death. Ultimately, however, Freud prefers to connect the fear of death to the fear of being left alone, without that which gives life to us. As we mentioned before, the familiar games of hide-and-seek, and peek-a-boo are directly connected with a child's fear of losing (or being separated from) the parent; the provider and protector of life. And Monk has experienced this loss in some very traumatic ways, from his father's abrupt abandonment to the sudden death of Trudy.

The shock of such losses indeed seem to weight heavily on Monk, despite the overall sense of "lightness" to the show. Still, as the opening song suggests, there is a depressing cynicism to

Monk's demeanor, which often reflects the unrelenting rhythm and tempo with which his "garbage" seems to continually pile up. This is what gives Monk his likeness to Sisyphus, who was cursed forever to push a massive (yet hopefully very clean) boulder up a steep mountain, only to watch it roll back down again every time. And this struggle of Monk's with a never-ending repetitive process doesn't emerge purely from his rich history of childhood trauma, but from the process of mourning as well.

Mourning and Loss

Freud writes that "one of the earliest and most important functions of the mental apparatus"—that is, our instinctual mental processes—is to "convert freely mobile cathectic energy into a mainly quiescent (tonic) cathexis."[6] The word "cathexis" is an obvious stumbling-block in making any sense of this claim.

Aristotle wrote of a process of "catharsis," in which pent-up emotions could be safely released through watching plays—or, for our purpose, TV shows. By identifying with a character, when things happen to that character, we are able to release our emotional charge by using the character as a proxy. And so, when we watch violent films, we are able to release some of our own stored aggression, or at least so the theory goes.[7]

Cathexis is the opposite of catharsis—cathexis is an investment of emotion, not a release of emotion, and 'cathectic energy' is our ability to invest in and care about things in the world, including people. And so, in that confusing quote above, what Freud is saying is that we are instinctually driven to find things in the world to care about, identify with, and invest in. This produces a disturbance in the mind when the cathected object is lost—as was the case for Monk when his father walked out on him, or when Trudy's life was taken. In both cases, the beloved object is lost; in the second case literally, and in the first case "notionally;" that is, his *notion* of his father was lost to him, since his father proved himself to be unable to unwilling to be the man that the young Adrian had believed him to be. His father as a living person survives the death of the notion of the father figure—the real Jack

---

[6] *Beyond the Pleasure Principle*, p. 75.

[7] For more on Aristotle's theory of catharsis and tragedy, take a look at Chapter 17 in this volume.

Monk remains, hanging around in the world as a kind of embarrassing surplus.

When the love-object is lost, the mind is torn in two different directions. The pleasure principle—the mind's tendency towards what will meet our needs and satisfy our desires—does not wish to let go of the cathected object, but reality-testing determines quickly that the love-object is no longer in the world to be found. What's a mind to do? The healthy response is to 'de-cathect' the lost love-object, freeing the cathected energy to re-invest in the world. This is what we call *mourning*. Until we accept that the love-object is lost, and de-cathect it, the world appears to be a poor and empty place, because the beloved object is not in the world. And so, one who has not mourned his loss sees the world as valueless, and is unable to "move on" with his life by finding new things to care about—Monk is still mourning Trudy, and so is unable to form new romantic relationships; and Ambrose is still attached to his notion of his father as a caring father, and so is unable to let go of his childhood home, even though it is little else but a shrine to the man he believed his father to be.

A Haunted Man

The process of de-cathecting is very painful, and can leave one feeling a bit like an amputee; as if a crucial part of oneself has been cut off. This is not an experience specific to those, like Monk, who have been diagnosed with some classifiable disorder. Rather, the degree to which mourning is painful, and the degree to which one never quite feels completely "over" a loss, is the degree to which the cathected object was valued and needed, or, in short, loved. Understanding Freud's theory of mourning in this way should thus give us pause in casting people's expressions of grief as either "weak" or "strong." The person who appears to have grieved "painlessly" and quickly is a prime suspect for someone who has repressed, or pushed away, the reality of the loss. In this sense, the person who is "weak" in the face of loss, and nearly consumed by grief, may prove to be the more honest one, and may be stronger in his ability to face up to and admit the extent to which the loss is real, permanent, and life-changing.

Although Monk appears to have a more honest view of his father than his brother Ambrose, in dealing with the death of Trudy, he seems to have great trouble with "moving on." To grieve Trudy's

death is painful, but to stop grieving seems even worse. Writing
about Freud's theory of mourning, the French philosopher Jacques
Derrida (1930–2004), wondered whether in some cases it might be
impossible to ever completely de-cathect, detach, and mourn a
highly-loved loss.[8] This may be what often gives Monk the feeling
of being *haunted* by Trudy's death; always wrestling with his memory of the case of her murder, as well of her in general.

Whether this is Monk trying to repress the reality of her death
or his inability to completely de-cathect, it clearly speaks to the
pain involved in mourning, and the desire to not have to be without that which had previously been a source of life, love, and
energy. There is a parallel in Freud's theory, then, in *all* losses and
deaths, with a person's earliest losses (how early we may never
know)—for example, mother's attention and care.[9]

Here we reach an important connection with anxiety. Recall that
Freud hypothesized that anxiety based in traumatic neurosis was a
mental preparation for an approaching perceived danger that had
already happened. In Monk's case we have someone who is terrified that all the world's dirt, disorder, and confusion will overtake
him. But, we *also* have someone whose *thoughts* are endlessly in
disorder, and who is endlessly confused by the meaning of Trudy's
death, and how to deal with it. It is highly significant that this is the
one case Monk cannot solve, or "put in order." *Here* he is haunted.

Repetition

He carries Trudy's loss around with him constantly; a hole in the
world instead of a memory of loss. Until he is able to de-cathect
her—that is, complete the process of mourning—he won't be able
to move on with his life. Unable to transform the hole in the world
into a memory, and unable to move forward until he does so, he
is stuck where he is, and the only thing that his unconscious sees
to do is to try to repeat the traumatic experience over and over
again, until somehow he is able to stop it from happening.
Impossible, of course: the mind can't change the world, no matter
how much we wish it could, and we cannot change the past, but

---

[8] See Jacques Derrida's *The Work of Mourning*, and *Specters of Marx*.

[9] And with this we come back to weaning, and what Jacques Lacan called "le
petit objet 'a'." Perhaps we are closer to cracking the traumatic core of Monk's phobic milk fixation than we had at first thought . . .

the unconscious doesn't understand these basic facts about how the world works.

Adrian's anxiety dream in "Mr. Monk is On the Run (Part 1)," is a dramatic version of the kind of solution his mind is trying to find. He dreams he's watching Trudy get into the car. He tries to warn her, but she can't hear him, and as fast as he runs forward, he can get no closer. And then the inevitable end comes. By trying to return to the scene of the crime—but this time, *knowing what is going to happen*—his unconscious is attempting to experience the loss of Trudy as something he was prepared for. The problem, of course, is this: if he had really been prepared for it, he would have prevented it; but if he prevented it, it wouldn't have happened. How can you be psychologically prepared for the loss of your beloved? If she is your beloved, this means you have invested psychologically (cathected) in her as a love-object, and that means by definition that you are not prepared to walk away from her!

When Monk had anxiety around nudity, he was experiencing after the fact—remember, the unconscious does not understand how time works—the anxiety that would have made his frightful experience as an infant bearable; that would have made it merely *unpleasant* rather than traumatic. His unconscious is trying the same trick here, but in this case it is even more ineffective; for no amount of mental preparation, through anxiety, would have made her loss just "unpleasant."

Until he is able to finish the mourning process, and allow Trudy to be a person in the past that he merely *remembers*, her absence is the most glaring, obvious, and objectionable fact about the world. Until then, every time he straightens a set of blinds, evens out the amount of ink in two pens, or solves a murder, he is engaging in displacement behavior caused by his frustrated desire to fix that *one*, that *only* really important thing wrong with the world: that *she* is *not in it*.

The Death Drive

Adrian Monk, it seems, always had his repetition compulsions and traumatic childhood neuroses, but it was with Trudy's death that these problems began to make him unable to function. At least three different things drive these compulsions, and the strength of all three, in congress, was almost enough to remove him from the world entirely.

The first, which we discussed using his fear of nudity, is the use of repetition to build the anxiety which would have shielded the psyche from past trauma; just like how children play games in order to re-enact and gain control over frightening events that they were subjected to. This set of compulsions and phobias presumably pre-existed Trudy's death and Monk's breakdown.

The second, as we have just discussed, is Monk's subsequent use of these compulsions and phobias as displacement behavior: following Trudy's death, it seems that Monk has unconsciously seized upon his pre-existing compulsions as a safe and satisfying way of "fixing" the world. By creating perfect order in every way under his control, he uses his compulsions as a proxy for creating order in the realm beyond his control; the realm of human value and meaning. The boxes in a perfect row stand in for the things out of place which *cannot* be put back in place—namely, that Trudy is no longer in the world. Through this displacement behavior, Monk is able to subvert and divert the process of mourning; the process by which he would otherwise be forced to recognize unconsciously what he knows consciously: that Trudy is gone.

There is, though, a third kind of impulse giving rise to Monk's repetition compulsions; contained within the other two and intensified by them, but more fundamental and universal than either. This is what Freud called the death drive. We have, he said, a basic instinct to flee from life. Life is dangerous, unstable, uncertain. It's a jungle out there. We always, in some way, wish we could leave it all behind. We wish we could just give up, let go, quit.

In children, we see this expressed in a basic fear of change and desire for repetition. Children repeat unpleasant experiences in order to gain mastery over those experiences, but they repeat pleasant experiences as well—and in a way that, in adults, seems neurotic and obsessive-compulsive. Children want to eat the same food at every meal. They want to hear the same jokes time and time again, and delight in them though they hold no surprise or novelty.[10] As Freud said,

> if a child has been told a nice story, he will insist on hearing it over and over again rather than a new one; and he will remorselessly stip-

---

[10] You might remember this one from "Mr. Monk and the Airplane:" Pete and Repete were on a boat. Pete fell off. Who was left?

ulate that the repetition shall be an identical one and will correct any alterations of which the narrator may be guilty—though they may actually have been made in the hope of gaining fresh approval. (*Beyond the Pleasure Principle*, p. 42)

The desire for stability, certainty, and safety is a way of trying to protect oneself from having to move forward in time, having to change, and, generally, having to be alive.

As adults, when we have been hurt, are afraid, or wish otherwise to retreat from the world, we engage in this kind of childish repetition as well, and for the same reasons. So-called "comfort food," for example, seems to consist of an exact replication of the highest-fat-content things eaten as a child. The troubled mind wishes to retreat to a stable past, safe from change, and so we obsessively seek to recreate exactly our past childish food-obsessions; the high-fat dishes presumably serve this function best because they bring about a physiological sluggishness that helps to further quiet the mind. Thanksgiving is perhaps the most conservative and fearful of our contemporary rituals: we return to our families, we eat the exact dishes eaten every year at this time (and only at this time), and then we collectively pass out in a bloated corpse-like torpor, aided by the mind-deadening effects of television and gravy. We eat to forget that life moves on; we eat until there's no more room for uncertainty.

Even when we try to move forward, it seems that there is an impulse, sometimes almost demonic, to recreate and re-enact our history. As Freud points out, quoting Nietzsche, there is a kind of "perpetual recurrence of the same thing" (*Beyond the Pleasure Principle*, p. 23), in which we seem to go through relationships with the same rhythm, phases and outcomes; "the benefactor who is abandoned in anger after a time by each of his *protégés*," "the man whose friendships all end in betrayal by his friend," or "the lover each of whose love affairs with a woman passes through the same phases and reaches the same conclusion." Pessimistically and masochistically re-creating an expected and familiar bad fate has the advantage of freeing us from anxiety. We know how to suffer with the pain we choose for ourselves, and it's safer, easier, and more comfortable to wallow in our distinctive misery than to risk the uncertainty of a life that may present us with fresh possibilities for both pleasure and pain. Monk's distinct and comfortable misfortune seems to be abandonment, and he knows it, but still drives others to repeat that fate again and again. He speaks of this many different times, but for example, in "Mr. Monk Gets Lotto Fever," he says "I can't blame Natalie for leaving. I'd leave me too if I had the chance," and then, after Stottlemeyer wins the lottery and announces his immediate retirement, "Everybody leaves." It's hard not to think that he's like the child who says "fort" and throws his toy away. If he can't have his father and wife back—well, he'll drive everyone else away as well. At least, then, he's in control, and the pain will be a safe familiar pain.

In this way—in addition to being a reactive anxiety response, and a form of displacement behavior—Adrian's repetitive-compulsive behavior is also clearly an intensified form of a universal desire to escape from the pressures and uncertainty of life itself. The death drive pulls us all towards stability and safety, but it pulls Adrian more so than most. And why not? The world has given him more trouble and loss than it gives to most.

This also gives Adrian his child-like qualities. Like a child, he is ready to insist that things be done a certain way. He makes everything his business. He is self-centered and self-serving—not because he is cruel or unkind, but because he is too busy trying to keep his environment stable and safe to be thoughtful about others. Nobody is allowed to touch him, but he can touch anything he likes if he sees it's not in the order he would prefer.[11] He is a grown man who has chicken pot-pie Tuesdays.

The Strength to Mourn

And so, Monk regresses to childhood security-blankets, experiences phobic obsessions, and engages in compulsive behavior in order to avoid moving forward in time, to avoid going through the mourning process which would allow his life to move forward without his lost wife. Certainly a healthier reaction than a psychotic break, but not really a sustainable way to live. Adrian is a tightly-strained bow—perhaps this is how his mind, his genius, has been

---

[11] And Marc Zaffran is right when he says that we wish we could be such a self-indulgent childish genius! See Chapter 10 in this volume. Although Marc recognizes that there's a humanitarian side to this as well, even if it gets obscured by the self-importance of Monk's compulsions. As Monk put it, "I happen to believe that all men are brothers. Every man's bent antenna diminishes me." ("Mr. Monk Gets Cabin Fever")

able to shoot his arrows of genius so far—but if he's going to survive, he must find a way to loosen the tension.

As we leave him, at the end of the series, he begins this process. He solves the crime. Inevitably, it is a disappointment. Knowledge of Trudy's killer does not "solve" the crime in any meaningful sense; the primary problem hadn't been the cause of her death, but her death itself, and neither knowledge of that history nor retribution against the killer will change this fact. The solution on its own leaves Monk feeling empty, just as getting his badge back had. Even for us, as viewers, any realistic story about her death would seem like a bit of a let-down: by building his life around it, he had made her death larger than life. But most things in life are simple, and often repeated. They become important, interesting, significant, and meaningful mostly because they happen *to us*.

Monk built his life around these problems, these absences. He invested them with the weight of all the things his life might have been, or would have been. Once he has a badge, or an answer, his life loses its purpose, and he is forced to confront the fact that filling these holes is not enough to make a full life. This experience of emptiness gives him an opportunity to realize that happiness is not found in possessing objects of desire, but is instead found in developing new objects of care and concern—in the process of cathexis, and the danger of choosing to care about the elements of life that are changing, uncertain, and alive. He must learn to make new emotional investments, and leave his fearful conservatism behind; to build a new life of uncertainty and openness to the unknown.

Mr. Monk may not be a tragic hero exactly, and *Monk* may not be a comedy exactly, but it ends as a comedy traditionally does, since Shakespeare at the least: with marriages rather than murders. But not for Adrian Monk. He is left with a life not too unlike the life he's lived throughout the series. He's a widower, and a former police officer. The difference is this, and almost this alone: He has learned, and chosen, to pay attention to his unknown future as a potential source of value. All things in life are subject to change, temporary, and not to be counted upon or controlled, and the view that this may be a *good* thing is the primary change that Monk gains by the end of the series, and it has a simple name: Hope.

Case Files

JENNIFER CULVER is finishing her Ph.D. at the University of Texas at Dallas. While finishing her doctoral work, Jennifer teaches English, Creative Writing, and Science Fiction at a high school, preferably only to classes that round up to the nearest ten.

MICHAEL S. DODGE is a Boeing Fellow of Air and Space Law at McGill University. His interests are primarily in logic and the philosophy of science, and he is currently Vice-Chairman of the Philosophy and History of Science Division at the Mississippi Academy of Sciences. He has written on ancient skepticism, the nature of time, the history of biology, the concept of sovereignty, and on how science and law influence one another. Like Monk, he has mastered the fine art of hand-wiping, and enjoys the occasional glass of foot wine.

ANDREW B.R. ELLIOTT has written elsewhere about the Middle Ages in film and television, and teaches film and medieval literature at the University of Exeter in England. He often wishes that his life could approach Monk's level of organization, but his desk currently bears a closer resemblance to Stottlemeyer's. However, he has once been banned from a dry-cleaner's—apparently they won't thank him later.

MICHELLE GALLAGHER, a graduate student at UCLA working on a dissertation on Hume's theory of reason, has been told she has a "mild" case of OCD. Luckily for the neighbors, she can easily wait till morning to vacuum. However, on a bad day, in the cold, dark of night when the shower "needs" to be scrubbed, I would not recommend knocking on her door with a pressing murder case.

RONALD S. GREEN teaches Buddhism at Coastal Carolina University. He is currently working on applications of the "Zen Sherlock Holmes thing" as research methodology, and to finding the remote control.

MICHAEL KAGAN is the author of *Educating Heroes*, a book about Ernest Becker's philosophy of education, and Associate Professor of Philosophy at Le Moyne College. He brings his training as a rabbi and as a philosopher, and his work on strange stories, to courses such as "Heroism and the Human Spirit" and "Philosophies of Judaism." He loves watching people do things well, whether it's paper folding or crime-solving, and understands why Monk sent fan mail to the excellent Clothing Inspector #8.

JULIE KANE is an obsessive-type organizer of information—in her current iteration she's the Head of Technical Services for the Sweet Briar College Libraries. She will never shop in a disorganized store, willingly enter a large crowd, or partake in messy displays of emotion. She does not carry disinfecting wipes at all times, but may or may not have a compulsion to use a very particular hand lotion (Orange Ginger, mmm) and keep it in stock at all times.

ZERRIN ORAL KAVAS studied sociology and philosophy at Middle East Technical University in Ankara, and teaches sociology and political communication at Eastern Mediterranean University in North Cyprus. She has just completed a chapter on Mr. Monk after cleaning the house and is now trying to avoid clothespin marks while hanging laundry at 03:00 A.M.

LINDA LEVITT is an assistant professor of communication studies at Stephen F. Austin State University. She is a devoted fan of jelly beans, and although she doesn't separate them by color, she does count them out in even numbers before eating. She has never won a prize for doing so.

COURTLAND LEWIS is a philosopher, a gardener, a musician, cook, avid reader, and co-editor of *Doctor Who and Philosophy*. He is organized, punctual, and compulsive to a certain degree, but nowhere near as obsessive as Monk. He is one part Dr. Kroger and two parts Randy Disher; a little serious, but mostly silly.

DANIEL P. MALLOY teaches philosophy at Appalachian State University. He's published a number of papers on popular culture and philosophy. Like Monk, Daniel has a long list of phobias; it begins with clowns and gets more embarrassing from there.

NICOLAS MICHAUD teaches philosophy at the University of North Florida and Jacksonville University. He would spend much more time teaching in the classroom, if it weren't for the fact that the desks are never in straight and even lines. He finds that, once having fixed this oversight, class time is over. Grades are largely dispersed based on the students' assistance with the straightening-up process. Oddly enough, he's a very popular teacher.

E. DEIDRE PRIBRAM is the co-editor of *Emotions: A Cultural Studies Reader* and the author of *Independent Film in the United States, 1980-2001*. She is an Associate Professor of Communications at Molloy College, Long Island, New York. She cannot decide if, given the choice of being stranded on an island with one annoying person, it should be Mr. Monk or Dr. House.

SYLVIA RANDALL is a clinical psychologist of too many decades to mention. She specializes in couples therapy, founded *The Couples Resource Center* in Palo Alto, California, and now practices in West Linn, Oregon. She does feel a need to straighten out off-kilter pictures on the wall of her office, but, unlike Mr. Mead, has learned to contain the urge for the full fifty-minute therapy hour.

NILS CH. RAUHUT is author of *Ultimate Questions: Thinking about Philosophy* and teaches in the department of philosophy at Coastal Carolina University. He suffers from ophidiophobia and has not given up on his dream to organize his office like Adrian Monk.

GIANCARLO TARANTINO is an M.A. student at Loyola University, Chicago. His familiarity with Monk began with hearing his family sing the opening theme song in unison. His apartment was cleaned twelve times in the making of this book. There were no survivors.

TALIA WELSH has published in phenomenology, psychology, and feminist theory, and teaches Philosophy and Women's Studies at the University of Tennessee at Chattanooga. An avid fan of *Monk*, she has watched all the episodes (in order, of course) three times so far, and is working her way to a nice, round 100.

D.E. WITTKOWER is also editor of *iPod and Philosophy* and *Facebook and Philosophy*, and teaches Philosophy and Interdisciplinary Studies at Coastal Carolina University. He wears a suit and tie every day, but not to the beach,[1] and he does not own 'sand shoes'—unlike Monk, he's apparently got an "off" switch *somewhere* in that head of his.

MARC ZAFFRAN was a practicing Family Physician in France from 1983 to 2008. Under the pen name "Martin Winckler," he has published numerous novels (including the international best-seller *The Case of Dr. Sachs*) and cultural criticism books on (Medical) Television Drama. Since February 2009, he has been studying how ethical values related to patient-doctor

---

[1] usually.

relationships are taught to medical students as a guest researcher at the Center of Research in Ethics of the University of Montreal (CREUM). Marc is currently designing an ethics course for med students based on TV shows such as *ER, Northern Exposure, Six Feet Under, Scrubs, House, M.D.* and *Monk.* His own Dr. Kroger said it would be good therapy.

I Organized Everything by Topic Alphabetically. You'll Thank Me Later.